Birmingham

Belhaven World Cities Series

Edited by
Professor R. J. Johnston and Professor P. Knox

Published titles in the series:

Forthcoming titles in the series:

Other titles are in preparation

Birmingham

A Study in Geography, History and Planning

Gordon E. Cherry

JOHN WILEY & SONS
Chichester • New York • Brisbane • Toronto • Singapore

Published 1994 by John Wiley & Sons Ltd,
Baffins Lane, Chichester,
West Sussex PO19 1UD, England
Telephone National Chichester (0243) 779777
International +44 243 779777.

Other Wiley Editorial Offices

John Wiley & Sons, Inc., 605 Third Avenue,
New York, NY 10158–0012, USA

Jacaranda Wiley Ltd, 33 Park Road, Milton,
Queensland 4064, Australia

John Wiley & Sons (Canada) Ltd, 22 Worcester Road,
Rexdale, Ontario M9W 1L1, Canada

John Wiley & Sons (SEA) Pte Ltd, 37 Jalan Pemimpin #05–04,
Block B, Union Industrial Building, Singapore 2057

Library of Congress Cataloging-in-Publication Data
Cherry, Gordon Emanuel.
Birmingham: a study in geography, history, and planning / Gordon E. Cherry.
    p. cm. – (Belhaven world cities series)
  Includes bibliographical references and index.
  ISBN 0–471–94900–0
    1. Birmingham (England) 2. City planning – England – Birmingham.
I. Title. II. Series.
DA690.B6C48 1994   93–46899
942.4'96 – dc20   CIP

British Library Cataloguing in Publication Data

A catalogue record for this book is available from the British Library

ISBN 0–471–94900–0

Typeset in 10/12pt Sabon by Florencetype Ltd, Kewstoke, Avon
Printed and bound in Great Britain by Biddles Ltd, Guildford, Surrey

University of Hertfordshire

Hatfield Campus Library
College Lane Hatfield Herts AL10 9AD
Tel (0707) 284673 Fax (0707) 284670

This book is in heavy demand and is due back strictly by the last
date stamped below. A fine will be charged for overdue items.

ONE WEEK LOAN

To our grandchildren
Jaimie
Robert
Alistair
Kirsty
and
Joshua
for the pleasure they give us

Contents

Contents

List of figures

List of figures

List of tables

Acknowledgments

The merits of the fusion of geography, history and planning are often proclaimed in academic circles, but interdisciplinary teaching remains remarkably elusive in practice. I am pleased to have had an association with one teaching programme at the University of Birmingham, where my own specialism, planning history, came to full expression because of the uninhibited borrowing from its contributory disciplines: the B Soc Sc in Geography and Planning, joint degree offered by the School of Geography and the Centre for Urban and Regional Studies. I express my thanks therefore to a generation of undergraduate students who allowed me to explore the course of urban change and planning practice with them. It has also been a pleasure to guide and work with higher degree students whose PhDs broke new ground in planning history.

In the School of Geography I have been helped by the presence of kindred spirits. Professor Jeremy Whitehand and his colleagues in the Urban Morphology Research Group provided an academic frame of reference which was always conducive to my own work. The UMRG sponsors the Urban Morphology Newsletter, edited by Dr Terry Slater, again networking an international readership with whom I have much in common.

In retirement years it is a privilege to have such supports to one's academic pursuits. I am grateful to the School of Geography for having me as an Honorary Research Fellow; equally to the Institute for Advanced Research in the Humanities for their Honorary Fellowship.

Having engaged on this work of planning history, it is sobering to reflect on the accumulated debt I owe to friends and colleagues in the International Planning History Society. Over the years we have shared freely the insights from research communicated at conferences, expressed in papers and books, and debated in personal contact. *Birmingham* could only have been written on the back of this wealth of reflected knowledge.

Professor Anthony Sutcliffe, co-worker with me for so long on these matters, was particularly helpful in showing me some early papers from his work 20 years ago on the History of Birmingham project.

I am grateful to the School of Geography, University of Birmingham for help on typing services.

Many thanks are due to the School of Geography, Bournville Village Trust, the City Architects' Department, Housing Department and Planning Department of the City of Birmingham, and the International Convention Centre for help in providing illustrations.

To Editor and Series Editors I extend my thanks for the invitation to write the book in the first place, and their helpful guidance thereafter.

I am indebted to Beryl Bryant for having transformed my written pages into a quite beautifully typed manuscript. It has been a pleasure to work with someone who takes such a lively interest herself in my subject matter.

To my wife Margaret, renewed apologies for the mountain of paper which quite defeats normality in house and home, but many thanks for striving once more with the index.

The Author and Publishers are grateful to the following for permission to reproduce photographs.
School of Geography, University of Birmingham 1, 3–10, 12.
Bournville Village Trust 2, 14–23, 25, 27–31, 35, 37, 42, 45.
Housing Department, City of Birmingham 11, 13, 24, 26, 32, 33.
Planning Department, City of Birmingham 34, 36, 41, 43, 44.
Architects' Department, City of Birmingham 38–40, 47.
International Convention Centre 46.
Louis Macneice's poem Birmingham (1934)
(*source: The Collected Poems of Louis Macneice* edited by E. R. Dodds) is reproduced by permission of Faber and Faber Ltd.

Gordon E. Cherry
University of Birmingham
October 1993

1
Introduction

This volume, *Birmingham*, stands as one in a series which deals with cities of major international significance. The series' editors wisely permit considerable latitude in the way in which particular cities are depicted, but in making certain requirements they do in fact establish a common framework: they ask for authors to convey a 'sense of place', they look for an 'insider's' view of the city, duly reflective of insights and experiences, and they suggest the coverage of certain themes, broadly captured by the field of urban studies. The editors anticipate a wide readership among students in geography, economics, planning and architecture, political science, and sociology.

Birmingham follows this remit very closely. As author I have worked in the city and lived in its environs for 25 years, long enough to become familiar with its traits, but as an outsider unfettered by emotional ties of deep attachment. As an academic (geographer and town planner) I bring to bear the synoptic view that the editors seek, ranging appropriately over both time horizons and subject matter. The city portrait is thereby drawn, suggesting a place and community which is distinctive, very different from other cities with which it might be compared, its character emergent over time, structured from the warp and weft of social and economic change, and articulated through its institutions and political processes.

This city image of Birmingham is presented as a study built particularly upon geography, history and planning. From geography we have a picture of place and space and their physical attributes: a settlement on a sandstone ridge overlooking a small river which afforded a modicum of water power in an upland tract with abundant coal and iron resources. Its history suggests a slow start in a rather inhospitable environment, quickening with economic progress in metal working. Transformation came from the

1

middle of the 18th century as Birmingham was established as a premier manufacturing town; the town and its region figured large in the unfolding of the Industrial Revolution.

History and geography were increasingly intertwined in a process whereby a complex industrial city superseded the manufacturing town. Its transport arteries of road, canal and rail made up the sinews of an expanding urban area containing a central district, distinctive residential areas, industrial quarters, and, from the middle of the 19th century, parks and open spaces. A local community assumed important characteristics: hard working, inventive, independent, radical in politics, dissenting in religion. Birmingham remained stubbornly different from its rivals; it was not a factory town, as the Lancashire and Yorkshire mill towns were, preferring to proclaim itself in its metal trades and small workshops.

At this point the boundaries of historical geography overlap those of social history, economic history and political history as the threads of a local culture emerge, and dominant urban features appear. The picture of the growing town is also formed from the influence of another factor first evident in the last decades of the 18th century, of increasing importance as the 19th century unfolded, of massive significance from the 1860s onwards, and then of huge importance throughout the 20th century. This development was the activity consequent upon the setting up of forms of town governance whereby public bodies had authority to engage in matters of housing and sanitary regulation, to provide public buildings and other facilities, and to engage in development projects of all kinds. Local government progressively became a key factor in the growth and shaping of Birmingham. Unimagined power in environmental regulation and influence in determining the future pattern of development came with the successor activity, town planning.

Birmingham today is inexplicable without an appreciation of the formative elements in its development, found particularly in geography, history, economics, politics and town planning. Their influence helps to construct the 'spirit of the place', the *genius loci*: the physical appearance of the city, its economy, its community groups and their attitudes and aspirations, its political structures, religious affiliations, its sturdy provincialism, its capacity to adapt. This book tries to capture this cultural picture, not as a snapshot in time but as the result of a historical sweep, the present day representing an accumulation of sequential images. The volume is therefore synoptic, ranging widely over history and geography and their cognate disciplines; it is neither simply a history nor just a geography of Birmingham; it is both and much more besides. While it retains an emphasis on the physical appearance of the city, its manifestations of built form and the way the urban environment has been shaped and guided by public bodies, we do not neglect the people of Birmingham, its leaders, its captains of industry and its communities. It is a narrative, descriptive for the most part, but with an explanatory capacity; it is enlivened by excursions into related matters which set physical development and community response into context.

In one sense, then, this book is an exercise in planning history, a city portrait coloured by an approach which the multi-disciplinary perspective brings to bear. Planning history is eclectic in that it borrows freely from a variety of sources. But in the process of borrowing it fuses, and develops an insight of its own; within its catholic embrace there is an absorbent function whereby disciplines, viewpoints and perspectives are brought together in an interactive process which becomes a catalyst for outlining another approach. Hence the interests of those in historical geography, economic history, and social and political history converge with those in the applied fields of public health, housing, technology, architecture and town planning. In the process of inter-relating disciplinary and professional interests, new understandings emerge.

A planning history of Birmingham is particularly apt. The city's development is largely a story of the last 250 years, and planning history has itself been most applied to this period, because during this span of time the environment (and especially the built environment) is demonstrably different from anything that has gone before. The agents and processes of change in the creation of that environment are socially, politically and technologically distinct from those in earlier years; so they are in Birmingham.

The planning historian locates his subject matter in environmental change and forms of planned development; when the focus is a particular city the interest will be on changes over time in built form, spatial patterns and particular construction projects. The explanation will be within social, political and economic history, especially where there are insights into the influence of ideas, the interplay of power structures, the force of particular personalities and the currency of fashion in the application of wider norms and values. In most countries, but especially Britain, an important context will be the force of the local and national planning system; town planning in Britain has had a particularly formative influence on urban growth, notably post-war. Furthermore, the strengthening hand of local government for most of this century has gone far to determine the nature of urban development, massively so in terms of housing provision, road construction and land use generally. In Birmingham both these features (local authority power and town planning) have been supremely important in the 20th century story.

The planning historian, of whatever first disciplinary training, is obliged to develop a wide historical perspective in which 'public history' figures large. The planning historian of Birmingham is particularly favoured by the availability of an abundance of historical material over the last two hundred years. Little had been published on the earlier history of Birmingham. Leland, Henry VIII's topographer, devoted a few lines in his *Itinerary* (1538);

Camden in Elizabeth's reign hardly gave it more attention in *Britannia* (1586). William Dugdale's *Antiquities of Warwickshire* (1730) gave Birmingham a dozen pages. This scanty treatment was rectified by William Hutton. Born in Derby in 1723, he was established in Birmingham as a stationer and bookseller by 1770; he became one of the elite of the growing town, building a country house at Washwood Heath. His *History of Birmingham* was published in 1782, with a second edition a year later adding considerably to the detail of the first; a third edition followed in 1793, a fourth in 1809, and there were other editions after his death in 1815. It was republished in 1976, with an introduction by C. R. Elrington.

Thereafter, *A Century of Birmingham Life, 1741–1841* was published in two volumes by John Alfred Langford (1868). Rather more scholarly, almost a century after the first appearance of Hutton's work, the first of two volumes of the *History of the Corporation of Birmingham* by J. T. Bunce was published in 1878, and the second in 1885; further volumes were added by other writers (C. A. Vince (1923), J. T. Jones (1940) and H. J. Black (1957)) to bring the story up to date (ultimately to 1950). At about the same time, Robert K. Dent's *Old and New Birmingham* was originally published in weekly numbers between 1878 and 1880; it was reprinted in three volumes in 1973. Dent's *The Making of Birmingham* followed in 1894.

In the 20th century short historical surveys appeared including J. H. B. Masterman's *The Story of the English Town: Birmingham* (1920) and *A Short History of Birmingham* (1938) by Conrad Gill and Charles Grant Robertson, written for the city to commemorate the 150th anniversary of the incorporation of the borough. More important, however, were the city's three commissioned histories by Gill (1952), Asa Briggs (also 1952) and Anthony Sutcliffe and Roger Smith (1974); respectively *Manor and Borough to 1865*, *Borough and City 1865–1938* and *Birmingham 1939–1970*, they are indispensable companions for the local historian. This does not of course cast Volume VII of the *History of the County of Warwick*, edited by W. B. Stephens in the Victoria County History series, published in 1964, in any lesser light.

These weighty, authoritative volumes have been followed by a torrent of less substantial works, some derivative but some contributing to a quirkish, anecdotal genre of local urban history. Vivian Bird's *Portrait of Birmingham* (1970), *Birmingham Heritage* (1979) by Joan Zuckerman and Geoffrey Eley, Victor H. T. Skipp's *A History of Greater Birmingham – down to 1830* (1980), *The Making of Victorian Birmingham* (1983), and Chris Upton's *A History of Birmingham* (1993) are informative and entertaining. Biographies, church histories and accounts of districts within the city have been prolific in their number; so too are a plethora of yearbooks, directories and handbooks (the British Association for the Advancement of Science met five times in Birmingham before 1914). The city is favoured by historical journals: the *Transactions* of the Birmingham (and since 1967, Warwickshire) Archaeological Society, *Midland History*, and the recent *Birmingham Historian*, the news journal of the Birmingham and District Association of Local History Societies.

Birmingham was photographed in profusion. Thomas Lewis (1844–1913) became one of the country's first commercial and architectural photographers, and was responsible for a valuable collection of negatives and prints. The Henry Whitlock studios (first in New Street and then in Corporation Street) specialised in portrait and group photography, and the two collections came together in 1962, when the studios closed, and were acquired by John Whybrow, the successor director of the firm which had begun with Thomas Lewis. John Whybrow's *How Does Your Birmingham Grow?* (1972) was a collection of old and new photographs which stimulated an outpouring of illustrated publications ranging from Dorothy McCulla's *Victorian and Edwardian Birmingham from old Photographs* (1973) and John Whybrow and Rachel Waterhouse's *How Birmingham Became a Great City* (1976) to compilations of postcards as exemplified by *A Postcard from Bournville* (1992) by Joe and Frances Brannan, and visual attempts to reconstruct the past as for Selly Oak by Dowling, Giles and Hayfield (1987).

Such is the wealth of available material, it is quite impossible to suggest more than a guide to what has already been written. Much of it follows fairly familiar territory after a while. One historical sweep however takes an ideologically aligned, left wing view (Barnsby, 1989). His thesis is that 'working people are the central core around whom the history of Birmingham has been made' (p. 495). He advances the view that secularism was the bridge over which the Birmingham working class movement crossed from the revolutionary innovative and pioneering structures created in the developing phase of capitalism, 1815–50, to the re-emergence of socialism in the 1880s.

Meanwhile the economic historian has explored the regional laboratory in which the Industrial Revolution was forged, accounting for the rise of Birmingham and the Black Country; the business historian has traced the fortunes of individual enterprises; the social historian has examined the community's response to housing and social conditions; the architectural historian has provided a valuable inventory of the city's buildings, their design and the conditions under which they were constructed; and the regional geographer has drawn on the interplay of environmental factors over time and in space. These many academic writers explore specialist perspectives as history has fragmented into many disciplines; their many titles are invaluable to understanding the growth of Birmingham and are drawn heavily upon in this volume. The planning historian weaves his own canvas from the threads offered by all these perspectives in presenting a composite portrait of the city.

We therefore describe and explain a modern industrial city. This term is apt because Birmingham traces its formative development unambiguously to the economic and technological transformations of the Industrial Revolution. It is a product of those stirring events which have marked the period from the close of the third quarter of the 18th century to the present day. Although the town clearly experienced a quickening in the tempo of industrial life during earlier centuries, Birmingham before the 1770s had not really made a decisive mark in either the national economic league table or the hierarchy of city munificence. It can therefore be set apart from Glasgow and English provincial cities, such as Liverpool and Bristol, with their proud commercial history and commensurate corporate power pre-dating a rise to manufacturing fame. Birmingham was not the archetypal urban and industrial product of the last two and a quarter centuries in this country, because as a manufacturing town based on metal trades it was very different from the north country mill towns, but it bore well its 19th century appellation as a city of a thousand trades and as a workshop of the world.

Birmingham is also modern in the sense that apart from occasional buildings and areas of past association, there is relatively little of the past in the physical make-up of the city: village centres and their churches now swallowed up in the outward march of suburbia, old halls, homes of the gentry, an old inn or farm house, the remnants of a pre-urban landscape and the industrial archeology of past centuries. Otherwise very little, and Birmingham is a city that does not readily look back; its city motto 'Forward' is undoubtedly apt. Birmingham has, without much regard, torn down or ill-used its past; it has almost a transatlantic penchant for renewal, as befits its performance in post-war central area redevelopment.

Its implicit association with modernity has been helped by a readiness to espouse innovation. The evidence is at least variable and certainly not consistent over the years, but the culture of the city has allowed its institutions, and by and large the attitudes of its citizens, to be 'progressive'. Scientific invention has rarely been in short supply, and over some periods very much to the fore. Political pragmatism, breaks with the past and the search for new ways of doing things can be seen to mark the city's development in administrative arrangements, housing policy, and a long-standing love affair with the motor car. Both the 20-year-old National Exhibition Centre and the more recent International Convention Centre have served to reinforce its modern image, derived through civic boosterism, designed to establish a claim to the league of international respectability.

To flesh out the substance of what may lie behind these impressionistic glimpses of Birmingham, and to get under the skin of the city, requires an examination of the component factors of its make-up. As we have suggested, the *genius loci* of Birmingham is formed from its geography, history, economic background, social and demographic features, changing technology, class relations, religion and political leadership. It is usually argued that industrial cities are very similar, but it all depends at what level of generality the proposition is debated. It can equally be asserted that industrial cities are very different, and with a deeper penetration of analysis, the more this is seen to be so. Indeed we shall see that Birmingham has a distinctive character and 'feel', in spite of the fact that popular sentiment elsewhere would aver that the city is at the heart of the most bewildering, amorphous urban areas of provincial England.

While an exercise in planning history, in another sense the book is an exercise in cultural geography. It argues that we understand the city through the processes by which it has acquired its culture. The appearance of the city, together with its layout, form and structure, reflect its people, its community institutions, power structures, economic and political muscle, its demographic form, social relations between and amongst its major groups, and their attitudes to their own city and the rest of the country. Birmingham has generated its own local culture, which in turn has helped to shape the city. Local traditions, and their renewal over time, have helped to express the city in a spatial form and provide its distinctive buildings. In this way a city becomes important for its people because they relate to it and share its fortunes; at its best it becomes a source of pride and inspiration.

The last decade of the 20th century is seeing a renaissance in the notion of 'urbanity'; the unique interaction of people and space in cities of distinction and quality is once more being recognised after many years of a general indifference to cities and their potential. European cities, after some very unfortunate decades of destruction, by both bomb damage and reconstruction, followed by bland architecture and obliteration of past forms and meanings, are rediscovering the importance of their physical form, their spaces and buildings, and the preservation of the past, in the setting for the everyday lives of their citizens. The more complex an urban tissue, the more interesting a city: it becomes a city which attracts and stimulates; it provides comfort because it is familiar, though a touch of the unknown about it will stimulate the curious; and it provides a setting for casual encounter.

There is sufficient about Birmingham for its landscape to be thought of as a palimpsest, literally a historical record of past physical forms whereby street patterns, development blocks and buildings are superimposed one on another over time. There are favoured landmarks which have become points of identity for local people. A combination of traces of the past and today's familiarity becomes an important feature of urbanity. But more important in Birmingham's case is its social dimension rather than its physical. A local middle-class structure has dominated, with identifiable bourgeois and proletarian roots; it has meant an open society with a capacity to absorb external influences, to adapt and to adjust. Country dwellers have been assimilated into an urban setting for over two centuries and more; immigrants from the West Indies and the Indian subcontinent have found their home here for over forty years. New occupational trades have been learned as old ones passed into obscurity; new occupational relationships have been forged as capitalist production systems evolved. Nineteenth century religious dissent, itself founded on earlier traditions, and political radicalism, are now much more muted, but the open society which they engendered still obtains. Institutionalised racism has weakened and, by and large, a spirit of tolerance and openness within the limits of a very broad middle class is a feature of the city.

Birmingham as an independent city force was prominent in the last quarter of the 19th century and up to 1914. In many ways 19th century Britain was dominated by its provincial cities: Birmingham and Manchester in politics, Glasgow and Liverpool for their commercial wealth, and a host of medium-sized towns with economic vitality expressed in mills and factories, and their growing political power reflected in magnificent town halls. London of course remained the seat of national political power and centre of Empire; it was also a growing manufacturing centre with the largest local consumer market anywhere in the world. But provincial cities were not yet reined in by a central bureaucracy; there was a sturdy independence about them, and their economic motors were driven locally.

During the 20th century national and international forces conspired to weaken much of this provincial vigour. National legislation increasingly imposed common obligations upon local councils; room for independent action progressively narrowed. The stature of local politicians declined. Economically, local enterprise bowed before the requirements of wider responsibilities of international capitalism. Decisions, made locally in the 19th century, were now made in the board rooms in centres elsewhere in the country and overseas. The industrial city seemed to have become a pawn in a global economy.

By the end of the 20th century, however, we may be in a position to acknowledge the importance of certain trends which run counter to these features. The European scene increasingly displays the significance of city regions which are just as important as the nation states of which they are part. The West Midlands forms an economic heartland of five million people, the central core of which is a population cluster dominated by the city of Birmingham. The post-war urban geography of western Europe has thrown up a pattern of metropolitan areas which now dominate a sub-continent extending from southern Norway and Sweden and eastern Denmark to midland and south east England, through the Rhine Valley and south west Germany, including Switzerland, northern Italy, the axial belt of France from Normandy to Provence, and north east Spain (Hall and Hay, 1980). Some of the major centres remained attracted to tidewater locations on estuaries (a favoured 19th century setting), but most of the faster growing cities are inland, though all are on natural corridors of transportation. In this huge tract of rapid urbanisation, where people have left the land to concentrate in a relatively few, dominant centres, Birmingham and the West Midlands take their place.

Geographical clustering within and across nation states is occurring within the context of conflicting institutional and political trends. Powerful forces of centralisation operate at the same time as pressure for decentralisation. The notion of a federal Europe cemented by the bureaucracy of Brussels within the European community has the perceived effect of imposing a uniformity on many features of individual nation states. In particular countries, notably in Britain in recent years, national requirements have significantly contributed to a centralising of power. Yet regional distinctiveness persists and individual cities have shown a capacity to do things their way; individual enterprise can flourish as ingenuity takes advantage of opportunities presented. Birmingham's exploitation of European money to pump prime its International Convention Centre and other ventures is a case in point. One suspects that the processes of regeneration, allied to the quirks of civic boosterism, will permit individual cities to extend their role in local leadership and entrepreneurial development, rather than simply fade away as anonymous agents of the state.

To establish the identity of the city we must first (Chapter 2) explain Birmingham's wider geographical and historical setting in the Midlands. This is important because the area's relative isolation kept Birmingham as a fairly insignificant economic backwater until in the 17th century the district's metal-working trades established a robust regional reputation. In Chapter 3 we describe the rise of Birmingham in a Midland context from the 1760s up to the middle of the 19th century, the growth of its manufacturing trades, the development of its urban form, and the ways in which the city was governed and administered. We then proceed in Chapter 4 to consider Birmingham's full-blown industrial development, housing and urban growth in the second half of the 19th century when the essential stamp of the city was forged. We examine the importance of socio-politico-religious institutions in the city and the emergent role of local government; the 'civic gospel' and the heady years of town improvement in the last third of the century are highlighted. Continuing the historical sequence, in Chapter 5 we review the environmental conditions of Birmingham around the turn of the century, and the impetus for change; the influence of new approaches subsumed under 'town planning' is examined in the 15 years or so before the outbreak of the Great War. Chapter 6 is a self-contained story of the inter-war period, 1919–39, in which we focus on the city's housing and economic development. Chapter 7 is the account of the war years and the aftermath of reconstruction. This unfolding historical background then enables us in subsequent chapters to consider Birmingham post-war: its economy (Chapter 8) in two distinctive phases separated by the watershed years of the mid–1960s; its housing (Chapter 9) covering aspects of both redevelopment and additions to the housing stock; work resulting from the operation of the planning machine, including road development (Chapter 10); and (Chapter 11) a focus on changes in the central area. Finally, Chapter 12 allows us to draw the threads together and consider Birmingham in profile, a product of geography, history and planning, a modern industrial city of singular character, a city of opposites and inconsistencies.

It will be apparent from the above that *Birmingham* addresses a number of different audiences. These include the general reader, interested in cities, their history and their planned development; students of urban geography and planning; planning historians; and residents of Birmingham and the Midlands – both a lay public and students, particularly of the three city universities and other colleges, who come for higher education. In order to meet the interests of such a disparate readership a common denominator has been adopted. The profile of the city is depicted in narrative form, a sequential story of a settlement from the earliest times to the present day, in which we identify its particular periods of growth and its various historical landmarks. For ease of readership, copious referencing and foot-notes have been avoided, though source material is properly identified. In the interests of stressing broad themes, and of keeping to a manageable framework of understanding over such a broad canvas, detail (though available in abundance) is selectively introduced. There are occasions when a wealth of information relating to street names and district terminology has to be supplied; local Birmingham readers will find little difficulty here, but for others it is hoped that the maps will always be helpful. Finally, the story of Birmingham has to be seen in context. Events locally were usually mirrored in other big cities and against a national backcloth of social, economic and political change; hence an illustrative bibliography points the reader, where appropriate, beyond Birmingham to a wider frame of reference.

2
The Midland Setting: Birmingham's Origins and Early Development

The profile of Birmingham is shaped essentially by a raft of formative developments which took place over a period from the close of the third quarter of the 18th century to the present day. These factors propelled a thrusting community, already benefiting from the quickening transformations of the Industrial Revolution, into an assertive leader of an urban constellation extending over an area co-terminus with one of the nation's economic heartlands. Neither coal nor iron underlay the streets of Birmingham, yet from the earliest days it managed to be parasitic on the raw materials of its surrounding region, capturing an entrepreneurial and service function to give it an ever-increasing edge in the wider urban hierarchy.

The events of the last 200 years and more have therefore to be put into context; Birmingham is only explicable in its Midland setting. But even this is not enough, for the rise of Birmingham has to be seen against a lengthier historical perspective. Over a period of many centuries the values inherent in the geography of the Midlands were totally reversed; what was a sparsely settled, rather inhospitable upland core, with established towns and more prosperous agrarian communities around the fringes, became a powerhouse of manufacturing industry with an ever-growing population. The facts of economic and settlement geography were turned on their heads.

In this chapter, therefore, we set the scene: Birmingham in regional context, and Birmingham's growth from hamlet, to village, to market town, and to a manufacturing centre which by the close of the 18th century was the fourth biggest town in Britain. The physical structure is sketched briefly; where necessary, further detail is afforded by Warwick (1950) or in the case studies given by Millward and Robinson (1971). Having established the facts of geology and the physiography of the landscape, the human imprint then becomes more important for our story. Skipp (1979) gives an all-embracing environmental history of the region; Rowlands (1987) provides a very full regional history from AD 1000. There are many historians of an antiquarian kind, but Slater (1981) offers a summary historical geography of Warwickshire. Settlement evolution is treated in detail by contributors to the Scientific Survey prepared for the meeting of the British Association for the Advancement of Science held in Birmingham in 1950: Thorpe for the pre-Norman period, Kinvig for Domesday times, Pelham for the period to 1700, and Wise and Johnson for the 18th century. Court (1938) affords an indispensable account of the rise of Midland industries. For a national context, Darby (1973) and his contributors sketch the historical geography of England.

The Midlands and its early history

Birmingham is located in the heart of Midland England, further from the sea than any urban centre of note in Britain. An area roughly triangular in shape, the region is bounded in the west by the Welsh Marches, in the south east by the Cotswolds and their northward limestone extension, and to the north by the southern reaches of the Pennines and the Peak District. In the centre lies the Midland or the Birmingham Plateau, roughly above the 300ft contour. This higher land comprises two units, one centred on South Staffordshire and the other on East Warwickshire, which merge in the middle on their southern flanks. The plateau is highest around the margin, particularly in the south west, where an indented steep face is presented towards Worcestershire, the rim broken by the valleys of three rivers: the Stour, Alne and Arrow. To the north east the River Tame drains the plateau and opens out into a broad lowland. The plateau is thus a distinctive watershed in Midland England, catchment areas draining via the Avon and the Severn to the south west and via the Trent to the north east.

Within this area the site for Birmingham's early development lay on the left bank of the River Rea, about two miles from that river's confluence with the Tame. A keuper sandstone ridge, running south west to north east, provided lighter soils than the clays of the often-flooded Rea valley. Soft water springs issued from the lower slopes, easily tapped by shallow wells. The river, relatively insignificant though it was, gave a flow strong enough to turn a wheel. The steep sides of the Rea valley at this point provided the easiest crossing point in its lower reaches. But these natural advantages remained unexploited for many centuries.

The plateau with its relatively high edges was unattractive to early settlers. The soils on the plateau were less fertile than on the surrounding lowlands, and heathland and forest precluded much penetration. To this day the Birmingham area contains a significant number of place names incorporating the word 'heath': Balsall Heath, King's Heath, Washwood Heath and many more. In pre-Roman days the plateau could only have been very lightly settled, and farming predominantly pastoral, for the seasonal pasturing of animals. Archaeological remains of cutting tools and other instruments suggest human presence, but little more, and the region was probably an indeterminate zone separating the dominant Celtic tribes: the Cornovii who controlled land to the north west, the Coritani whose domain was to the east and the Dobunni whose capitals were to the south west. The Belgae who dominated most of south east England also exercised influence in the south.

A consequence of this geographical setting was that major routes and the earliest settlements were confined to the edges of the plateau and beyond. The Roman Watling Street, approaching from the south east, avoided the plateau until it crossed it at a fairly narrow section near Cannock. The Fosse Way, functioning as a military supply road, servicing a 30-mile-wide defensive zone, ran diagonally from south west to north east, picking out the drier limestone terrain. On the other hand, the lesser known Ryknield (or Ickneild) Street ran through the centre of the region, north–south from Burton on Trent to Bourton-on-the-Water, where it met the Fosse Way. It is virtually obliterated as it traverses modern Birmingham, earthworks of the temporary Roman habitation at Metchley, close to the site of Queen Elizabeth Hospital and the Medical School, successively destroyed by canal, railway and building development. The camp was made shortly after the middle of the first century in the western advance of the Roman forces. The main Roman towns were at Wall (Letocetum) and the more substantial Wroxeter (Viroconium).

Following the withdrawal of the Romans, England fell prey to invading settlers from mainland Europe; over a period of three or four centuries a new agrarian population with permanent centres of habitation provided a formative imprint to our national, man-made landscape history. The Midland story has this context. Including some Saxons and Frisians the Middle Angles spread westward from the Wash, utilising the Rivers Nene and Welland; they proceeded to occupy territories around the upper Avon. The Western Angles, or Mercians, settled to their west and north, following the Trent and its tributaries into Staffordshire and north west Warwickshire. Another stream of invaders, essentially Saxon in origin, headed north from the Thames valley, across the Cotswolds into the lower Avon and lower Severn.

The chronology of settlement followed three main stages: first the Trent and Avon valleys, then the Severn valley, and last a penetration into the central wooded areas of the Birmingham Plateau. It may have been that the Anglian settlement at Birmingham was founded early in this expansion, not later than the early 7th century, when it must have represented a particularly deep penetration into the plateau. The first parts of many village names refer to early owners or group leaders in the settlement process: Birmingham, the settlement of Beorma's people, bears the family name of the principal inhabitant or the leader. English settlers learnt to use the Celtic names of rivers, such as the Tame, Avon and Rea. This suggested that some Britons remained in the settlement process, but the new villages and hamlets all possessed English names, the commonly-found Aston and Norton indicating locations (east and north respectively).

Both before and after the Roman period a large number of trackways criss-crossed the Midlands, salt from Droitwich to the south being a much needed commodity; river crossings proved easily surmountable obstacles as the prevalence of the suffix 'ford' in place names readily testifies. The region for long remained a lightly settled one, frequently fought over by competing powers, but a settlement pattern gradually emerged, characterised by small clusters of houses, widely dispersed.

By the 10th century, however, Edward of Wessex had established suzerainty and guarded the area with fortifications at Tamworth and Stafford. During this period, too, the administrative units of shire and hundred were put in place. The Church had already established its own units of jurisdiction and administration, and these maintained their centres off the plateau. The bishopric of Lichfield, originally based on the Kingdom of Mercia, dated from the 7th century, though in 1075 the See was transferred to Chester. To the south the Diocese of Worcester was formed about AD 680, its area extending from Gloucestershire to south west Warwickshire. By the 11th century the geography of the region's settlement pattern, economy and its institutional structures of governance were largely in place.

The Midlands and Birmingham: 1086

The Norman invasion, its impact felt in the imposition of a new, governing elite, did little to disturb these features, so William's national stock-taking, the Domesday survey of 1086, conveniently provides us with a snapshot record then obtaining of the settlement geography of the area. The King's commissioners collected data from a total of 334 villages in Staffordshire and 279 in Warwickshire; but detail for the higher and more wooded parts of the region was meagre. A crucial aspect of the geography of the

Midlands was highlighted: the distinction between the forested Arden, and the more open country on lighter soils to the south, the Feldon. The results showed that much of Staffordshire and the Warwickshire Arden was poor, whereas in the south the Warwickshire Feldon was prosperous, as too were the valleys of the Trent and the Tame. In Arden the settlements were widely scattered, but some filling in was in progress as the woodland on the heavier soils was cleared.

By 1086 the local hamlets had all become manors or parts of manors; each was subject to a lord, and from the inhabitants he received various services and payments in return for the right to hold their houses and land. No mention of a free layman is made in Domesday returns for the whole of the Birmingham area. Apart from two priests (in Aston and Northfield) we read only of the 'unfree': villeins, bordars, cottars and slaves.

Particulars are given of 15 manors, or parts of manors, in this area. For Birmingham, where the original settlement was probably centred around what is now the Bull Ring and St Martin's Parish Church above the crossing point of the River Rea, the survey revealed an unflattering assessment:

> there is land for six ploughs. In the demesne is one, and there are five villeins and four bordars with two ploughs. Woodland half a league long and two furlongs broad. It was and is worth twenty shillings.

The adjoining manors of Aston, Selly Oak and Erdington, now districts within the city, were larger in population size and had greater agricultural value. The largest manor was Aston with 44 tenants. Whereas Birmingham had nine and was assessed at 20 shillings, Aston paid one hundred. But the manor of Aston included several other hamlets (for example Castle Bromwich, Little Bromwich, Water Orton, Saltley, Bordesley, Duddeston and Nechells) and may not have been all that different from its neighbour. Perhaps the largest compact settlement was at Northfield where 33 tenants were recorded. Only two mills were mentioned (at Aston and Erdington), but it is likely that this figure was exceeded.

But the real comparison lay with the rich Feldon in south east Warwickshire: here the detail for Brailes shows land for 60 ploughs, there were 100 villeins and 30 bordars, there was a mill and the whole paid 55 pounds and 20 loads of salt. The contrast in economic prosperity was profound. The Birmingham Plateau and the area of Birmingham itself was impoverished, of low productivity and lightly settled, while the centre of economic gravity lay on the periphery, particularly to the south east. The Birmingham area is estimated to have had a population density of about four persons per square mile; it was even less in the South Staffordshire area around Cannock and the tract that later became known as the Black Country, but south of Arden, densities were uniformly higher, up to twice and three times higher in the favoured Feldon.

The three counties of Warwickshire, Worcestershire and Staffordshire had adjoining boundaries along the Birmingham Plateau. Birmingham itself lay near the convergence of the three shires; the original settlement was in Warwickshire, but other parts now within the city belonged to other counties – King's Norton and Northfield in Worcestershire, for example, and Harborne, Handsworth and Perry Barr in Staffordshire. The very fact that the Birmingham area lay athwart county boundaries testifies to its peripheral importance: focal points, economic strength and political power lay off the plateau, rather than on it.

More local administrative arrangements confirm the relative insignificance of the Birmingham area. At the time of the Domesday Survey counties were subdivided into territorial divisions called 'hundreds'; below the hundred was the 'vill'. The name of the hundred was derived from the place where its court was held. Warwickshire was divided into ten hundreds, the largest being Coleshill which extended over the area drained by the River Tame and its tributaries the Blythe, Cole and Anker, the catchment area of the north eastern part of the Birmingham Plateau. The settlement of Birmingham was tucked away in the upper reaches of this system towards the headwaters of a network of small streams. Immediately to the south west, the Came hundred in Worcestershire lay astride the watershed between Trent and Severn, including the Bromsgrove district and the basin of the upper Rea containing King's Norton, Northfield and Selly Oak. Once again we see the settlement of Birmingham confined to the periphery of things, tangential to any geographic centre of gravity.

Quite apart from its physical setting, an abundant tree cover emphasised Birmingham's isolation. A broad area of wooded country covered northern Warwickshire north of the River Avon. The East Warwickshire Plateau, the Anker basin and the Tame-Blythe lowlands supported the Forest of Arden, the limits of which were even more extensive. The soils of this area were varied, including sandstones and clays of the Upper Coal measures (east Warwickshire) and of the Keuper Marls (central Warwickshire), some glacial deposits and outcrops of Arden Sandstone. It was not continuously wooded and by the time of the Domesday Survey settlement and land clearance was taking place. In the area drained by the Blythe and the Cole the largest settlements were Hampton-in-Arden, Coleshill and Kingsbury, with recorded adult populations of 69, 44 and 39 respectively. In the upper reaches of the basin Aston had 44 adults, Northfield 33 and Sutton Coldfield 26; in this group Birmingham had just nine. To the north west, Staffordshire's economic position was inferior to that of the other two counties, many estates described as waste, and settlements were few and thinly spread on the South Staffordshire plateau. The conclusive evidence is that the area of Birmingham and its immediate region was of little geographical significance at the end of the 11th century.

Seven centuries of change

After the Norman Conquest the larger secular landowners took possession of their estates, while the Church continued to exercise its power based on ancient property. Two of the villages in Worcestershire (King's Norton and Moseley) belonged to King William as detached parts of the great manor of Bromsgrove. Yardley belonged to Pershore Abbey and was part of the manor of Beoley. All the rest were held by lay lords, and were included in the huge estates of Fitz Ansculf, the baron who held Dudley Castle. Over the next two centuries modest growth and prosperity attended the region, but the relative position of the Birmingham heartland within Warwickshire and Staffordshire changed little. The population of England perhaps trebled during this time, a rate of increase at least matched by that of the two counties. The woodlands were opened up, often by single houses, moated for drainage purposes and to keep out deer and forest animals, and in time hamlets were established. Assarts, land taken in from the wood-land, constituted permanent clearings, the larger requiring capital and labour on a scale not previously available.

Greater wealth from the land permitted a growth in urban development. This occurred over the next 200 years, though admittedly from a very low base. Of the 112 English towns recorded in the Domesday Book only four were in Staffordshire and Warwickshire: Warwick, the largest with administrative and market functions; Tamworth, a royal mint town in Mercian times; Stafford of little strategic significance; and Lichfield, its See transferred to Chester. But between 1100 and 1300 140 new towns were established in England, and 40 of these were in Staffordshire, Warwickshire and North Worcestershire, lay lords being equally as active as the clergy in the process. Numerous grants of market charters were being made at this time, churches were built and rebuilt, and Cistercian and Benedictine foundations were established. All this is evidence of a more established and intensive settlement pattern. Some growth in the region must have seemed remarkable; Coventry, for example, grew from the manor of 1086 to a town of 4000 people by 1280.

During this period Birmingham and its surrounding local settlements remained in relative obscurity; the direct and indirect benefits of town building were conferred elsewhere, the fringes rather than the interior of the plateau still the more geographically favoured. But Birmingham was not without change. The original township was small – less than 3000 acres in extent – but it soon took a lead in the constellation of settlements of which it was part.

After Ricoard of Birmingham, the Domesday lord, the descent of the lordship shows Peter in possession of the manor around 1150. He was steward to Gervase Pagnell, whose family had acquired the barony of Dudley. Some time between 1154 and 1166 Peter de Birmingham was permitted by Pagnell to hold a weekly (Thursday) market; as was then legally necessary, the grant was confirmed by a charter from the King. This right to take tolls and hold jurisdiction over the market, which remained in force until the 19th century, was significant locally because it was the earliest market on the whole of the Birmingham Plateau.

With the increase in trade (and the income derived from it) successive lords made a return to the community: St Martin's was rebuilt, and the Hospital of St Thomas of Canterbury endowed. Round them, a large enclosure was placed between the village and the arable fields stretching as far as Congreve Street, named after the Prior's rabbit warren or conigre. After Peter came six or seven successors all bearing the name William; the second or third of them was allowed in 1251 to hold an annual fair for three days around Ascension Day.

The next century and a half, let us say until the middle of the 16th century, did not change the relative position all that much, although towards the close, a quickening of commerce and of industrial development foreshadowed important changes. The Black Death struck the Midlands in the spring of 1349, the plague and other epidemics persisting with other visitations over the period to 1375. A depleted population did not recover until the next century. But Coventry continued to surge, probably peaking with a population of about 10 000 by 1430, though by the early 1500s its slump was well advanced.

Changes were apparent however. The hamlet of Birmingham in 1086 was different from the village of the early years of the 14th century. The Augustinian Priory of St Thomas the Apostle was founded in 1285, with land in Aston, Saltley, Bordesley and Birmingham. The Birmingham land was that upon which the Hospital or Priory was built, extending from Chapel (now Bull) Street eastwards along Priors Conigree (now Steelhouse Lane). Further endowments later extended the site. Two subsidy rolls in 1327 and 1332 suggest that in Warwickshire only Warwick and Coventry (massively so) had a larger number of taxpayers than Birmingham. It is true that Sutton, Alcester, Stratford and Solihull ran Birmingham close, but Aston had been left far behind. Trade was prospering, 14th century endowments to churches reflecting growing wealth. In 1381 the inhabitants of Deritend were allowed to build their own chapel, and in the following year a licence was granted to the burgesses of Birmingham to found the Guild of the Holy Cross, which undertook road and bridge repairs as well as acting as a charity. The crossing point of the River Rea at Deritend brought traffic along the slope of Digbeth and through the Bull Ring, and the village took on a small-scale industrial function. But it was still relative: as Gill (1952) observes, 'while Coventry was sending its famous blue cloth to all England and to countries across the sea, the traders of Birmingham knew little of the world beyond a day's journey from their doors' (p. 20).

However, the balance of population and taxable wealth was shifting to the Arden and the coalfield parishes of North Warwickshire and South Staffordshire. The market towns and their industrial hinterlands were showing increasing signs of prosperity. The number of taxpayers listed in 1525 is instructive: Coventry had 713, but increases in smaller towns elsewhere suggested widespread growth: Walsall and Coleshill both had over a hundred, Wolverhampton and its surrounding villages had 168 and Birmingham in a much smaller area had 153. Trade in food, raw materials and manufactured goods was extensive both within the Midlands, and between it and the rest of the country. The granting of fairs attracted merchants from wider distances. Textile manufacture (the wool trade supporting carpet weaving), leather making and leather working, and metal goods all figured in the industrial profile of the growing towns, and coal was mined and ironstone dug in South Staffordshire and East Warwickshire.

Birmingham itself continued to exercise some dominance in the network of settlements on the plateau. The manor, roughly rectangular in shape (2½ miles east to west, 1½ miles north to south), had Birmingham and adjoining hamlets of Bordesley, Duddeston and Nechells in the south east corner. A barren and uninhabited heath lay to the north west. There was simply one long street running through the village, Deritend hugging higher ground beyond the river to the south. By the mid-16th century Birmingham boasted a population of around 1500, rising perhaps to 2000 by the end of the century. Woollen manufacture was a staple trade and leather working was also important, but by 1600 metal manufacture was dominant, with swords, scythes and cutlery well to the fore.

However, it is significant that nearly half the 16th century had passed before Birmingham was visited and described by any stranger. In the reign of Henry VIII, John Leland, when he made his famous journey through England, came through the main street of Deritend where

> dwell smithes and cutlers, and there is a brooke (Rea) that divideth this street from Bermingham, and is an hamlet or member belonginge to the Parish therebye. There is at the end of Dirtey (Deritend) a propper chappell and mansion house of tymber, hard on the rype (bank) as the brooke runneth downe . . . The beauty of Bermingham, a good markett towne in the extreame parts of Warwike-shire, is one street going up alonge, almost from the left ripe of the brooke up a meane hill by the length of a quarter of a mile. I saw but one Paroch Church in the towne. (*Itinerary*, 1538)

It was apparent that the village was taking on a distinctive form, its principal features enduring for many centuries (Figure 2.1). North of Digbeth the road diverted around St Martin's Church. The western arm, called Mercer, or Spicer, Street contained several houses of well-to-do merchants. To the south west of the Church stood a moated manor house, which later became neglected, and another moated house was St Martin's Rectory. The eastern arm formed the Corn Market. The open space of the village green had long been encroached upon; private houses were built around the churchyard and a line of butchers' shops, The Shambles, ran straight through the Bull Ring. Further up the hill was the High Cross where dairy produce was sold. Beyond that, the area around the junction of New Street and High Street was obstructed by encroaching buildings, so much so that only a narrow footpath remained and vehicles had to pass through an archway. Here was located the Toll House, an early Public Office. High Street was used as a cattle market, and to the east, after a short distance along Dale End, there was open country.

This cartographic description readily suggests Birmingham as essentially a one-street town in late Tudor times. But important changes in land control would subsequently permit a more rounded urban configuration to replace the linear. The dissolution of the Priory in 1536 was the most important of these changes. From its original endowment, greatly extended by later gifts, the Priory had come to dominate much of the upper slopes of the ridge to the north west of the town. The Priory escaped confiscation in 1537 when smaller priories and religious houses were suppressed, because for many years it had been regarded as belonging to the free chapel, and was a recognised benefice. But the chapel was seized in 1547 and the spoils soon divided into several ownerships. The confiscated land later fell to developers, although for 150 years the ruins of the Priory remained. Eventually the Priory land was built upon, and by the beginning of the 18th century the fashionable Old Square took shape, itself later to fall victim to rebuilding (Hill and Dent, 1897). A different estate had already fallen into new hands: the demesne of the manor, which the de Birmingham family forfeited in 1536. Never again did Birmingham have a resident lord.

From about the middle of the 16th century the national population began to grow for the first time for 200 years. Between 1560 and 1640 the population of England increased by about 45%. Evidence from parish registers in Staffordshire and Warwickshire suggests that the rate of increase in the Midlands was considerably greater than the national average. A quickening of trade and commerce was based increasingly on the industrial growth in the scattered settlements of the two counties, alongside which Birmingham itself developed. There were growing links between the Midlands and the London market for both food and manufactured goods, and in spite of poor communication routes, trade with London, Southampton, Bristol and the East Anglian ports flourished. Birmingham and other merchants successfully challenged the monopolies of the London trading companies.

Metal working developed rapidly on the South Staffordshire coalfield, with specialisms in nailing, lock making, scythe making and metal parts for harnesses; following the lead set in south east England (in the Weald of

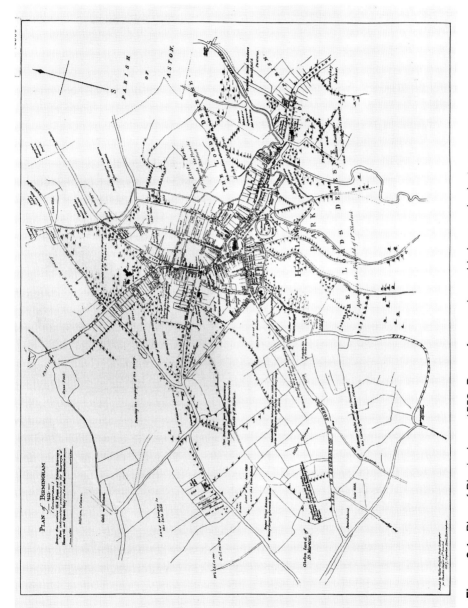

Figure 2.1 Plan of Birmingham, 1553. Drawn from various old plans and private surveys.

21

Kent and Sussex) blast furnaces had made their appearance at Cannock Chase by 1560 and with in the next century there was a network of furnaces, forges and slitting mills in the southern part of the county. Birmingham itself gained from this growth in metal working. When the Tudor topographer, John Leland, visited Birmingham in 1538, he observed in his *Itinerary* that:

> There be many smiths in the towne that use to make knives and all mannour of cuttinge tooles, and many lorimers that make bittes, and a great many naylors. Soe that a great part of the towne is maintained by smithes, who have their iron and sea-cole out of Staffordshire.

The visit of William Camden in 1584 confirms Leland's account; in *Britannia* (1586) (precisely 500 years after Domesday) he describes the town as 'swarming with inhabitants and echoing with the noise of anvils'. We may conclude that, by 1600 the metal trades in Birmingham were firmly established as the basis of the small town's prosperity.

By the second half of the 17th century the extent of urban growth in the Midlands was unmistakable. Between 1662 and 1679 assessments for payment of Hearth Tax indicated that the number of households in Staffordshire and Warwickshire in any one year was about 40 000. This was equivalent to more than a quarter of the total for England and Wales in a geographical region that was about one tenth of the whole. During the Civil War Birmingham had been a centre of opposition to Charles I. In 1643 the town was attacked by the King's German nephew, Prince Rupert of the Rhine; after plunder, the Royalists used gunpowder and burning coals to set it on fire. But a normal way of life was soon restored and by the 1680s Birmingham was enjoying a full share of the country's advancing prosperity and had gained at least two new industries – gun making and brass manufacture.

Birmingham's population, perhaps around 2000 at the beginning of the 17th century and approaching 5500 by mid-century, was rising sharply by the end: in the 1690s the number of baptisms each year averaged 172, and by the 1720s this had increased to 279 – figures which did not include the immediately adjoining district of Deritend which was in Aston parish. Natural increase of births over deaths was supplemented by immigration from surrounding parishes – largely industrial in nature, rather than rural – and from further afield. Birmingham's expansion during the Stuart period was impressive. As Gill (1952) summarises:

> When James I came to the throne this little town, with between two and three thousand inhabitants, was still as much rural as industrial. By 1714 the population was five times as great; Birmingham had become one of the chief centres of manufacture in England, with brass- and copper-working added to its older industries; St Philip's Church, the present Cathedral, was almost finished; and there was already a movement to secure a municipal charter. (p. 48)

Growth continued apace and during the first half of the 18th century the town broke its old confines. Just before the end of the 17th century urban development had spread up the hill, away from the Bull Ring, up and over the sandstone ridge which forms a watershed between the Rea and the Tame, and into open country. Much of the old Priory land was purchased around 1700 by John Pemberton who opened it up as an attractive residential district focused on the Old Square, and on the other side of Bull Street construction of the new church of St Philip was started in 1711. This striking church was built to a design supplied by a local architect, Thomas Archer. The field in which it was erected ('Mr Phillips' barley close') was presented by the owner, gratitude for the gift no doubt helping to decide the choice of a patron saint. Apart from the church (now the Cathedral), nothing today remains of this development, though Temple Row, even then, was noted for its elegant appearance (Figure 2.2).

More was to follow as streets and houses spread north, east and west from the older part of the town. From 1746 the Colmore family developed the New Hall Estate with a grid of streets around the central axis of Newhall Street. These developments are well recorded on two maps of Birmingham in the first half of the 18th century, one by William Westley, printed in 1731 (Figure 2.3), and another by Samuel Bradford in 1750 (Figure 2.4). Much later, by 1779, St Paul's church was completed in a setting of graceful Georgian brick houses – over the hill and a far cry from the overcrowded Digbeth and Deritend with their old industrial establishments.

But while Birmingham was expanding territorially, in one other way there was no change: Birmingham was still a manor. The lord had his rights as landowner, head of the manorial court, and controller of the markets. However, in addition, the town was governed as a parish, administered by church wardens, overseers of the poor, constables and surveyors of highways. In 1716 there had been a movement to gain incorporation for Birmingham, but there was no result to a presentation of a charter to the government. Thus it was that in the very early days of the Industrial Revolution, when Birmingham had a population of perhaps 30 000, the town still had the institutions of a rural parish, and with boundaries which were increasingly irrelevant. The ancient parish of Birmingham, comprising 2996 acres, lay in Warwickshire. On the north lay Handsworth parish in Staffordshire, with its hamlet of Perry Barr. To the east lay Aston parish, comprising the township of Aston, Witton, Erdington, Water Orton, Castle Bromwich, Little Bromwich, Bordesley, Deritend, Duddeston with Nechells and Saltley with Washwood. Edgbaston was to the south, and Harborne, with its chapelry of Smethwick, was to the west. Boundaries centuries old would not be able to contain the new geography of an expanding Birmingham.

At the beginning of the 18th century the industrialising part of South

Figure 2.2 The east prospect of Birmingham, plate by William Westley.

Staffordshire and Warwickshire still assumed a scattered, fragmented appearance, half urban, half rural with common fields and pasture interspersed with small settlements of cottages and gardens, coal pits, quarries, forges, mills, tanneries, glassworks and metal manufacturing establishments of all description. In the Birmingham area there were between 20 and 30 mills for metal working located in the valleys of the Cole, Rea, Tame and their tributaries; the last surviving reminder of this period is the restored Sarehole Mill, Hall Green. Birmingham itself by this time was unmistakably a manufacturing town. Textile industries remained important, the River Rea providing water for processing; tanneries were concentrated in the lower part of Digbeth, and just west of the Rea Bridge a short street known as Tanner's Row was appropriately named. But emphatically metal working had assumed dominance; textiles were failing and leather manufacture, once a staple trade, had almost left the town.

Around Birmingham some townships, such as Bordesley, Nechells and Duddeston were swallowed up to become industrial suburbs. Elsewhere an open field community remained for much longer, as at Erdington, unenclosed until 1802 and Saltley, open until 1817. The process of enclosure in fact was a protracted one, the last open fields in the Midlands to be enclosed by Act of Parliament located at Yardley in 1847.

The basis of this new prosperity was of course industrial development both within Birmingham and across the surrounding region. During the 18th century growth and diffusion of innovation marked the metalwork trade, glass making, brewing and coal mining. The pulsating heart lay in a tract of poor quality land, interspersed by heaths, to the north west of Birmingham. Rectangular in shape, approximately 10 miles by 12 in extent, it was centred on Dudley, with Wolverhampton in the north west, Walsall to the north, and Stourbridge and Halesowen to the south. It would become known as the Black Country, as its wastes and commons were taken over by a thickening scatter of industrial development.

Minerals were easily won: coal, ironstone and fireclay (often quarried from the same adits and pits) and limestone. Water power was available from the streams which drained northwards to the Tame and southwards to the Stour. From the blast furnaces the pig iron was converted into bars of wrought iron; in the slitting mills it was then rolled into sheets and cut into rods. These rods provided the raw material for the large numbers of smiths who in domestic workshops fashioned a multitude of small metal objects, typically nails, but supplemented by a host of specialist metal products. It was a highly distinctive area of small workshops, very different from the East Shropshire iron working district centred on Ironbridge and Coalbrookdale.

The commercial capitalists were the ironmongers who managed systems of extended credit, the centre for which was Birmingham. Specialisms developed, none more striking than the Birmingham gun-making trade which spread rapidly in the parishes of Wednesbury, Darlaston, Harborne and Dudley. Toy making (the making of small fancy goods in metal) also extended to a number of different centres, and the trade diversified further with the introduction of enamel box manufacture. The toy trade expanded the trade in malleable metals including copper, brass, lead, tin and zinc. By 1746 Birmingham had its own brass house in Coleshill Street, with nine furnaces producing 300 tons of brass a year. Specialist suppliers of oils and acids and decorative materials such as gold, silver, dyes, also made their appearance. Having established this lead in manufacturing supremacy the ironmongers were keen to retain the secrets of local success, and they reacted adversely to an act akin to industrial espionage when a Birmingham button maker, Michael Alcock, in 1753 was attracted to France in an attempt to transfer technology to La Charente (Harris, 1986).

As part of this industrial expansion vast numbers of people were engaged in the carrying trade, professional wagoners being found in all the Midland towns. As a consequence of the increase in the volume of goods carried, the need for speed and the search for reduction in transport costs, turnpike trusts were formed from the 1720s, covering the main roads such as those from Birmingham to Banbury, Oxford, Bristol and Holyhead. The need for improvements was demonstrated by the fact that access to Birmingham by stage coach and horse-drawn wagon was along 'holloways', deepened by the constant passage of wheels and hoofs; Holloway Head as a Birmingham central area street name is a reminder of them.

At the beginning of the 18th century Birmingham had three posts a week to London, but by mid-century this figure had doubled. Road services were progressively extended. In 1767 55 different carriers advertised at least weekly services in Birmingham, the wagons setting out to regular time-tables from 17 of the town's inns. As we shall see later, two transport revolutions, canal and rail, would soon establish a very different situation.

Birmingham's economic stirrings

In the previous section we have established that by the 17th century the Midland counties formed a region of small market towns, villages and hamlets. During that time it was a countryside in the course of becoming increasingly industrialised. Court (1938) describes it thus:

> a strung out web of ironworking villages, market towns next door to collieries, heaths and wastes gradually and very slowly being covered by the cottages of nailers and other persons carrying on industrial occupations in rural surroundings. Birmingham, especially towards the end of the century, is the main exception to this phenomenon of an industrial population not yet divorced from the soil. Even here, till a far later date, rural surroundings and even country occupations remained persistent. (p. 22)

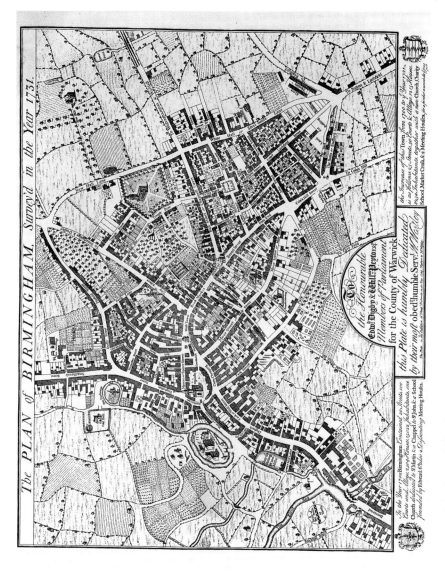

Figure 2.3 Plan of Birmingham, 1731. William Westley.

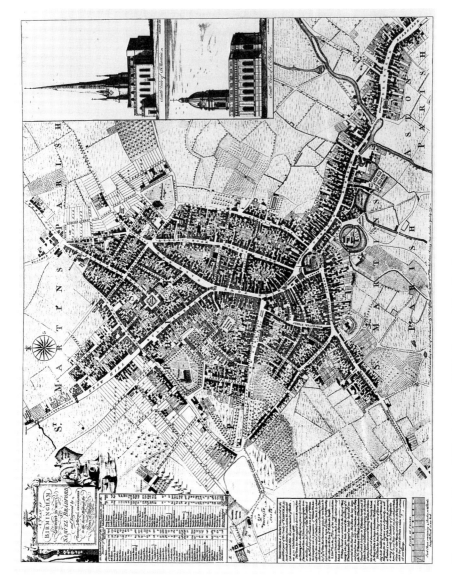

Figure 2.4 Plan of Birmingham, 1750. Samuel Bradford.

It is necessary for us to explore in a little more detail the circumstances which propelled Birmingham forward to new economic fortunes. Court's seminal work reminds us of the main factors. For centuries Birmingham's industries had rested mainly on tanning and the woollen cloth trades; Tudor men of consequence in the town were tanners, and cloth working reflected the Warwickshire staple of wool. The town had a leather hall where business was conducted, but this had gone by the late 18th century; cloth working also died. It may be that the leather industry was instrumental in stimulating certain branches of metal working in view of the association with saddlery and harness, but for a variety of reasons during the 17th century metal replaced wool and leather as the town's staple.

Originally its metal-working trades had been largely of a simple, iron-smithying type, but new trades, many requiring high skill, were soon introduced. During the Civil War Birmingham took its stand by the Parliament, supplying swords to leaders of the Parliamentary forces, refusing swords for the King. The town paid a severe price for this stance, as we have seen. But in the long run Birmingham (and indeed other industrial centres elsewhere in the country) benefited from the conflict because the outcome of the struggle removed the possibility of an extension of government supervision of economic affairs of a kind which had been pursued by the late Tudors and early Stuarts.

In fact Birmingham was to benefit a great deal from local economic freedoms. The old established industries in Midland towns had been closely tied to guild life. Guilds were urban institutions and they carefully regulated the business of industry and employment within their towns. They could not suppress industry within the surrounding district and, as a consequence, the newer Midland industries remained free of general guild influence. The coal-mining and iron-working districts were widely scattered and distant from the old medieval centres of population; moreover the relative simplicity of the processes of early smithying, and the part-time nature of the occupation itself, presented difficulties for towns to control or even monopolise the industry. Thus, while metal working was controlled by guilds in Coventry, the practice of guild control over industry in Birmingham (and Wolverhampton for that matter) never obtained. There were other freedoms too: the justices did not seek to control local industry through wage rates of labour, nor was there control over entry into the metal trades through any apprenticeship system. Neither was Birmingham subject to the religious impediments imposed by the Clarendon Code during the years after 1660, so that there was a strong inducement to non-conformists (particularly Quakers, who suffered most severely of all the sects exposed to the harsh laws) to settle in the area.

But the absence of institutional restrictions would have counted for little had it not been for the region's resources of two basic raw materials: coal and iron. During the 17th century there was a growing dependence on coal fuel. Because of its bulk and weight, it was only profitable to transport coal over land for short distances, perhaps 10–15 miles; hence the presence of easily workable seams was very important. The Midlands was well endowed in this respect, and the manufacturers of Birmingham and its industrial region developed close business links with the coal districts of East Shropshire and South Staffordshire. Connections were developed with the Warwickshire coalfield between Nuneaton and Coventry in the 18th century.

For iron working the change from charcoal smelting to the use of coal at the forge was made decisive with Abraham Darby's discovery of coke smelting. (Shropshire had limestone for the flux, but the area around Dudley provided the best quality.) Early coal mining centred around the outcrops adjoining Wednesbury, Tipton and Dudley, the move to deeper mining being dependent on a capacity to pump underground water. The Newcomen engine first met this demand and was used in the Midlands in the 1710s. The late 18th century was a period of great expansion for the South Staffordshire coal-mining area, feeding on the demand which came from the expansion of iron working and other industries and the general introduction of the use of steam power in the collieries.

The basis of the coal-mining area was the Thick Coal, a 30 feet thick seam stretching south from Bilston for seven miles to the neighbourhood of Stourbridge, with an average breadth of four miles. The coal country therefore extended over an area of 28–30 square miles, and its full development formed the basis of 19th century prosperity.

As we have seen in the previous section, the iron industry was well represented in the Midlands and for some centuries certain specialist trades had become established in particular localities. Nail making was widely distributed, particularly between Dudley and Bromsgrove, and an early concentration was around Rowley Regis. Scythe grinding and scythe making centred on Belbroughton, buckle making around Bilston, and saddlers' ironmongery at Walsall.

Birmingham as a small town had but general metal trades initially: in Henry VIII's time Deritend housed its smiths and cutlers and across the Rea and up the hill Birmingham's smiths made knives, its lorimers made bits, and its nail makers complemented a regional product. By the time of Elizabeth this village of smiths was taking off, and between Elizabeth and Anne Birmingham's community of iron workers was transformed into a community engaged in metal. A growth of skill and enterprise encouraged the development of four specialist trades during the 17th century: jewellery making, button making, gun making and the brass trade. Demands on capital were met and organisational capabilities were proven. Birmingham's products gained access to London markets and there was no little rivalry between the two centres, as London accused Birmingham of shoddy goods and deceitful practices.

Meanwhile iron making in the region was experiencing technological change, the 17th century seeing the introduction of the slitting mill. Introduced into England from abroad, this engine replace hand labour; it cut or slit hammered strip and flat bar into hoop iron and rod for nail making. Water power from two streams was especially important to the iron slitters: the Stour, and particularly the Tame. By the end of the 17th century iron forges and furnaces, rod mills and blade mills were located along the length of the Tame and its tributaries. Bescot became a seat of iron making, and nailing came to dominate the parish of West Bromwich.

But the iron industry turned away from the water power of the Tame and the Stour. The new factors were steam power and coal. From about 1760 coke began to be generally substituted for charcoal in smelting, and the last years of the century saw a rapid concentration of capitalist industry in the Severn Valley around Ironbridge. Shropshire supplanted the Forest of Dean as a supplier of iron. In the next century Staffordshire would become more important than Shropshire, Henry Cort's puddling process, patented in 1784, which accelerated the process of iron manufacture, helping such centres as Tipton to achieve pre-eminence, in company with other productive regions, notably Lanarkshire and the West Riding.

In the meantime the economic surge depended on improvements to communications. We have already noted the importance of the 18th century road and water transport schemes, and we should elaborate a little on this. The Midlands had only one eminently navigable waterway: the River Severn. Larger boats traded to Shrewsbury and smaller craft to Welshpool. A major feature was that it was a free river, with only Gloucester having the right (seldom exercised) to take tolls from passing vessels; navigation was therefore open to all. From the 16th century Bewdley emerged as an important centre in the organisation of river trade; the oak woods of the Wyre Forest nearby provided timber for boat building. By the 17th century the river became one of the busiest in Europe as the coal and metal industries of Shropshire, Staffordshire and Worcestershire began to stir.

Other rivers were of much less navigable importance, and improvements could only achieve modest results. In the 1630s an improvement scheme for the Avon permitted 30-ton barges to proceed from Tewkesbury to Stratford. Later in the century improvements to the Stour permitted navigation from Stourbridge to Kidderminster, and there was also an improvement of the Salwarpe to help Droitwich and its coal-consuming salt trade.

But the settlements on the higher plateau had no such river access; transport by pack horse and wagon and the carriage of heavy, bulky goods (like the coal and iron on which the region was increasingly depending) was slow and expensive. Salvation lay with the canal. Nationally, the beginning might be marked with the opening of the Sankey Navigation in 1757, constructed from St Helens to the Mersey, the objective (significantly enough) being the cheaper transport of coal to Liverpool. It was followed by a more important canal project, built in 1761 at the expense of the third Duke of Bridgewater, to transport coal from his mines at Worsley to Manchester, master-minded by the engineer James Brindley. The scene was set for other regions to benefit from this transportation revolution; the West Midlands received the new technology before the decade was out. The advantages to Birmingham were soon apparent.

3
The Manufacturing Town
1760s–1851

During the last quarter of the 18th century Birmingham became the third largest town in England and Wales, surpassed only by London and Bristol. As Bristol was a port as well as an industrial centre, it could be claimed that Birmingham was then the largest industrial town outside London. Its manufacturing base already rested on efficient productive methods, and expanding markets suggested prosperity to come. Birmingham was poised for growth.

The population of the town grew dramatically, more than tripling in half a century, from an estimated 23 600 in 1750 to a census figure of 73 670 in 1801. This increase in numbers was the most obvious single feature in the West Midlands' experience at this time, but it would be wrong to see the rise of Birmingham in the second half of the 18th century (or indeed subsequently) as a self-contained phenomenon. Money (1977) has argued that Birmingham was not an independent centre; rather, because it was at the meeting point of three counties (Warwickshire, Worcestershire and Staffordshire), a balance had constantly to be struck between the new centre and the older influences of the county capitals, the cathedral cities of Lichfield and Worcester and the city of Coventry. It was in this context that an urban culture of Birmingham developed, based on the experience of its citizens and the perceived identity of the town.

To begin with, canal building exerted a major influence on the self-consciousness of both the town and the region. It was impossible to ignore the interdependence of different parts of the West Midlands, and the region became increasingly aware of its relationship with other parts of England. Long distance travel was attracting greater numbers: by 1777 52 coaches a week, each carrying six passengers left Birmingham for London (a journey of about 19 hours). There were 16 coaches a week to Bristol, four to Coventry and four to Sheffield.

Birmingham aspired to future greatness, but found it necessary to share it with its surrounding region. The founding of the General Hospital was a major initiative, supported by triennial festivals of oratorio which turned it into an important and fashionable charity. The New Street Theatre further enhanced the reputation of the town and reinforced its social and political connections. Science flourished. Libraries were established and local periodicals circulated. But all these features were also assimilated into the life of the surrounding area, and interconnections correspondingly strengthened. The Birmingham Bean Club provided a long-established link between the leaders of the growing town and the landowners of the neighbouring counties. Birmingham consolidated its position in the established wider structure of society and politics. Independence and interdependence within the region were, and remain, recurrent themes in Birmingham's recent history.

This chapter looks at the period from the 1760s to the middle of the 19th century when the town successfully established itself as a premier manufacturing centre concerned largely, but by no means exclusively, with the making of metal goods. The first section appropriately focuses on developments in manufacturing industry, beginning with the transport revolution foreshadowed in the previous chapter. Second we examine critical features of the growing town, particularly its housing development and the advent of the railway. The third section considers how the town was administered during this period, and reviews the work of the Improvement Commissioners up to their demise in 1851. These were fundamental years in the town's history, when its future was definitively shaped as never before. As Gill (1952) observes: 'In many respects modern Birmingham may be dated from this period: the beginning of railway communications, modern credit and investment, great factory buildings, world wide connexions in commerce; and in matters of government, the municipal charter.'

Industrial expansion

Until 1770 the whole of Birmingham's trade was carried by road. Several of the roads outside the town had been improved by Turnpike Trusts, but the high cost of road haulage remained a critical deficiency. The advantages of the early north-western canals, as described in the previous chapter, were seized with alacrity.

The first canals were constructed in the Midlands in the years 1766–9. In 1766 work was begun on the Trent and Mersey Canal, and another leading from it near Stafford to Stourport. An Act was obtained in 1767 for the Birmingham Canal, a 22-mile waterway, to join the Grand Trunk system. Clearly facilitating the transport of coal into the town from the Black Country, construction began the following year, and the first boat-load of Wednesbury coals entered Birmingham on 6 November 1769 at a site close to Newhall Street. Two years later traffic came to a new wharf at Brick Kiln Piece (later Easy Row), now the site of the Holiday Inn. Tipton coals came in May 1770, Bilston coals in October, and the price of coal in Birmingham immediately nearly halved; coal which had sold at 13s a ton dropped to 7s 6d. In the same year Brindley's Staffordshire and Worcester Canal communicated with the Severn and Stourport, the Birmingham Canal as a branch feeder opening in 1772. Other canals followed, to Fazeley (1789), Stratford (1793) and Warwick (1800); the complex story of rivalries, expansions and new waterways is recounted by Broadbridge (1976). An additional connection with the Severn, the Birmingham and Worcester Canal, was begun in 1792, though not completed until 1815.

Meanwhile a national canal system was emerging. The Trent and Mersey Canal ran from Wilden Ferry in Derbyshire to Preston Brook and Runcorn on the Mersey, and the Staffordshire and Worcestershire Canal joined the Trent and Mersey at Great Haywood to Bewdley on the Severn; this was the Grand Trunk, completed in 1777. A link with London was afforded by the Grand Junction from Brentford to Napton in Warwickshire from where there was a link to the Midland system. Within a heady ten years or so Birmingham's communication links had been transformed, and with them the economic prospects for the growing town and the Black Country. Birmingham became encircled by canals, and the wharves adjoining Suffolk Street, Gas Street and Newhall Street were the veritable centre of a remark-able, new communications network. Factories were inevitably attracted to the canal banks: by 1811 there were no less than 124 works and wharves lining the two-mile stretch between Bordesley and Aston (Wise and Johnson, 1950).

We have already observed that Birmingham itself had no endowment of natural resources in the form of coal and iron, and that its water power was very limited. Yet 'the first manufacturing town in the world', as Arthur Young described it, grew to industrial pre-eminence. It is appropriate, therefore, by way of explanation, to start with the exploitation of its human resources – the inventiveness and entrepreneurship of its citizenry. William Hutton first saw Birmingham in 1741. He was later to write:

I was surprised at the place, but more so at the people. They were a species I had never seen. They possessed a vivacity I had never beheld. I had been among dreamers, but now I saw men awake. Their very step along the street showed alacrity. Every man seemed to know and prosecute his own affairs. The town was large, and full of inhabitants, and those inhabitants full of industry. I had seen faces elsewhere tinctured with an idle gloom void of meaning, but here, with a pleasing alertness. (Hutton, 1782, p. 63)

These features of vivacity, alacrity and alertness were already apparent in the Lunar Society of Birmingham (1766–1809), that remarkable club whose members met for discussion, to report scientific experiments and to exchange information (for further reading see biographies of individual members, a bicentennial celebration by Cadbury (1966) and Schofield's (1963) more expansive history of the Society). It frequently met in the house of Matthew Boulton; his first business was that of a silversmith and buckle maker, but he also experimented with steam engines and, in association with James Watt, designed and sold rotary engines for driving machinery. Erasmus Darwin was a physician but had many interests including that of designing mechanical devices. William Small was a doctor of medicine with wide interests in engineering, chemistry and metallurgy. John Whitehurst built precision instruments. Josiah Wedgwood, the potter, was a promoter of the early canals. Richard Lovell Edgeworth was a designer of carriages, Thomas Day an educational reformer, James Keir a glass and chemical manufacturer. James Watt was a metallurgist and designer of steam engines. William Withering, another doctor of medicine, was also a botanist with an interest in geology and chemistry. Jonathan Stokes shared this interest in botany, and Robert Augustus Johnson in chemistry. Samuel Galton was a gunmaker; as a Quaker he was disowned by the Society of Friends 'for fabricating and selling the instruments of war'. Joseph Priestley, a minister of religion, appointed to the Unitarian New Meeting House in Birmingham in 1781, was also a scientist; he had already written a history of electricity and in chemistry he studied the nature and composition of gases.

Science, industry, medicine and transport were all influenced by this club. We might be surprised that such a constellation of luminaries was present in Birmingham at this time. But a reading public had existed for many years. A local newspaper, *Aris' Gazette*, was published as early as 1743 and it provided a focus for cultural and intellectual life. When Baskerville published his first volume in 1757, and was appointed printer to Cambridge University the following year, Birmingham's printing and publishing soon became of more than local significance. Be that as it may, the fourteen members were unusually distinguished and eleven became Fellows of the Royal Society.

But while this list in no way exhausts the enterprise of local people at this time, Gill (1952) considered that four remarkable people did as much as anyone to establish Birmingham's manufacturing reputation during the second half of the 18th century. John Taylor, John Baskerville, Henry Clay and Matthew Boulton were all pioneers of modern production who maintained at the same time the old traditions of craftsmanship. Taylor was a button maker who introduced to the town the making of gilt and plated small wares; with Sampson Lloyd, the Quaker ironmaster, he was a founder of Lloyds 'Old Bank' in 1765. (The availability of credit was of crucial importance to the growth of manufacturing enterprise; three other firms were in competition with Lloyds by 1791 and three more banks appeared in 1793, 1804 and 1805.) Baskerville was a printer and an expert in japanning. Clay discovered and patented a material known as paper board, later papier mâché, suitable for the manufacture of panels, trays and snuff boxes. Boulton supported James Watt in carrying through and perfecting the invention of the steam engine; the story of his Soho Works is traced below.

A feature of this collective enterprise was that industrial innovation was being advanced on the basis of scientific discovery. Around the end of the 18th century there was a veritable ferment of invention in the Birmingham area, a remarkable constellation of luminaries (none of them Midland born) gathering in the town, as Court (1938) reminds us. An indication of the intellectual liveliness of Birmingham industries at this time is given by the number of patents taken out by residents. Until the Patent Law Amendment Act of 1852, Birmingham led the provincial towns as regards the number of grants of letters patent.

Much of all this came together at the beginning of the century in the Soho Manufactory, Handsworth (Gale, 1948). Matthew Boulton, son of a toy-maker, inherited his father's business in 1759. He decided to concentrate a number of branches of the hardware trade into one organisation and a site was selected at Soho in the parish of Handsworth, two miles from his Snow Hill premises. An existing water mill was demolished and a three-storey factory erected in 1761 (Figure 3.1). With a partner, John Fothergill, a Birmingham merchant, he expanded his business and concentrated the whole of the manufacturing in the new premises. Water power was available from the Hockley Brook and the factory followed advanced principles of industrial organisation. A huge output of steel jewellery, watch chains, buttons and buckles demanded extensions to the factory, and adjoining he built a new residence, Soho House – where the Lunar Society frequently met.

From the cheap toy and allied trades, Birmingham expanded into the market for jewellery and plated goods of high quality. The town's new position was confirmed with the establishment of an Assay Office in 1773. Until this time Birmingham silver products were sent to the Assay Office at Chester for hallmarking, and the inconvenience demanded a local facility. Boulton's near neighbour at Sandwell Park, West Bromwich, was Lord Dartmouth, a Secretary of State in Lord North's Government: he advised the promotion of a Private Act. With support from Sheffield trade and elsewhere, the counter-petitions from London were overcome and Boulton's Bill was successful (1773). The Birmingham Assay Office opened its doors in August just three months after the Royal Assent, in a modest suite of three rooms at the King's Head Inn, in New Street. By 1790 it had moved to offices of its own, and the present Newhall Street premises were acquired in 1877.

Figure 3.1 Soho Manufactory, Handsworth.

In 1775 Boulton entered into partnership with James Watt for the supply and erection of a steam pumping engine, and further developments in engine manufacture followed. By 1792 William Murdock, a Scot, then working in Cornwall, was experimenting with gas lighting; he returned to Birmingham before the end of the decade. Meanwhile, land a mile from the Manufactory was bought and new premises, the Foundry, constructed for the work of engine building; it was opened in 1796. The Manufactory continued to prosper and Boulton developed his interest in coinage by supplying coining machinery. It was the Manufactory which was first lit by gas light, in 1802 by Murdock, in celebration of the Peace Treaty of Amiens in that year.

But this industrial enterprise, housing large numbers of workers, and dependent on technological innovation, was remarkably untypical of the growth of the Birmingham economy at this time and indeed for the early decades of the 19th century. Hopkins (1989) emphatically demonstrates that the great expansion of Birmingham industry owed little to large-scale technological change; neither was it based on water or steam-driven machinery housed in factories; it was not like the Lancashire spinning industry. Steam power in Birmingham was of relatively little importance until the 1830s, its countless small workshops making small use of it. It was largely inapplicable to gun making, the jewellery trade, toy making and the glass industry, and where it was of utility (in the primary metal industries), iron and brass founding did not really start to expand until well into the 19th century. Birmingham was not the steam-powered, factory cradle of the Industrial Revolution.

Moreover, Birmingham remained very much a mixture of the old and the new. Alongside the great factory at Soho, the small businesses survived. It was a case of tradition and the influence of existing industries *versus* innovation and the rise of new manufacture. It is a nice point to recall that as late as 1843 the tithe map of Edgbaston Parish still showed Speedwell Mill and Edgbaston Mill on the Rea, Pebble Mill on the Bourn Brook, and Over Mill below Edgbaston Pool on the Chad Brook, as blade mills.

At the onset of the 19th century the industrial structure of Birmingham was provided by its specialist craftsmen housed in small workshops; they employed hand tools largely without powered machinery. The gun trade became concentrated in the streets around St Mary's to the north of the town centre; it was a typical metal-working industry employing a wide range of skilled workmen in small establishments. Gun barrels and locks were made elsewhere, the barrels requiring machinery. Huge numbers of guns were made: over 1 740 000 for the Board of Ordnance between 1804 and 1815 in the Napoleonic wars, more than double the number made elsewhere in England during that time.

The brass industry expanded rapidly with widening demand. An 18th century market for brass fittings for carriages and harness, cabinet accessories, cocks, taps and gauges for steam engines and plumbing requisites grew in the 19th century, and production accelerated with the use of gas lighting and the need for associated brass appliances. Local manufacturers started to make brass on their own account; a site was commemorated by an old street name, Brasshouse Passage, off Broad Street. Brass bedsteads became a notable product of the 1830s and brass making became the most important industry in Birmingham, leading the world in this trade. While Manchester led in cotton, Bradford in wool, Sheffield in steel, Birmingham's forté was brass, its products found in all countries in gas fittings, railway and ship engines, coins and ornaments of every description.

The toy industry was subject to the vagaries of fashion. The buckle trade collapsed by the end of the 18th century but was replaced by growth in the button trade. In due time one form of button plating was replaced by the introduction of electroplating from Sheffield after its invention in 1838, but by the 1840s the button trade itself had peaked. Pin making dated from the middle of the 18th century; made by hand in a process whereby the work of fourteen different individuals went into the making of a single pin, the manufacture gave employment to numerous women and children, but by the 1840s mechanisation was widespread.

The older part of the toy industry was absorbed by the jewellery trade; relatively insignificant at the beginning of the 19th century it was one of the most prominent by mid-century, specialising in middle-class jewellery and cheap trinket ware. The early years of Victoria's reign saw the wearing of jewellery become more fashionable, but it was the discovery of an effective method of electroplating which marked the real increase in trade for Birmingham (Gledhill, 1988). John Wright with George Richards Elkington, co-partner with his cousin Henry of Elkington's Works, discovered the new method which was less erratic and cheaper than the previous one. Still typically workshop based, mass-produced plated, cheap jewellery could now be marketed. Specialised services followed: gold chains, studs and links, official insignia, and the making of watch cases.

Alongside the three metal industries, there was a multitude of smaller concerns. The manufacture of flint glass was important, though never on a scale attained in Stourbridge, with specialist trade in window glass, plate glass, lighthouse lenses and optical glass. The local firm Chance Bros won a contract for the supply of nearly one million square feet of window glass for the Crystal Palace in 1851 (and for 750 000 square feet more when the Palace was moved to Penge). The making of papier mâché, pioneered in Birmingham, gave rise to the production of a variety of goods including cabinets, tables and tea trays. Some decorative finishes were applied, such as that of japanning, popularised by the printer Baskerville. The minting of coins became well established. Other metal trade derivatives included screw-making, and the making of umbrella frames and machine made nails. Birmingham also took the lead in introducing steel pens. Machinery was introduced in the 1830s, Josiah Mason, who formerly worked in a buckle-maker's shop in Kidderminster, being the pioneer as Briggs (1988) recounts in his inventory of 'Victorian things'.

All this development in the first half of the century was achieved not through factory development but through the multiplication of small work-shops. The physical development of Birmingham industry was markedly different from the textile industries of Yorkshire and Lancashire, and the finished iron industry of the nearby Black Country. A small factory may have consisted of a row of converted dwelling houses; workshops were similarly in domestic premises. At mid-century the smaller workshops were still predominant over the larger industrial establishments which employed steam power, and they were concentrated around the town centre. The scene was vividly captured by de Tocqueville when he visited Birmingham in 1835:

> These folk never have a minute to themselves. They work as if they must get rich in the evening and die the next day. They are generally very intelligent people, but intelligent in the American way. The town itself has no analogy with other English provincial towns . . . It is an immense workshop, a huge forge, a vast shop. One only sees busy people and faces brown with smoke. One hears nothing but the sound of hammers and the whistle of steam escaping from boilers. (Briggs, 1964, p. 223)

A growing town, and an increasingly prosperous one in spite of the pro-longed setback of the Napoleonic Wars and disruption to world trade, meant an expanding trading and service element in the Birmingham economy. A demand for housing meant more construction workers. Food suppliers such as butchers, bakers and tea dealers multiplied. A widening middle class required the services of tailors, mercers and drapers. A service sector took root.

Important consequences for the social history of Birmingham can be seen from these features of economic development. A local middle class was emerging by the late 18th century. A directory of 1770 listed 68 merchants and factors; another directory in 1802 listed 140 such men. The historian Hutton reckoned that in 1783 209 inhabitants possessed upwards of £5 000; of these, 10 had £50 000 and three had £100 000. An analysis in 1828 was that 301 persons had £5000 of property, of whom 26 had £50 000 and 15 £100 000. But there was no capitalist aristocracy in the town. Industry was carried on by small manufacturers, with no unbridgeable social division amongst the workforce. Another important aspect was that a large proportion of the Birmingham labour force was skilled: the census of 1841 assigned only 11% of adult males in the town to the category of unskilled labour. All this contributed to a set of conditions in which a political alliance could be struck between the working and the middle classes. Later in the century a prominent middle class, with a distinctive cultural and intellectual force, assumed an undisputed leadership.

In the meantime we can emphasise again that the course of social and economic development in Birmingham (and throughout the West Midlands for that matter) was marked by no drastic discontinuity from the past. Whereas the processes of change in manufacturing towns in the north and north west were attracting concern, there were no such polarities in the Midlands. Birmingham achieved an altogether happier adaptation of traditional values to urban and industrial life than did many of its rivals. There was no great gulf between workman and employer, and in this respect the social and political state of the town differed markedly from, say, Manchester.

The growing town

During the last 40 years of the 18th century Birmingham's population more than doubled, while that of the Midlands increased by about 60%, and that for the country as a whole by 45%. The town was taking on an urban supremacy within its region, while the region itself was surging faster than the nation. A new shift in national population distribution, based on migration from rural to urban, was unfolding.

Birmingham's population rose by another two and a half times in the first 40 years of the 19th century (73 670 to 182 922). The town's growth was not quite so fast after 1801 as that of some other large towns, but parallels are difficult to draw because of the incidence of town boundaries: Birmingham was tightly hemmed in and growth may have been accredited to adjoining townships.

In the unprecedented surge of new building, new ways of raising capital to build houses were devised. Richard Ketley, proprietor of the Golden Cross Inn, just below Bath Street, founded the earliest known building society, established in 1775, and others soon followed in the region, as at Dudley, Wolverhampton, Handsworth and Coventry. Typically these societies would bring together a group of people, perhaps up to 50 in number, who would contribute between four and six shillings a week to a common fund, the security allowing them to borrow sufficient capital to build. As the houses were completed, the members balloted for ownership; when all had been provided with houses, the club was wound up. In the 1780s one in ten of the stock of new dwellings in Birmingham was provided by building societies. Five building societies were founded between 1780 and 1800, buying land for development and letting out either houses or sites for houses.

The growth in the number of houses was mostly accommodated in courtyard arrangements; in the 1830s Birmingham had over 2000 courts. But beyond the edge of the town new streets invaded the adjoining fields. Typically in 1799 when all that remained of Birmingham Heath was enclosed, eight new streets were quickly laid out on the previously open and waste land. The building societies themselves made new streets and extended others in Deritend.

Within the town large gardens were still common. In fact Birmingham had a relatively plentiful supply of open land in the form of allotments. Known as 'guinea gardens', from the fact that they were originally bought for a guinea (£1.05), they were handed on from one generation to another. (They were gradually extinguished by the middle of the 19th century, though a sole survivor exists today in the Westbourne Road Leisure Gardens Association.) Hence, in addition to housing development at the periphery, there was scope for infilling to higher densities. In these various ways the town expanded with estates forming distinct enclaves.

As we have already seen, before 1750 the Colmore Estate was developed in the district between Snow Hill and Congreve Street. To the east was another estate occupied by Dr Ash, a leading local physician; after his departure for Bath in 1788 his land was sold and developed to become the suburb of Ashted. Additionally there was expansion westwards, spacious houses in Easy Hill appearing in the 1760s (Figure 3.2). Baskerville's house (Figure 3.3) nearby was sold in 1788 and development proceeded on the seven acres of land adjoining. Summer Hill, over the top of the sandstone ridge, became the site for a small district of elegant houses built in 1790, but they were later overcome by manufacturing premises. On another estate the names of its successive owners are commemorated in Sherlock Street and Gooch Street. The land had been bought in 1730 by Dr Sherlock, Bishop of London; his successor Sir Thomas Gooch inherited the estate in 1766 and developed it. Peripheral estate development of this kind increasingly constituted the main form of Birmingham's territorial spread. It was popular with the well-to-do and by the early years of the 19th century a high proportion of the professional and ruling classes were living beyond the bounds of the old parish.

The rates of population increase, which all the growing towns experienced, were fuelled by in-migration with a consequent inevitable pressure on housing stock. As Hopkins (1989) puts it, for the country as a whole: 'Lodging houses multiplied, older middle-class houses were divided up into tenements, attics and cellars were used as living quarters, and row upon row of new and sometimes jerry-built housing were rapidly constructed' (p. 118). But all towns were not alike and Birmingham avoided the worst excesses to befall some rivals. It did not have the high density of Dublin, the tenement style of building was confined to Scottish cities, the cellar dwellings of Liverpool and Manchester were nowhere replicated in Birmingham, and the oddity of the 'two-up and two-down' terraced flats was concentrated on Tyneside. The town did, however, have large numbers of back-to-back houses, perhaps two thirds of the population being housed in them at mid-century; it was a form of housing construction which was

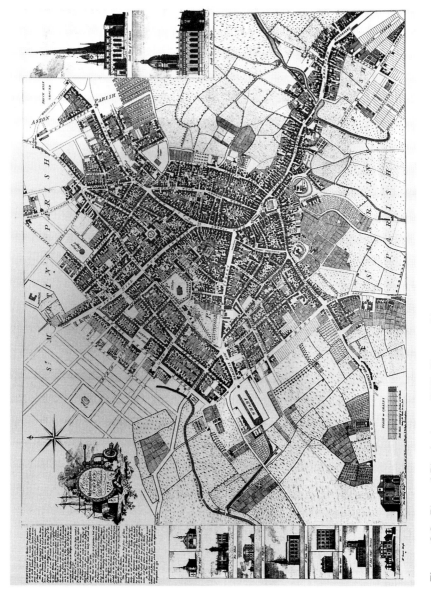

Figure 3.2 Plan of Birmingham, 1778. Thomas Hanson.

Figure 3.3 Baskerville House.

Drawn by P.H. Witton Jun.

Engraved by W. F.

warm, cheap and relatively popular with both occupant and builder. But it also had its courts, the older ones of which were narrow, ill-ventilated, badly drained and, as a consequence of inadequate privy emptying, filthy and unhealthy. Indeed, for much of the century adverse comment on Birmingham's housing stock featured health hazards rather than constructional deficiencies.

The anxiety rested within a wider frame of reference and was reflected nationally, and indeed internationally. Andrew Lees (1985) has argued that from the 1820s onwards British cities (and subsequently big cities in France, Germany and the USA) became primary objects of concern. These cities, 'rapidly growing concentrations of flesh, blood, stone and glass, of men and machines, of people and power' (p. 305) seemed to encapsulate within their boundaries a vast range of crucially important processes that went hand in hand with urbanisation. Novelists and men of letters; social theorists and sociologists; historians who sought to make sense of urban development; protestant clergymen, medical doctors, sanitary experts, municipal administrators, local reformers, architects and planners, essayists and journalists, all combined to awaken and shape public consciousness of urban life. Birmingham took its place in this. The targets were material and physical hardships stemming from overcrowding and poor housing, bolstered by fears about sanitation, urban mortality rates, crime and violence and the ugliness of cities. Sanitary reform was one of the early solutions to be adopted.

In fact the public health reports of the 1840s speak relatively well of Birmingham. The prevalence of separate dwellings was noted, as was the well-drained nature of the town. All main streets had underground drainage, though there were open sewers in Bordesley and Deritend. Chadwick's *Report* from the Poor Law Commissioners *On the Sanitary Condition of the Labouring Population of Great Britain* (1842) contained evidence that 'the houses . . . are on the whole built upon an improved plan. This town . . . is distinguished apparently by an immunity from fever, and the general health of the population is high' (Flinn, 1965, p. 89). But there were concerns. One was the state of the River Rea, 'a black sluggish stream' which received the town's sewers. Just before the railway terminus the Rea's water was 'not sufficient to dilute and wash away the refuse which it receives in passing through the town, and . . . in hot weather it is consequently very offensive, and in some situations in these seasons is covered with a thick scum of decomposing matters' (*op cit*, p. 363).

It was the common lodging house, however, which attracted anxiety as a source of contagious disease in almost every large town. Chadwick regarded them as 'stages for the various orders of tramps and mendicants who traverse the country from one end to the other, and spread physical pestilence, as well as moral deprivation' (*op cit*, p. 411). The evidence from Birmingham was that:

Lodging-houses for the lowest class of persons . . . principally exist near the centre of the town, many of them in courts; but great numbers of front houses, in some of the old streets, are entirely occupied as lodging-houses. They are generally in a very filthy condition; and, being the resort of the most abandoned characters, they are sources of extreme misery and vice. These houses may be divided into three kinds – mendicants' lodging-houses, lodging-houses where Irish resort, and houses in which prostitutes live, or which they frequent. (*op cit*, p. 411)

Incidentally, the Irish had for long been viewed as a factor in the generation and communication of disease: one witness before the Irish Poor Inquiry of 1836 commented that 'The Irish in Birmingham are the very pests of Society; they generate contagion' (*op cit*, p. 15).

The courtyards, representing a form of high density infilling within a street block, with access from a narrow entrance (an 'entry'), attracted most criticism. The houses were small and of the poorest construction. Single brick walls divided the properties, which were regularly infested with bugs and cockroaches. Pumps serving up to 400 people drew water from underground wells. A wash house, an ashpit for rubbish and privies framed an undrained open piece of ground. The custom of keeping pigs both in the courts and in areas of poor housing generally was evidently widespread: more than 3000 pigs were numbered in the borough in 1845.

The growth of Birmingham during the 19th century saw the continued extension of building estates on the belt of fields and gardens which formed the periphery of the town (Wise and Thorpe, 1950). To the east the suburb of Ashted took shape around St James' Church. To the north beyond the Fazeley Canal, St George's-in-the-Fields marked the layout of new streets. To the west of the New Hall Estate, now almost fully built up, Islington emerged as a fashionable suburb. To the south, new development in Deritend and in the Rea lowlands confirmed an eastward growth for the town.

But the most remarkable development, throughout the century, was the creation of Edgbaston in the early years of the 19th century. The Edgbaston Estate had been bought by Sir Richard Gough in 1717, for £20 400. A wealthy merchant and director of the East India Company, he settled at Edgbaston and engaged on the rebuilding of Edgbaston Hall; in 1719 he enclosed the grounds as a deer park. His son, Henry, married Barbara Calthorpe, heiress to a clutch of estates elsewhere in the country. The second Sir Henry became Sir Henry Gough-Calthorpe; he was ennobled in 1796 as Lord Calthorpe. Previously he had moved his family from Edgbaston Hall to the Calthorpe home at Ampton in Suffolk. Never again was any member of the Calthorpe family to live in Edgbaston; the Hall was leased out to distinguished tenants (and was converted into a golf club in the 20th century).

The third Lord Calthorpe, who held the title from 1807 to 1851, initiated a series of changes which transformed the estate. The story provides a classic example of the way in which the aristocracy engaged in town development at that time (Cannadine, 1980). The estate originally acquired totalled 1700 acres, but other lands adjoining were also purchased to bring the total to 2500 acres. It was Birmingham's largest single land holding and as the town embarked on its dramatic growth, the geographical qualities of the site became apparent. It had a sunny aspect and, with rolling topography, was well drained; its location south west of the town protected it from industrial and residential smoke. As a site for building development it was well nigh perfect.

Between 1810 and 1813 Lord Calthorpe and his agent John Harris decided to begin the systematic development of Edgbaston as a building estate. The guiding principles proved highly significant for the future development of Birmingham: speculative builders, working class housing, industry, manufacturers and trade were excluded, while the industrial elite of the town were welcomed. There was astute vigilance in estate management. When the Birmingham and Worcester Canal crossed the estate, clauses in the Act prohibited the building of factories, workshops or warehouses, forbade the construction of reservoirs on the land, and ensured that the towpath was on the west side, furthest away from the Hall.

Building leases were granted in increasing number, after a slow start. Agricultural tenants were moved to other farms as and when they became vacant. Churches and other amenities were encouraged. Educational and charitable institutions, suitably reflecting prestige, promoted Edgbaston's successful image. Favourable terms were extended to the Deaf and Dumb Asylum in 1814, the Botanical and Horticultural Society in 1836 and the General Institution for the Blind in 1851. Roads were laid out and plots marked. The fringes of the estate were variously developed, but the core area between Hagley Road and Bristol Road was laid out with wide, curving roads as a suburb for the wealthy of Birmingham. Restrictive covenants in the building leases (normally for 99 years) extended to building materials, the setting back of frontages and prohibitions of certain uses. By the 1840s a peak building period had begun.

Edgbaston was exceptional; urban expansion for new housing usually came haphazardly, street by street. Birmingham, decade by decade, was pushing out into open country, as Gill (1952) describes. By 1831 the northern limit of housing was New John Street. Beyond it was open country to Aston; Hockley Brook was still a rural stream. Warstone Lane marked the north western boundary. In Edgbaston development was largely confined to Calthorpe, Frederick and George Roads (or Streets as they were known then), Wheeley's Road (Lane) and the lower end of Wellington and Sir Harry's Road. In the north east Duddeston Meadows and Vauxhall Gardens were still open. To the south there was housing beyond Moseley Street, eastward to the newly built Trinity Church at

Bordesley, as far as Duddeston Row. Bordesley itself was still a district of gardens and open fields, as the name Bordesley Green suggests. To the south west, along Bristol Street and Pershore Road, the outer spread of housing had reached Benacre Street (Figure 3.4).

By 1850 expansion could be seen on every side. To the north new streets were marked out in the fields between New John Street and Lozells Lane. A solid belt of urban development formed the northern boundary of the Borough extending into Aston Manor, Lozells and Handsworth along Soho Hill. In the east housing had progressed down Garrison Lane and St Andrew's Street, and Balsall Heath grew out along the Moseley Road and the Birmingham and Gloucester Railway. Vauxhall Gardens were closed. In the south Stratford Place marked the edge of the built-up area. Towards Moseley several roads now ran westwards: Belgrave Road, Sherbourne Road, Balsall Heath Road. Along Bristol Road there was housing as far as St Luke's Church. Beyond Bath Row housing now covered an area previously devoted to gardens.

The sustained rise in population, the increase in numbers of houses, the laying out of new streets, the emergence of new fashionable districts removed from the squalor of the older areas, and the mushrooming of the town's manufacturing capacity all pointed to a dramatic change in Birmingham's status as a growing town. But as its very appearance was being transformed a second transport revolution introduced a new urban feature, the effect of which would carry Birmingham from a manufacturing town to an industrial city. The railway age arrived.

A railway was planned to link London, Birmingham and Liverpool as early as 1824. The intention then was to build a line from Birmingham to Liverpool via Wolverhampton and Nantwich and to run branches to Dudley and Stourbridge, the collieries and ironworks of Shropshire, the Potteries and Chester; a line to London would follow. In the event the merchants of Liverpool made their priority a link with Manchester. The line having been made in 1830, the Grand Junction Railway Company project was undertaken from Birmingham to Newton-le-Willows where a connection was made with the Liverpool–Manchester line. The London link was under construction at the same time; there was opposition from interests in Northampton and from landowners with property on the route, but by 1835 two thirds of the land needed had been acquired. A site for a London terminus had also been secured at Euston Grove, instead of the original site at Camden Town.

The Liverpool line was finished in 1837; the one to London in 1838. Both lines approached Birmingham from the east (where the gradients were easiest) and the two companies agreed to share a common station: the impressive, dignified Curzon Street. This terminus had a number of disadvantages, notably its location on the edge of town and the poor road links with the town centre, but it was some years before improvements

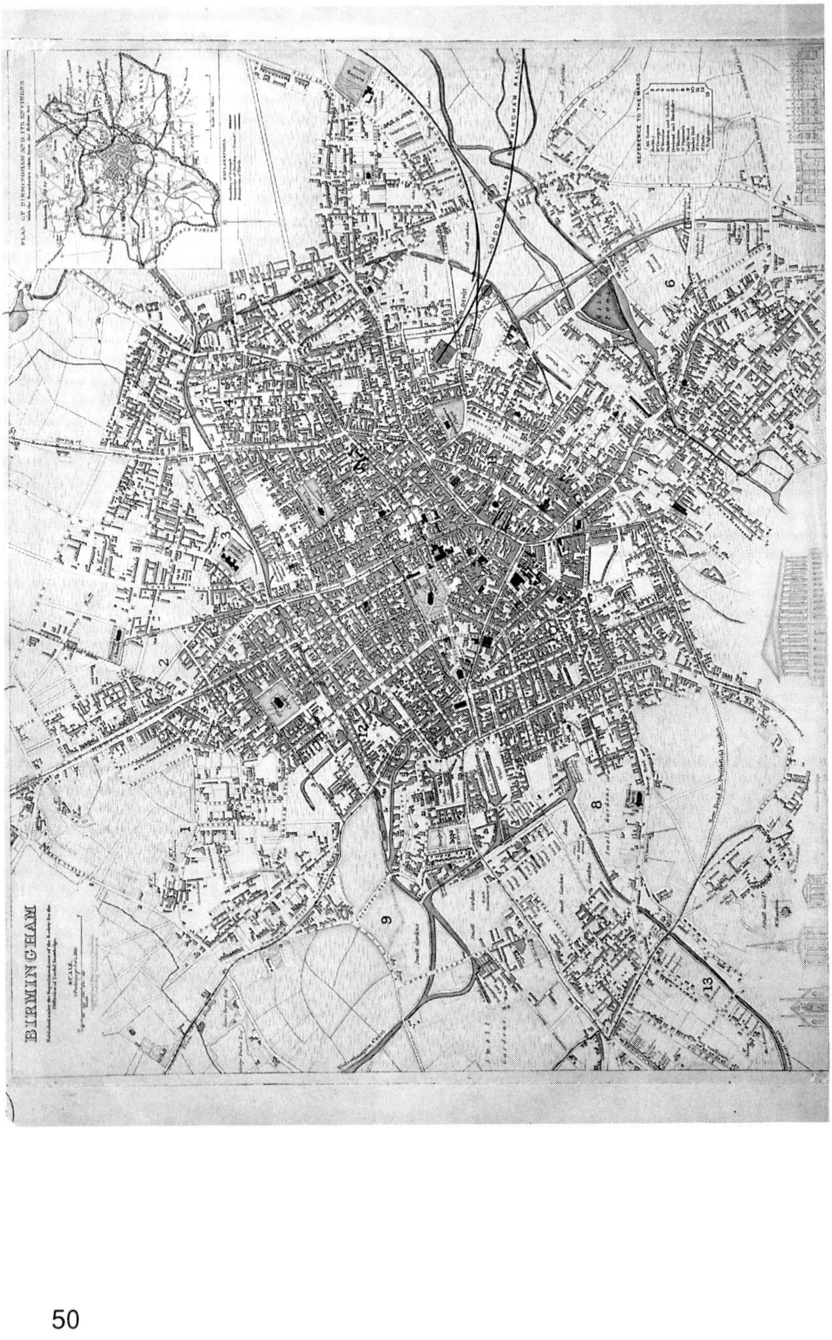

Figure 3.4 Plan of Birmingham, 1839.

could be made. Links were made to Gloucester in 1840, Derby in 1841 and Bristol in 1842, so quite early on Birmingham was joined to the four great English ports of London, Liverpool, Bristol and Hull.

Kellett (1969) emphasises the importance of land ownership in Birmingham's railway development. The railway lines to the north west discreetly skirted the Colmores' valuable New Hall Estate. To the east and south Sir Thomas Gooch was the most important landowner, but, an elderly man already in the 1840s, he raised no great objection. The other principal landowners with whom the railway companies had to negotiate included corporate bodies such as the Lench's Charity and the Free Grammar School, but some of their lands were already seedy and disreputable and it could easily be shown that railway development would actually improve them. Negotiations with the canal companies were also necessary. The Birmingham Canal Company had secured a perpetual lease on six acres of central land, just east of Paradise and Navigation Streets, which proved to be very valuable for long-term railway development in this area. Indeed looking at the history of railway construction in Birmingham the superimposition of railway routes onto the old canal pattern, and the absorption of the central canal warehousing and wharfage area, is a striking feature. Overall, however, the essential impact on the urban form of Birmingham was to leave Edgbaston in the west scarcely disturbed, but to admit the wholesale intrusion of railway yards and associated trades in the east.

The mania of railway construction came to a head in the years 1844–6. No less than thirteen projects for railways running into Birmingham were awaiting official approval when the Board of Trade suspended its consideration of plans in November 1845. Several new companies were proposing to build stations in other parts of town. Up to 1851 there was only one station site, at Curzon Street. To this terminal came the lines from the south east (London), the north east (Derby), the north west (Crewe) and the south west (Gloucester). The Birmingham and Derby Railway Co. opened a separate, low-level station a little further out, at Lawley Street. The Grand Junction Railway (from Crewe) also built its own station, first a temporary one at Vauxhall and then its own separate station facing Curzon Street. Hence there were really four stations under one name.

The caution which had made Curzon Street a terminus was abandoned (relegated to a centre for heavy goods traffic) in favour of Navigation (later New) Street Station, accessible through tunnels at either end. Here, a network of streets was purchased; poor housing in Peck Lane, Old Meeting Street, the Froggery and a number of other streets and alleys was cleared in the town's first concerted attempt at redevelopment. Squalid property was swept away: 'cul de sacs or alleys along which it was not wise to venture, packed with brothels and thieves' nests, breeding grounds for typhoid, cholera and crime' (Kellett, 1969, p. 140). Both New Street (opened in

1854) and Snow Hill (1852, in a project which also involved housing clearance) gave access to the Stour Valley and the Black Country. New Street station was particularly well sited, within 100 yards of Birmingham's best hotel (The Royal), and near the Post Office, banks, professional quarters and the markets. The central terminus, with underground through transport, made Birmingham a model of its kind; when it was enlarged to 15 acres in the early 1880s it was the nearest approach in any of the major cities to a single grand central station.

Remarkably, compared with many other cities, Birmingham had little difficulty in accommodating the railway and all its associated activities. Fortunately, the railway companies compromised early on with regard to sites and lines. No great warehousing problem emerged. Birmingham was a manufacturer of imperishable small wares, and goods traffic was handled without undue consumption of urban space.

Implications for the life and trade of Birmingham can hardly be exaggerated. Canal traffic was affected belatedly, 50 years or more elapsing before an absolute decline set in: the tonnage on the Birmingham Canal Navigations rose steadily from 4½ million in 1848 to 8½ million in 1898, and only later fell to 7½ million in 1905. But the daily coach trade collapsed almost at once. The original railway time-table showed that the London journey time took 5½ hours; to Liverpool it was 4½ hours (though the first train completed the journey of 97 miles in 3 hours 17 minutes). But there were six trains daily each way on the London line and twelve to Liverpool. Geographical time and distance changed abruptly.

Town governance

We have already observed that at the beginning of these years of change Birmingham still had its manorial court, though it had little share in the administration of the town, with the parish the principal institution to supervise local affairs. But increasingly it was a new body, the improvement commissioners, which was entrusted with the regulation of the thrustful manufacturing centre. An unfolding story, described in detail by Gill (1952) can be summarised as follows.

There was clearly a national problem; Birmingham was in no way unique. As urban populations burgeoned, the ways in which the growing towns were administered required radical reform. Unprecedented problems were encountered as towns expanded in size and grew in internal complexity. Roads needed more frequent repair as traffic volumes increased with buoyant trade. New streets were laid out and houses built to accommodate the growing numbers of people. Streets were widened as they became congested; encroachments onto narrow thoroughfares had to be removed. These tasks required a supervised workforce, but compulsory labour, managed by untrained surveyors and supervised by amateur justices, could not be relied upon to be effective. Increased population numbers made it more difficult to deal with law breaking: apprehending the individual felon or dealing with riots were tasks increasingly beyond the parish constables and manorial courts. Birmingham as much as anywhere found that the town's inherited institutional structure for local administration was increasingly unsuitable for the environmental and community affairs with which it had to contend.

Reform, when it came, proved piecemeal and *ad hoc*, and progressive measures were protracted over a period of almost a century before the elements of a local government system, as we would know it today, were in place. The initial device was the Improvement Act, sought by interested parties of town residents; the powers provided for the setting up of improvement or street commissioners. Nationally, between 1785 and 1800, more than 200 Improvement Acts received Parliamentary approval, each providing for specified improvements to particular towns. Five Acts for Birmingham between 1769 and 1828 established new arrangements for dealing with the issues of the growing town, and over time the manorial court and the parish passed into oblivion. The commissioners had duties originally in cleansing and lighting, but these widened to include the maintenance of a force of watchmen and the improvement of market facilities. Ultimately the commissioners functioned with *ad hoc* powers over streets, markets, scavenging, the Poor Law, highways and public order.

The purpose of the first Act (1769) was to make the streets of Birmingham cleaner, safer and more convenient. Birmingham joined Manchester as one of the first of the new provincial centres to remedy the deficiencies of its ancient manorial and parochial administration by establishing a statutory authority with specific powers. Fifty commissioners, named in the Act, were entrusted with the task, and they were given limited powers of removing nuisances, street cleaning (undertaken by officials) and of demolishing nearly a dozen houses which, at the lower end of New Street, left only an archway for vehicles and pedestrians. Other dwellings were listed for clearance in the area of the Bull Ring – the first of a number of actions over a period of many years to deal with the market problem, both in terms of congestion and location. (Markets were held out of doors, there being no market hall; cattle were sold in the High Street, fish in Dale End, and farm produce and general merchandise round the Old Cross in the High Town where the Bull Ring approached High Street.) The commissioners also had the power of installing lamps in the streets, hence the legislation was commonly known as the Lamp Act.

The second Improvement Act 1773 saw 29 new commissioners nominated. They were given new powers to make fresh regulations for the use of the streets and to undertake improvements in five places listed in a schedule. They were also given the right to appoint watchmen – the right, but not the power, it should be added, because their cost could not be afforded. Little work was done by these commissioners.

The third Act 1801 met a fresh demand for the public endowment of the watch. This was the time of general unrest during the time of the French Wars, and there was still the memory of the riots in the town ten years earlier. The context then had been the deteriorating relations between Anglicans and dissenting elements, when there was agitation for the repeal of the Test and Corporation Acts. But the precipitating factor in Birmingham's riots was political, not religious. Dr Joseph Priestley, sympathetic to the French Revolution, aroused mob hostility; his house on Sparkhill and the Old Meeting House (of which he was Pastor) were both destroyed and big houses set on fire, including those of John Taylor, a leading button manufacturer, William Hutton, bookseller and local historian, and John Baskerville, the printer. The riots lasted a week and the local magistrates proved powerless to hold them in check. The new Act gave the necessary powers to levy the higher rates required to maintain the Watch. The commissioners (50 in number) were given the power to build a public office for commissioners' meetings and for the use of local magistrates. There were also new powers of street regulation, a new schedule of street improvements and a list of buildings for clearance.

The commissioners duly appointed a watch committee and built a public office (in Moor Street, completed in 1807). But their primary interest proved to be in market trading. The general market was transferred from High Street to the Bull Ring and the levying of tolls was leased from the manor. Thus it was that the work of the improvement commissioners progressively assumed a greater importance than that of the manorial court and the parish. But any notion of town governance was a very limited one: in 1804 the commission's local services were maintained on a budget of £2700 – and that for a town of more than 70 000 people. Moreover administration was geographically cramped: the town's boundaries were much less than that of the ancient manor, and less even than that of the parish.

The incremental path was slow. The fourth Act 1812, a consolidating Act for the previous three, named 99 persons as commissioners, Thomas Attwood becoming chairman. They became the sole authority for making, paving, draining and repairing all highways in the town. Their main interest, however, still lay in markets (Figure 3.5) and, after a new meat market (Smithfield) had been built on the site of Birmingham's moated manor house in 1815, the planning and building of a market hall became their prime concern. With schemes also in hand to enlarge the public office and build a town hall it was necessary to prepare a new bill for enlarged borrowing powers. A fifth Act was passed in 1828.

At this point the painfully slow progress of local reform was eclipsed by national movements for parliamentary and municipal reform, in which Birmingham played a large part. It took a further 20 years for the

Figure 3.5 High Street Market, 1829.

consequences of political agitation and no little turmoil in the town itself to work their way through to the establishment of a local government structure which would serve Birmingham well for the rest of the century and beyond.

The scene now turned to Thomas Attwood. From the library of his house in Harborne he drafted a general plan for the mobilisation of mass support for parliamentary reform. As the movement spread across the whole country he worked out a detailed constitution for a 'Political Union for the Protection of Public Rights'. It is not necessary to go into the details of the success which attended the agitation which was fomented; suffice to say that a general election followed the passing of the Reform Act in 1832 and Birmingham sent two Members to the new House of Commons, Thomas Attwood and Joshua Scholefield, both radicals, elected without opposition.

One important consequence of the Reform Act (for our story) was that a parliamentary committee and then a royal commission proceeded to inquire into municipal government. But let us return briefly to the improvement commissioners, who after 1828 showed rather more vigour than some of their predecessors. The increased money at their disposal, and their right to all the market tolls, enabled the commissioners in 1831 to buy the rectangle of land between Philip Street and Bull Street for a new market hall (Figure 3.6). A contract was let and the building formally opened in 1834. The architect was Charles Edge. With a 500ft long roof, a classical rectangular building with a great Doric porch supporting the central arch of the entrance, it was reputed to be the finest market hall in England. There were markets elsewhere for livestock, meat and fish, but the new central facility, large enough for 600 stalls, was a welcome boon. The central streets were now gas lit (since 1818 in fact) and the town centre began to take on an appearance more in keeping with Birmingham's growing size and importance; Christ Church (by Charles Norton, 1814), was impressively sited at the corner of New Street and Colmore Row, and Charles Barry's Gothic buildings for King Edward VI's School provided a classical facade for New Street between 1834 and 1838.

The germ of a modern civic centre was sown when the commissioners began to buy up land at the western end of New Street and Colmore Row. Land with a frontage to Paradise Street enabled the Town Hall (really an Assembly Hall) to be built. This neoclassical interpretation of the Temple of Jupiter Statore in Rome was designed by Joseph Aloysius Hansom and his partner Welsh, as a result of an architectural competition, the first to be held in Birmingham. The building was started in 1834 but the financial arrangements between the commissioners, their architects and the contractors led to Hansom's early bankruptcy. Work on the building continued at least until 1849.

We return to the national scene in order to explain later events in Birmingham. The Municipal Corporations Act 1835 repealed the old

THE MARKET HALL _ BIRMINGHAM.

Figure 3.6 The Market Hall.

municipal charters, and a total of 178 reformed cities and boroughs came into existence in November of that year, the Act prescribing a new constitution for the towns. Birmingham of course had no charter and, together with some of the other largest and fastest growing towns in the country, was excluded from the new arrangements. But the same arrangements for the new type of town government were there for Birmingham to aim at: a council elected by resident householders and a division of the area into wards.

The Government's intention was that the populous towns, especially those which were parliamentary boroughs already (and Birmingham figured under both categories) should be granted charters individually, if application were made. The initiative rested with the towns concerned. There was no prospect of a general Act transferring to the new councils the powers of *ad hoc* bodies, such as the Birmingham street commissioners. Locally the Liberals favoured a charter while the Tories opposed it, arguing that the town was well governed already, increased costs would result, and that the powers of the new council would actually be less than those of the improvement commissioners. But the tide of argument was in favour and a local petition was supported. The Charter of Incorporation was received in 1838, municipal government extending to a wider area than that exercised over by the commissioners: Birmingham was now administered as one area in conjunction with Edgbaston, Deritend and Bordesley, Duddeston and Nechells. The Borough was divided into 13 wards, governed by a Council comprising a mayor, 16 aldermen and 48 councillors. Ten wards elected three councillors each; three wards elected six each. This arrangement survived until 1873 when the number of wards was raised to 14, each electing three councillors.

More was to happen yet before the emergent local government structure was finally put into place. The Charter, having been received, was soon the focus of discontent. Opposition came to a head over the cost of policing, the context provided by the rise of an organised Chartist movement. Early stirrings were seen in Birmingham at a meeting held at Holloway Head in August 1838, and less than a year later (July 1839) Chartist riots wrought havoc in the Bull Ring. The new Council prepared to levy a rate on the borough with the object of setting up a police force. But the overseers and church wardens refused to accept the precept to collect a rate. There was an impasse and for some time a quite impossible position obtained. The governing body of the town, penniless and without power, saw Birmingham governed by other authorities: the street commissioners remained in office and the Government took over responsibility for the police.

Chartism violence passed, however, and by 1842 the situation was calm enough for Birmingham's control over the police to be restored and for its processes of municipal government to finally begin in earnest. The rest of the decade was in effect a period of apprenticeship in public administration for the new Council. The Paving Department, directed by the Surveyor John Piggott Smith, brought about much needed improvement. In 1840 local residents were freed from the payment of tolls at Five Ways, as a consequence of which a very extensive suburban district was opened up. Meanwhile the commission exercised responsibilities over the railway lines: a new road was proposed, in effect a continuation of New Street across Dale End towards the Curzon Street terminus. It was constructed as far as Moor Street but the project was abandoned when New Street station replaced Curzon Street. The commission also projected new sewerage schemes with an outlet into the River Tame at Saltley.

The two bodies were working in parallel, but the duality came to an end at the close of the decade. The opportunity for this came with the Public Health Act 1848. The Act specified that if one in ten of the ratepayers in any borough so approved, an inspector from the General Board of Health should visit the town. A local board of health would be approved if a recommendation in favour were made; that body would normally be the Borough Council. The required signatures were readily forthcoming in Birmingham and an inspector strongly recommended a local board. Discussions between the Council and the Commission were not productive and the council determined on a local Act. Its promotion was successful (the Improvement Act 1851) and the commissioners' duties were transferred to the council at the beginning of 1852.

It was the end of an era and the beginning of a new one. A system devised to meet the needs of an 18th century town was finally replaced by one to cope with the complexities of a modern city. The financial resources of the new Borough Council were trebled. They could be directed to an extensive programme of improvement: widening, levelling, clearing and paving streets, providing a good water supply and implementing the ambitious scheme of drainage just begun. Moreover recent legislation had encouraged the provision of parks, recreation grounds, libraries, museums and art galleries. The manufacturing town was in transition to an industrial city and a new body for local government was in place to assist in its progress.

4
The Industrial City 1851–1890s

By mid-19th century some of the raw edges of town life had gone, or at least were eased. Sanitation and housing improvements were on the way, and new administrative arrangements were finally in place for more effective town governance. The future was full of promise: industry was flourishing, rail links conferred great benefits, population growth continued apace, and Birmingham's status was at last being reflected in some imposing buildings in the town centre. By the close of the century the potential of the manufacturing town had been realised. An industrial city of premier rank emerged; its manufactured products were known across the world. It enjoyed an enviable administrative reputation; it was hailed for its ambitious improvement schemes; and it stood on the threshold of boundary enlargement that would give it elbow room to house its growing number of citizens for upwards of 50 years.

We can give a flavour of the progress made during the second half of the century by featuring three elements: industrial expansion, the spread of new housing, and town improvement undertaken by an energetic town council. But there was more to it than this. By 1900 it is possible to sketch Birmingham as a city almost in the terms that we would use today, hence, finally, we touch on some further elements of its appearance, structure and life: its transport (the tram network), the city centre and its parks and open spaces.

Industry

In 1850 Birmingham's manufacturing staples were guns, jewellery, buttons and brass products. During the second half of the century the industrial output diversified, with a vast array of metal products including tools of all description, light castings, hinges, fenders and grates, engineering and wood screw manufacture. Birmingham became the workshop of the world (Briggs, 1952). The service sector widened too. Banking developed; the Midland, founded in 1836 as the Birmingham Exchange Bank expanded to become the 20th largest in England and Wales by the 1870s. Commerce flourished; it was somehow appropriate for the penny post, introduced in 1840, to be the innovation of Rowland Hill, the son of a Birmingham schoolmaster.

Changes in fashion and the consequences of innovation led to the demise of some products and the emergence of new ones. It had always been so. In the previous century the buckle trade, which had peaked around 1770, was destroyed by the introduction of the shoe string. But there could be adaptation: metal buttons went out of fashion and in a constant search for alternatives buttons of glass, pearl, porcelain, and with fabric coating were produced. Quill pens were supplanted by steel pens. Tinplate and japanned-ware, famous in the 18th century for a wide range of commodities from trays to cash boxes, were challenged by electroplating. The japanned iron industry survived through the manufacture of such items as coal scuttles and baths, before it eventually gave way to products of sheet metal, copper and aluminium. The old-established wire-drawing industry was transformed in 1853 by the discovery of hardened steel wire; this led to new products such as piano wire, needles, hooks, springs, umbrella frames and wire ropes. Meanwhile the papier-mâché trade was altogether less successful in adaptation, and the trade had disappeared by the end of the century.

Some important developments had become apparent by the 1860s. Small workshops, while still thriving, were increasingly being absorbed in large factories. This was soon noticeable in the gun trade where large-scale production of military arms became centred in a number of pockets on the eastern fringe of the town. The largest single factory was that of the Birmingham Small Arms Company at Small Heath.

In 1853 the Government decided to set up its own manufacture of small arms, and a state factory was opened at Enfield (1854). The response from Birmingham, after the Crimean War, was given by a group of local gun-makers who built their premises on a 26-acre site at Small Heath in 1861. Birmingham's importance can be seen from the fact that of the six million weapons proofed nationally between 1855 and 1864, 4¼ million were produced in the town.

Birmingham became a centre for engineering in 1857. The Tangye brothers set up their works for the making of machines and after an early success in the making of hydraulic jacks, they later turned to such products as steam pumps and gas and oil engines. But it was with screw manufacture that Birmingham acquired a mid-century 'spectacular'. The key figure here was J. S. Nettlefold, initially an ironmonger in Holborn, London, where he set up a screw factory. He moved to Birmingham in 1842. At the 1851 Exhibition he was impressed by the efficiency of a new American screw-making machine which greatly increased productivity. With his brother in law, Joseph Chamberlain, he secured the English rights of working the machine. His son, also Joseph, came to Birmingham at the age of 18 to share in a business which grew rapidly: in 1850 the number of screws made weekly in the whole of England was 70 000 gross, while 15 years later Birmingham alone produced a weekly average of 130 000 gross.

Entrepreneurship and enterprise remained the gateway to prosperity. Some of it had very local origins indeed, and perhaps owed much to chance and perseverance. Take the Cadbury success for example. George and Richard Cadbury both inherited £5000 from their mother when she died in 1855; they took over the Bridge Street business in 1861 when their father retired (Gardiner, 1923). There were then only a dozen or so employees in a small concern, and they were approaching the end of their resources after three successive years of loss. Financial turnaround came with the discovery of making cocoa suitable for drinking. Up till then cocoa had been a gruel: cocoa, potato starch, sago flour and treacle, but with the cocoa butter taken out instead of flour added to counteract it, a palatable drink was the result. Within 15 years an expansion of the premises was necessary and a new plant at Bournville was constructed; the number of their employees soared – 300 by the late 1870s to nearly 1200 in 1889, and 6000 in 1914.

Equally, consider the Joseph Lucas story (Nockolds, 1976). From selling casks of paraffin around Hockley, he moved into selling buckets, shovels and pots. In a workshop in Little King Street he developed his first cycle lamp; by 1890 a five-storey factory on this site was then one of the tallest buildings in the area. The business successfully moved into producing a range of cycle lamps and accessories.

Meanwhile, Birmingham remained a centre for small units of production (Figure 4.1). In 1870 there were probably fewer than 20 firms in the town employing more than 500 persons, and many of these had existed before 1840. They included Gillott's and Mason's pen factories, Winfield's brass and engineering works, Aston's button factory and Elkington's electro plating business. There were also the three large railway carriage works at Saltley. In Smethwick there was Chance's glass works and Nettlefold and Chamberlain's screw factory. Several factories employed between 200 and 500 persons, but the great majority of establishments had fewer than 20 in their workforce.

By the beginning of the last quarter of the century Birmingham's position as workshop of the world entered a new phase: for the first time the performance of Birmingham and the Black Country was being challenged by foreign competition. It was masked for a short while by the boom years at the beginning of the 1870s. The output of pig iron in 1871 in South Staffordshire was the highest in any period in its history, equivalent to

Figure 4.1 The bedstead trade, cutting rods, Fisher Brown & Co. Ltd, Lionel Street 1902.

almost 11% of the total British supply. But depression followed, and the Black Country entered a long period of declining fortunes in both the coal trade and the mining of ironstone. In 1900 coal output was half that of 1865 and the decline was even more rapid after the turn of the century. There was also a change in the production of pig iron; the number of

63

furnaces fell, though output remained at 1875 levels until the Great War. Interestingly, the Black Country failed to become an important steel producer; except for the Bessemer plants in England, new steel districts had coastal locations because of imported iron ore. Birmingham therefore turned elsewhere for its supplies of crude steel, including Germany and Belgium before the end of the century. The consequences of this competition from other countries were seen less in Birmingham's immediate economic fortunes and more in terms of local and national politics: Joseph Chamberlain turned from free trade to a programme of tariff reform, with colonial preference. Birmingham remained the main centre for finished products, while the Black Country relied on the making of component parts for the finishing processes. But the new metal was steel, replacing iron and brass.

Meanwhile other changes were taking place. A distinctive social feature in the economic life of Birmingham had been the 'small man' arrangement in manufacture where the distinction between employer and employed was often indeterminate, with small masters recruited from the workmen. Subcontracting prevailed and home workshops were widespread, a consequence of this industrial structure being seen in the relative paucity of large factories and the spread of converted dwelling houses, thereby creating a mixed land use and cramped environment. But by the end of the century for most industries the original handicraft trades had been transformed. The factory became a more typical unit of production. New engineering trades demanded large numbers of small, standardised parts, and in a burst of mechanisation, machine tools superseded skilled artisans. Light and medium engineering replaced hardware manufacture. Furthermore, there was increasing use of new power machinery, including gas and oil engines, and later, electric motors. Birmingham industry at 1900 was undergoing yet another transformation.

Altogether new influences were playing on the industrial structure of the town, as Smith's (1964) wide-ranging review suggests. The traditional industrialism of the Birmingham workforce (either employer or worker) was undermined by various forms of cooperative activity, in groups such as trade unions, price and trade associations, mergers and joint enterprises. A growth in scale was a development which spread through the Birmingham economy in the last two decades of the century. The change was readily seen in the disappearance of small concerns or perhaps their expansion into larger firms. Meanwhile the economy was subject to the increasing influence of the government.

Even as these changes were happening the conditions were in place for the emergence of key industries which would form the basis of Birmingham's prosperity in the following century: cycle manufacture, the electrical trades and the motor car industry. Coventry was the first to benefit from the introduction of a bicycle with two equally sized wheels – the so-called 'safety' model – in 1885. But by 1914 Birmingham (including Aston) was the centre for their manufacture. In a parallel development the motor cycle found a ready home locally, James Norton setting up a small Birmingham factory in 1898 to produce the Norton 'Energette'. The electrical trades took off with the newly founded General Electric Company's 240-acre site at Witton. The car industry began with Wolseley Motors at Adderley Park, followed by the Austin works at Longbridge. Wyatt (1981) recounts the story that in 1905 Herbert Austin inspected a derelict factory there; built in 1892 it had been last used by a firm of metal workers who had vacated it some years previously. The buildings had a 200ft frontage, and the site, surrounded by fields on which there was an option, amounted to 2½ acres. The land fronted the Bristol Road and it was served by a railway branch line. Austin bought the site and the factory buildings in January 1906, for £7750. Within 20 years Austin's works was the largest motor factory in the British Empire.

The stage was set for the continued growth of Birmingham as an industrial city, but on increasingly different lines. As a manufacturing town it had possessed a variety of specialised trades, the products of skilled handicraft, where precision and measurement were all important. But the world of standardised engineering replaced it. The economies of large scale production were less important in the small metal trades, which produced specialised products, than in the textiles or in heavy engineering, so Birmingham had not been a factory town as Lancashire cotton and Yorkshire woollen towns had been (though brass foundries proved an exception to the general rules). Standardised engineering led to an increased scale of plant and the new unit of industrial organisation gave the city an increasingly different economic and social structure. Amalgamations transformed business relationships: Nettlefold absorbed competitors, Cadbury entered the world stage, Dunlop emerged from complex origins. A town of skilled craftsmen, small masters, outworkers and middlemen had its labour force remoulded into two groups – skilled workers engaged in making and adjusting tools, and semi-skilled machine operators.

It is clear that during the fourth quarter of the 19th century Birmingham and District was in transition, the depression years of 1875–86 forming a watershed in the area's economic development. The culminating point in the period of mid-century growth, when the area was the hardware centre of the country and a major seat of iron production, was reached in the boom coincident with the Franco–Prussian war. This marked the concluding phase of the old industrial era. Depression set in, to recover after the mid-1880s; significantly, expansion was connected primarily with industries other than those on which the area had been principally engaged in earlier years. The new industries were now concerned with finished articles of a different character from that hitherto associated with Birmingham's products (such as food and drink, or rubber), or with highly composite products (such as cycles, cars, machine tools, and electrical apparatus). By 1914 the district could claim to be an engineering, as much as a hardware centre.

In advancing this thesis, Allen (1929) traces three main periods in the evolution of economic change. From 1785 to 1860, 'the malleable iron age', the area's supremacy was as a hardware producing centre. Between 1860 and 1886 there was a period of readjustment and only slow growth; this was the end of the iron age and the beginning of foreign competition in the finished manufactures. From 1886 there was a change-over from hardware to engineering, during which time there was an increasing concern with composite products and finishing processes. In the years up to the Great War and beyond, there was a rapid advance of new industries and a slow decay of the old trades.

Locationally, too, changes were apparent. As newer industries were founded in the later 19th century an earlier tendency for peripheral clusters to emerge became quite a marked feature (Wise and Thorpe, 1950): to the north west beyond Ladywood, along the banks of the Birmingham Canal, to the south west at Selly Oak and Stirchley adjoining canal and railway, to the south east, again along canal and railway at Small Heath, Hay Mills and Greet, and to the north, similarly well served by transport facilities, where the flat land of the Rea Valley attracted larger establishments such as the gas works at Saltley and Nechells and railway wagon works. The Tame Valley, equally low lying, also welcomed larger industrial units, most noteworthy that of the General Electric Company at Witton in 1901, where there had been no industry before. By the end of the century, then, the industrial map had changed, with peripheral spread accompanying a trend to factory-style premises.

Housing

In the previous chapter we noted that a feature of the growing manufacturing town was the widening spread of the built-up area. Moreover, as increasing tracts of land on the outskirts were taken over by new streets, and as complete housing districts were formed, some of these areas attracted larger numbers of skilled artisans, clerks, and shopkeepers. As the century wore on, a sociological as well as a physical transformation was taking place: the outer areas were selective in their new occupants, by income and social class.

Doctors and lawyers continued to live in the centre, typical being the areas of Newhall Street, Bennett's Hill, the Crescent, the Old Square and the streets enclosing St Philip's churchyard. But the processes of redevelopment from the 1860s onwards removed some of these old quarters and the professional classes sought new areas elsewhere – Edgbaston, Moseley or further afield. A population transference began, the central districts losing population, the outer districts surging. As early as the decade 1861–71 the pattern was clear, with the population of the four central wards (St Peter's, St Philip's, St Paul's and St Mary's) decreasing from 51 000 to 42 000. The population of the central wards as a whole peaked in 1871, after which there was a steady decline. Densities fell and congestion was eased as Birmingham's expanding population sought out new living space. The old insanitary courts remained, and it was here that the poorest and the economically insecure families continued to live; the newer, healthier and better constructed housing in the recently developed districts commanded higher rents and attracted a different population group.

The seemingly haphazard, street by street addition to the periphery marked the growth of the industrial city throughout the second half of the 19th century, just as in the manufacturing town of the earlier years. By the 1860s Birmingham had expanded to its neighbouring villages (Figure 4.2). In the north west Winson Green was absorbed, houses reached up to and beyond the Soho works and there was a link with the southern part of Handsworth. To the north building was taking place beyond Lozells and new streets had been made as far as Aston Park. Beyond the borough boundary to the north east housing had progressed past Nechells and was spreading along Lichfield Road. Witton grew with industrial development nearby. In the east Small Heath expanded rapidly, again with the stimulus of a local manufacturing works, the BSA. To the south, Moseley and Birmingham were physically linked and building activity was pushing rapidly along Stratford Road. Westwards Pershore Road was a hive of development and Calthorpe Park marked the limit of expansion.

Thirty years later building had extended on either side of the Soho Road and into the southern part of Handsworth Parish. In Aston Manor the suburbs of Gravelly Hill and Erdington were established. Eastwards the town engulfed Washwood Heath and Saltley. Beyond Small Heath housing was attracted to an industrial area at Hay Mills. Balsall Heath was joined to Small Heath by the development of Sparkbrook and extended south to Sparkhill and King's Heath. In the years around the turn of the century the south western areas of Bournbrook, Bournville, Selly Oak and Stirchley received the greatest housing development, followed by areas in the south east, as at Acock's Green and South Yardley. The last expansion before 1914 absorbed Ward End and Little Bromwich.

The rise of 19th century suburbia was of course a feature of all big cities; Birmingham's experience was mirrored nationally. F. M. L. Thompson (1982) has observed:

> While it was going on, the process gratified landowners, developers, builders and the occupants of the new suburbs, or at least continued to lure them with the prospects of profits, status, and happiness, but pleased practically no one else. Contemporary social and

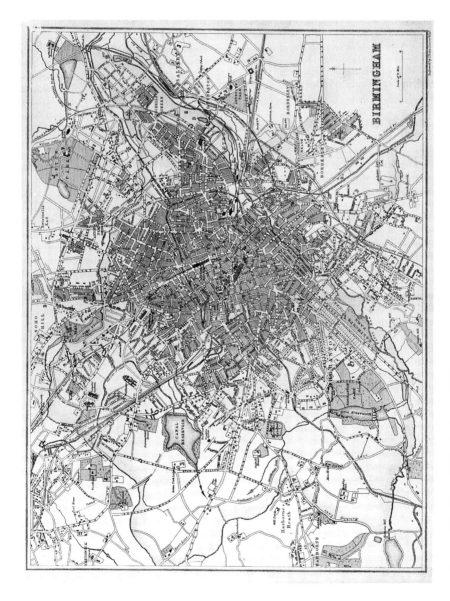

Figure 4.2 Plan of Birmingham, 1870.

architectural critics were fascinated and appalled by the mindless, creeping nature of the sprawl ... The ceaseless activity of the builders, the alarming rapidity with which they turned pleasant fields into muddy, rutted building sites, the confusion of hundreds of building operations going on simultaneously without any discernible design, the impression that little schemes were starting up everywhere at once and were never being finished, were in themselves frightening portents of disorder and chaos ... (p. 3)

Birmingham must have displayed these features too. In 1801 there were 1.6 million dwelling houses in England and Wales; by 1911 the total was 7.6 million. There was also a massive investment in other building and construction works associated with transport developments and new public and commercial buildings (Doughty, 1986). Birmingham shared massively in this boom, but we still know remarkably little about the processes whereby it took place, such as with regard to financing and contracting. There was no Thomas Cubitt, master builder, in Birmingham, and so it was the constellation of small, speculative enterprises and building societies that created the new residential districts of Birmingham. (The building of Edgbaston was a quite different operation.) Gradually the suburbs and their sub-districts acquired individuality and character, a lively street life marking out the terraced, 'tunnel-back' housing that predominated. It is sobering to reflect that Birmingham, in keeping with the largest English towns, was being suburbanised and socially segregated at least half a century before the arrival of cheap mass transit. In a voluminous housing historiography the background is well sketched by Rodger (1989) in a succinct review of urban housing between 1780 and 1914, by Burnett (1978) in a comprehensive social history of housing, and by Muthesius (1982) in a study of the English terraced house.

By the end of the century Birmingham had developed a capacity for swallowing up the life of its peripheral area. Whole new communities with different characteristics emerged. Moseley changed from a village into an exclusive suburb. Handsworth mushroomed as a respectable middle-class area; with 11 000 people in 1861 it expanded to 70 000 by 1911. Yardley developed, attracting businessmen from the centre, the extension of a tram line from Small Heath to the Swan Hotel particularly influential. Erdington, a late beneficiary of the opening of the Sutton Railway line in 1862, increased its population from 2600 in 1881 to 32 500 thirty years later. The Harborne Branch of the London and North Western Railway, just over two miles long, opened in 1874, tapping local traffic with stations at Monument Lane, Rotton Park, Hagley Road and the terminus at Harborne; the line closed in 1934. Further afield the Birmingham West Suburban Railway helped to open up King's Norton; its line from Granville Street was constructed in 1876 to a junction with the Gloucester Line at King's Norton via Edgbaston, Selly Oak and Stirchley. The Granville Street terminus was replaced by Five Ways when the line reached New Street in 1885. Acock's Green and Olton were opened up by the end of the century and in further-afield Solihull the railway helped in the development of Widney Manor and Dorridge Park estates. Greater Birmingham was emerging.

The role of the railway in late 19th century/early 20th century suburban development should not be exaggerated. The number of travellers attracted was small and the railway companies had very modest suburban intentions. The Great Western Railway opened stations for local traffic at Acock's Green, Solihull and Knowle (four, seven and eleven miles respectively from central Birmingham), but the Midland opened only one, at King's Norton, seven miles out. The attempt to capture local residential traffic, typified by the GWR's 'Homes for All in Rural Birmingham' campaign before 1914 was too late and too restricted in its appeal to the middle classes. But the late flourish did result in an additional central Birmingham station: Moor Street, opened in 1909 and built permanently in 1914. The disposal of a substantial area covered by the old Police Station and Public Offices presented an unusual opportunity which the Birmingham, North Warwickshire and Stratford-upon-Avon Railway was launched to exploit.

A distinct urban morphology took shape. A crescent-shaped area surrounded the old centre, extending from Perry Park in the north, through Aston, Lozells, Saltley, Small Heath and Sparkbrook to Selly Oak in the south west. Here, long rows of uniform terraced houses complemented a rather disjointed street pattern. Beyond, similar housing was engulfing outlying settlements as at Yardley and King's Heath. Further out still, the likes of King's Norton and Solihull retained a certain detachment. To the north and west beyond Harborne and Handsworth the Black Country may have seemed contiguous, but in many ways it was a world apart.

Roughly in the centre of this Birmingham spread was the highly prestigious residential suburb, Edgbaston. After a slow start building peaked in the period 1843–1880. The mid-century census recorded a population for Edgbaston of 9269; but by 1881 it had risen to 22 760. The commercial, industrial and professional capitalists, who boasted amongst their number the principal leaders of Birmingham society for perhaps half a century, found their home there. As Cannadine (1980) remarks, for the civic elite 'Edgbaston was but the Council House at home' (p. 83). Some of the finest suburban houses graced this elegant leafy suburb, readily presented today in architectural guides (Braithwaite, 1986). It was the premier area for the town's high status population, easily surpassing at least four other rivals in Handsworth and Handsworth Wood to the north, Erdington in the north east, Moseley in the south and the curiously truncated Selly Park to the south west: all these were beyond Birmingham's boundaries until 1911 (Giles, 1976).

Lord Calthorpe's agents continued their astute management; land for Calthorpe Park was given in 1867, and with the granting of land for the University in 1900 a highly protective *cordon sanitaire* in the southern quadrant of the Estate established a permanent buffer against the industrial and working class district of Selly Oak. But the late 1870s saw Edgbaston at the zenith of its fame, the Estate failing to share in Birmingham's building boom of the late 19th century. The tentacles of suburban development stretched out even further and Edgbaston found itself surrounded. It remained a premier suburb, the Belgravia of Birmingham, but at its edges the barriers of exclusivity were beginning to crumble against industry and commerce; in the south east, the Bristol Road area was patently in decline.

During these years of vigorous growth, the territorial spread of Birmingham was shaped by private, ground landlord considerations. Housing supply responded to perceived demand in a myriad of development decisions; urban form was created by building activity which was random and unco-ordinated. All this would change radically in later years as a result of public sector control and regulation, a process which began with the enforcement of drainage requirements and standards of construction for individual houses. During the second half of the 19th century Parliamentary Acts and local by-laws progressively extended the powers of the State in relation to housing and a wide range of environmental matters (Cherry, 1988). The Public Health Act 1848 required national standards to be observed by local authorities in matters of public health. Its observance was permissive and it was not until the Local Government Act 1858 that provisions were really effective. Building control powers were considerably extended to include regulations for the structure and stability of buildings and the space around them; powers were also extended for local authorities to make by-laws with regard to new streets and drainage.

Almost all the major towns of the country proceeded to issue by-laws according to the 1848 and 1858 Acts – an early hand of public regulation, successive strengthenings of which would in large measure shape and determine the spatial form of urban environments. Birmingham was no exception and quickly adopted the prevailing form of by-law control. The Public Health Act 1872 established sanitary authorities across the whole country, with obligatory powers, and in 1877 the newly established Local Government Board (1871) published its model by-laws. Adopted by the borough in 1876, they laid down that every dwelling should have a minimum air space on at least two sides, thereby putting an end to the building of back-to-back houses in Birmingham. By the mid-1880s the terms 'by-law house' and 'by-law street' came to typify much of late Victorian urban England. A uniformity was imposed. Streets exceeding 100ft in length were to be at least 36ft wide. For house construction specifications prescribed open space front and rear, habitable rooms with windows of regulatory size, and detailed sanitary arrangements. Birmingham adopted by-laws for buildings and streets and the resultant suburban layout gave the town a distinctive peripheral form very different from the building style of the past.

Local authority action with regard to housing was not confined to regulating new building. It was also extended to dealing with the insanitary condition or faulty construction of some of the poorer housing of the older stock. Again, there was a national context, central government extending power to local authorities to undertake clearance schemes through the compulsory purchase of dwellings and land. State intervention with regard to private housing matters was long resisted, the sanctity of property rights protected to the bitter end in some quarters, but legislation in 1866 (The Artizans' and Labourers' Dwellings Act) enabled local authorities to secure the improvement of dwellings by repair or demolition. Legislation in 1875 (The Artizans' and Labourers' Dwellings Improvement Act) gave permissive powers for local authorities to deal with areas of unfit housing, not just the properties themselves. The Act opened the way for measures of area-based clearance, from which Birmingham would profit.

Clearance of older property had already taken place in connection with other development projects. The building of first New Street and then Snow Hill Railway Stations between 1845 and 1854 had swept away some squalid streets such as Peck Lane, The Froggery and Old Meeting Street. In the 1860s and 1870s old property on the Colmore Estate was demolished for new development around Colmore Row, Edmund Street and Newhall Street (Figures 4.3, 4.4). Shortly after, the Council itself became an actor in what we today would call 'urban renewal' in the removal of some of the town's worst slums. St Mary's ward in the city centre provided the conditions for the most abject housing, with commensurate ill-health and high mortality rates; it was a collection of narrow lanes ('gullets'), home for more than 10 000 people. Under the 1875 Act the property was purchased and cleared. There was no provision for rehousing, but the scheme permitted the construction of a new road, Corporation Street, intended to give Birmingham a central area boulevard of distinction; this episode is recounted in later paragraphs.

There was no great enthusiasm for the Council to engage in the provision of dwellings for the working classes. Other large towns had already engaged in this practice, but Birmingham's efforts were lukewarm. In 1885 a proposal to erect flats in Dalton Street failed to secure support, but in 1889 a development site in Ryder Street (now part of the site of the University of Aston) provided the setting for the first council scheme: 22 dwellings were completed in 1890 at a cost of £182 each, and rented at 5s 6d per week. The following year a more extensive scheme provided 82 houses in nearby Lawrence Street (Figure 4.5). Legislation in 1890 (the Housing of the Working Classes Act) allowed the Council to widen its preparation of improvement schemes beyond the Corporation Street scheme area. The sanitary condition of two areas, Woodcock Street and Milk Street, justified compulsory acquisition and clearance. It was first proposed to build 116 houses on the sites, but the scheme failed to gain Council support on cost grounds and Woodcock Street was dropped from the plan.

Further dispute attended the proposals for Milk Street, but in 1898 agreement was reached for the construction of four two-storey blocks of tenements providing 64 two-bedroom dwellings in the form of 'dual houses', i.e. two-storey balcony access flats. Milk Street, off Digbeth, was in a highly unattractive industrial quarter, and by making no charge for ground rent and including shared sculleries, rents could be kept down to 4s 3d for the lower dwellings and 3s 9d for the upper. The Milk Street dwellings were completed in 1901, and with no particular political will to continue flat building in the city centre, the Council turned to other alternatives, which we consider in the next chapter. But for the moment Birmingham's experiments, first in model dwellings and then in flat building, had failed (Sutcliffe, 1974).

Figure 4.3 Edmund Street Clearance, c.1870. The Town Hall is to the right at the rear.

Figure 4.4 No. 5 Court, Thomas Street, demolished as part of the Improvement Scheme of 1876.

The civic gospel and town improvement

In the previous chapter we traced the steps by which the administration of local affairs was radically changed. In 1852, when the new Borough Council took office, old restraints were removed. But for much of the rest of the decade there was disappointment as financial resistance to expenditure prevailed. An 'economist' party, led by Joseph Allday, supported by the Ratepayers Protection Society, maintained strict financial control. Each year the Council levied three rates: one was the original borough rate, largely for police purposes; another (and largest) was the borough improvement rate, mainly spent on public works; the third was the street improvement rate, for the widening of streets. In all these matters the pursuit of economy dominated the desire for efficient service. The main object of the Council was to avoid spending money.

This inaction asserted itself in every branch of municipal business. The Surveyor, Piggott Smith, was removed from office; it was alleged that 'he was repeatedly at variance with the committee'. His former assistant was appointed in his place, at half the old salary. The Council did not take seriously its responsibility as a local board of health; it was 1860 before Dr Hill, a local medical man, was appointed part time Borough Analyst, whereas Liverpool had a Medical Officer of Health as early as 1848. In 1854 the Council became a burial board, but it was 1859 before land was purchased at Witton for a cemetery.

The Council reached a low level; Gill (1952) observes that it was 'factious in debate, narrow in outlook, mean and reluctant in public service' (p. 416). In 1858 it changed direction; when Allday failed to secure reappointment as alderman, he withdrew from local politics. The Council was forced to respond to the urgency of the sewage problem, and pollution in the Tame was overcome with the development of large sewage farms in the lowland between Saltley and Curdworth. Certain social projects were also embarked upon, notably with the provision of baths and wash-houses in 1862, the founding of the Central Lending Library in 1865 and the Central Reference Library a year later.

So far Birmingham had somewhat lagged behind other major provincial centres in expressing itself as a civic force. Manchester in particular had risen to national prominence in the late 1830s and 1840s. Yet Birmingham was not without the political radicalism that had featured in Manchester with its economic creed of Free Trade. The Birmingham Political Union, founded by the banker and industrialist Thomas Attwood in 1829, sought parliamentary and economic reform. In the 1840s the Quaker corn factor Joseph Sturge demanded the repeal of the corn laws and urged manhood suffrage. In 1857 John Bright changed his parliamentary constituency from Manchester to Birmingham after his defeat in Lancashire, and a radical tradition was confirmed; he was the acknowledged champion

Figure 4.5 Lawrence Street municipal dwellings. Built 1891, demolished 1971. Photo 1967.

of Liberal non-conformity. The scene was set for two decades in which Birmingham established a remarkable reputation in local and national politics, a period described in detail by Briggs (1952 and 1963) and Hennock (1973).

The Birmingham Liberal Association, founded in February 1865, cooperated closely with the Reform League which was active in the struggle which led to the Reform Act 1867. James Baldwin, a town councillor and one of the founders of the Association was first President of the League. The Association formed itself into a caucus with ward branches and fought the general election of 1868 with great efficiency. Three Liberal Members of Parliament, John Bright, George Dixon (who had become a Birmingham MP at a by-election the previous year) and G. F. Munz (Bright's colleague as sitting Liberal member) won substantial majorities. New political opportunities soon followed when the Municipal Franchise Act 1869 increased the number of electors. Nationally the electorate tripled (from 717 000 in 1832 to 2 226 000) with some representation of the working classes on to the register. Political parties adjusted to the emergence of popular politics and party machines, and some cities threw up new political leaders. Birmingham was one of them.

Locally, a network of Unitarian families mobilised their power and influence, providing 'a compact and tireless leadership in all branches of local life' (Briggs, 1952, p. 2). One of the national agitations they plunged into was the National Education League, founded in 1869. Begun as an effort to remove a local evil, it made non-conformity a militant political force in the country. Birmingham was the centre of the agitation.

The Education League launched Joseph Chamberlain into national politics, but his first impact was on local affairs, in the city he came to regard as his own. He grew up in north London where his father was in the wholesale boot and shoe business. He arrived in Birmingham in 1854, when he was 18 years old, sent by his father, who had invested in a screw-making business (John Nettlefold's) in the town and wanted someone to represent his interests in the firm. He soon established a reputation both in business and in the Unitarian Church as a forceful personality. He served a political apprenticeship in the Birmingham and Edgbaston Debating Society and the Working Men's Institute of his Smethwick firm. He was prominent neither in the Liberal Association of 1865, nor in the struggles of 1867, but entered full public life with his chairmanship of the executive committee of the radical and nonconformist National Educational League.

He entered the Town Council in 1869 as a militant Liberal member for St Paul's ward. His rise to power was dramatic. In Briggs' (1952) words, 'He caught the spirit of the times and hurried it forward, revelling in the exhilaration of responsible power' (p. 69). His St Paul's seat was not all that safe, but he was helped by cooperation between the middle and the working classes: the Working Men's Reform League merged with the Liberal Association. Within four years he not only took over the chairmanship of the School Board but was also chosen as Mayor. He served in that capacity for three years, 1873–76, a period which saw the practical articulation of a 'civic gospel' as Briggs, (1963) terms it, (though Hennock (1973) prefers the term 'municipal gospel') founded on the economic and social alliances forged over the previous decade and earlier radical stirrings. During this time Chamberlain successfully widened the scope of local government from which there would be no withdrawal for over a century. The Town Council would be an instrument of collective purpose. Quite simply he set himself the task of governing Birmingham in the interests of the whole community; he was a radical elected on a populist ticket.

He was assisted by a flood tide of religious endorsement, largely of a nonconformist sentiment, a number of Church ministers preaching the message of social politics. George Dawson came to the Mount Zion Baptist Chapel in 1844, only to open his own church, the Church of the Saviour, three years later, and occupied the pulpit there until his death in 1876. It was he, according to Hennock (1973) who was the creator of the municipal gospel; Joseph Chamberlain became leader of the movement. His successor at Mount Zion, Charles Vince, shared a similar interest in purpose. H. W. Crosskey, Minister of the Unitarian Church of the Messiah, arrived in 1869; unitarianism was the religion of many influential families in the town. Robert William Dale, minister at Carrs Lane Congregational Church for over 40 years (1854–95) praised the endeavours of reformist local government. Furthermore Quakerism was strong in Birmingham, though Methodism weak.

The civic renaissance, nurtured through municipal idealism, certainly owed much to these nonconformist spokesmen. Unitarians and Quakers in particular occupied important positions in both business and politics. Unitarian families held an extraordinary sway, notably the Chamberlains, Kenricks, Martineaus and Nettlefolds. Unitarian mayors held office almost without a break between 1840 and 1880.

By comparison the Church of England, though numerically strong, was tainted by an association with a Tory and generally conservative sentiment. Roman Catholics may not have had the force they could muster in Liverpool or Manchester, yet by mid-century Birmingham was an important centre for Roman Catholicism; St Chad's, consecrated in 1838, became a cathedral ten years later when Dr Ullathorne was enthroned Bishop. Perhaps we should not confuse numbers with influence: at the 1851 census of attendance at religious services, attendance at Church of England services almost equalled that elsewhere (20 000 as opposed to 21 500 dissenters of all kinds) – and this in a town with a reputation for non-conformity.

The new fervour for pro-active municipal governance of a kind which increasingly concerned itself with diminishing the disparities between rich and poor, first found expression in the sewage question. A total of 14 000 open middens and ashpits which drained directly into the sewers were removed. To pay for ambitious schemes such as these demanded new sources of income. Birmingham had no financial power beyond the sums it could raise from rates; it had no landed property or profits from commercial services such as port dues. But the town had to catch up with other authorities. Municipal gas was already manufactured by many municipalities and municipal water ownership was commonplace. Such profitable municipal utilities were soon identified for Birmingham. Chamberlain quickly acquired the Birmingham Gas Light and Coke Company and the larger Birmingham and Staffordshire Gas Light Company, Birmingham's private bill enacted in 1875. He then took over the Birmingham Water Works Company in 1876, parliamentary approval granted the previous year. A Medical Officer of Health (Dr Hill) was appointed in 1872 and the Council's first Health Committee was set up in 1875 with responsibilities ranging from the disposal of sewage and refuse to the inspection of milk and food. No less than 150 000 people in Birmingham were dependent on wells for their water in 1869, but within eight years more than 3000 contaminated wells used by 60 000 people were closed.

The period of public spending continued and the Improvement Scheme was launched in 1875. In July the Council agreed to set up an Improvement Committee; it reported in October with a representation by the Medical Officer of Health as to the insanitary area it was proposed to deal with. It included portions of St Mary's and Market Hall Wards, stretching in one direction from New Street to the Aston Road and in the other from Lower Priory to Steelhouse Lane. Part of the description ran:

> Narrow streets; houses without back doors or windows, situated both in and out of courts; confined yards; courts open at one end only, and this one opening small and narrow; the impossibility, in many instances, of providing sufficient privy accommodation; houses and shopping so dilapidated as to be in imminent danger of falling, and incapable of proper repair.

The results were:

> want of ventilation, want of light, want of proper and decent accommodation, resulting in dirty habits, low health and debased morals on the part of the tenants. (Bunce, 1885, p. 457)

It was a start on urban renewal which the building of New Street and Snow Hill railway stations had begun, and which the construction of the Law Courts ten years later would continue. The dominant theme in British housing policy from the time of Chadwick onwards had been the association of insanitary conditions with mortality rates; Birmingham was no exception and medical opinion was quick to justify the sweeping away of squalid slum land on health grounds. Urban death rates in the big cities improved greatly towards the end of the 19th century, but it is hard to show that the compulsory removal of unfit dwellings had very much to do with it. With regard to Birmingham, Woods (1978) has argued that administrative developments in hospital provision should be combined with public health improvements in any explanation of mortality decline. Additionally, it was poverty as much as sanitary conditions which was more closely associated with high mortality.

The population of Birmingham in the 1880s had a life expectancy at birth of about 43 years; 45% of deaths were to children under the age of 5 years. Birmingham was healthier than most cities and its housing stock was better, yet its health record still caused anxiety: no less than 43% of the annual deaths were attributable to seven major groups of air-, water- and food-borne diseases. The three great adult killer diseases of the time were cholera, typhoid and typhus, while water- and contaminated-food-borne diseases causing bowel disorders were responsible for high levels of infant mortality. But the situation would change appreciably over the last two decades of the century when isolation hospitals for infectious diseases were designated to complement the generally good health record of the town. (By the end of the 1870s Birmingham already had two extensive hospital complexes, the General and the Queen's, other specialised institutions, a sewage processing plant, water supply sources and a municipal cemetery.) Disease mortality had a tenuous link with sanitary conditions: the poorest people were living in the worst housing, they had the worst diet and were generally less healthy than the rest of the community. But nonetheless the promise of improving the town's high mortality rate underpinned the clearing of the slums in Chamberlain's project. The Council approved a scheme for clearing an area of 93 acres of dilapidated property in the central area.

After a Local Government Board enquiry, Parliament confirmed the acquisition of 43 acres in 1876. Properties were purchased without resort to compulsory powers and new building began in 1878. As we have already seen, the construction of Corporation Street, section by section, would transform central Birmingham, though piecemeal development meant that the boulevard lacked architectural unity. In April 1879 the first stretch, from New Street to Cherry Street was opened. By 1881 it had progressed to Bull Street, and the year following sections between Bull Street and the Priory and John Street and Aston Street were opened. Financial success was in doubt until at least 1892 but by 1889 it was lined with prestigious commercial buildings, though it took until 1900 before all the frontage land was let. A street nearly a mile long was finally completed in 1903.

The new power of municipal government required expression in a new meeting place. As early as 1853 a site had been purchased, but it remained undeveloped until 1870. In that year a proposal for the Council House (its title confirmed only after controversy) was approved; H. R. Yeoville Thomason was chosen as architect. Chamberlain laid the foundation stone in 1874 and the building was opened in 1879. Tellingly, depicted on the central pediment over the main entrance was a sculptured group representing 'Britannia rewarding the Birmingham manufacturers'.

The Council House stimulated other building nearby: Mason Science College was begun in 1875, a new School of Art followed in 1881 and an extension of the Midland Institute in the same year. New Reference and Lending Libraries were opened in 1882. Fittingly the area was chosen for the Chamberlain Memorial, inaugurated in 1889.

Chamberlain became Member of Parliament for Birmingham in 1876 on Dixon's retirement. Within four years he was in Gladstone's cabinet as President of the Board of Trade. His work in Birmingham meant that he had left a mark both on the city and in the conduct of its affairs. The reputation of the Council had been established and people of influence and position were attracted to play a part as councillors. Hennock (1973) puts great store by this social role:

> . . . it cannot be stressed too much that the Birmingham municipal reform movement was
> more than a successful attempt to provide a rather backward borough with necessary

municipal services. The crucial innovation was a new vision of the function and nature of the corporation. Because of this, it was also the recruitment to the Town Council of the social and economic elite of the town whose abilities made the actual administrative improvements possible. (p. 172)

The tradition of municipal service, once established, was effectively preserved into the 20th century among Birmingham's business and professional strata.

Birmingham acquired not just a national but international prestige in municipal governance. The city had become a byword for efficient city trading. In 1896 Chamberlain told a Birmingham banquet of like-minded citizens: 'I have always compared the work of a great corporation like this to that of a joint-stock company, in which the directors are represented by the Councillors of the City, and in which the dividends are to be found in the increased health and wealth and happiness and education of the community' (Perkin, 1989, p. 137). His harnessing of public-spirited capitalism to the affairs of Birmingham transformed the city. Chamberlain continued to live in his adopted town, building an opulent house on the outskirts at Moor Green; he called it Highbury in deference to his north London upbringing.

The century ended with local government strong and expanding, with the elected council exercising an increasing influence over the community it served. Birmingham had made striking advances in transforming a poorly administered authority. Its committees, council and departments were efficient. A start had been made on clearing away slums and on providing new housing. Health hazards were attacked and death rates were falling. The long-serving Birmingham, Tame and Rea District Drainage Board was set up in 1877. The Birmingham School Board became a model for educational authorities everywhere. A new Central Library was opened in 1882 after the earlier one had been demolished by fire. An Art Gallery followed in 1885. There was a succession of public parks. Graveyards were closed and turned into public gardens. Birmingham was increasingly shaped, governed and provided for by its Council. Bunce's eulogy of 30 years of improvement might today read rather extravagantly:

So, day by day, year out, year in, the vast machinery of local administration . . . works steadily and silently on . . . without pause, or hitch or serious flaw; equal ever to new duties imposed, never refusing new services required . . . (p. xliv)

but his paean of praise could justifiably range over a range of services including water supply, sewerage, street cleaning, health inspectors, markets, police, schools, baths and parks, libraries and gas supply.

These things would not have come to pass without a formidable political machine to accompany administrative competence. It began with the Liberal Party caucus and their use of ward politics. Liberal electors chose ward committees to organise the canvassing and routine business of their areas. Ward committees elected a central representative committee; they also chose parliamentary candidates and Liberal candidates for all the School Board elections. Criticised by opponents as a tyrannical organisation, and simply the iron rule of a little clique, Birmingham nonetheless 'stood for the most powerful political machine in the kingdom and the most active and adventurous brand of English radical liberalism' (Briggs, 1952, p. 175). In due time the Liberal caucus faded and the Conservative party machine was refashioned before the arrival of a new complexity in the form of a Liberal Unionist Association in Birmingham. When Chamberlain resigned from Gladstone's Administration in 1886, he took the Birmingham Liberal Association with him into the Unionist camp. In 1891 the Liberal Unionists had 29 seats, the Gladstonian Liberals 24 and the Conservatives 19. The Conservatives and the Liberal Unionists had by then already set up a joint committee, and, as they drew closer together, the politics of the council became increasingly Unionist and protectionist.

But the earlier experience was there: 20th century politicians and administrators would look with envy at what the Liberals achieved, and how they did it. Birmingham's tradition of powerful chief officers and committee chairmen has been of long standing, but it is the creation of the local party organisation that takes the eye. Chamberlain and the Liberals contributed to an outstanding quality of Birmingham's local government and its services. Yet there were plenty of observers to issue a justified word of caution: the local party machine could be regarded as the worst that could happen in a mass democracy. Elected representatives seemed to be responsible to the narrow and sectional interests of a small number of party members, rather than to the general public as a whole. A century later (though not in Birmingham) the militant left in a number of local government areas used the same tactic of party organisation – and attracted the same odium, though with rather greater justification.

Public health continued to be a major preoccupation, and the continued growth of population required an expansion of the town's water undertakings. In the 1880s Birmingham had 14 local reservoirs at its disposal. The Council looked to Wales for further supply, and the Birmingham Corporation Water Act 1892 empowered the building of the Elan Valley and Claerwent reservoirs and the laying of pipes to the Frankley reservoirs south west of the city. The waterworks were opened in 1904 by Edward VII and Queen Alexandra.

By this time Birmingham had amply confirmed its position as capital of the West Midlands. It became an assize town in 1884. The foundation of the new Law Courts was laid by Queen Victoria in 1887; a competition was won by Aston Webb and Ingress Bell and the result stimulated local architecture to 'an outburst of terra cotta' (Little, 1971, p. 33). In 1888 the town became a County Borough; the Local Government Act of that year created a new national system of county boroughs and a two-tier structure of counties and districts. In 1889 Birmingham was raised to the dignity of a city by Royal Decree. In 1896 the status of the mayoralty was raised to Lord Mayor. By this time he presided over a slightly enlarged area, the borough boundaries having been extended in 1891 to take in Saltley, Harborne and Balsall Heath, an absorption which brought another 50 000 people into the city (see Table 4.1). By the time of the census of 1901 Birmingham's population was 522 000 and a growing tributary population lay just beyond its boundaries. The scene was set for demands for far greater territorial aggrandisement, but this took another 10 years to achieve, as we see in the next chapter.

Table 4.1 Population of Birmingham 1851–1901

	1851	1861	1871	1881	1891	1901
1. Ancient parish of Birmingham Central wards	140 190	158 073	158 552	145 774	134 039	125 596
Western wards:						
All Saints	13 588	19 820	29 689	49 716	55 221	61 865
Ladywood	20 173	34 728	42 774	50 863	56 243	57 755
2. Other areas within the Borough of 1838						
Edgbaston parish	9 269	12 907	17 442	22 760	24 436	26 486
Part of Aston parish:						
Bordesley & Deritend	23 173	31 788	49 344	76 413	95 796	110 978
Duddeston & Nechells	26 448	38 760	45 986	55 248	63 433	65 572
Total for Borough of 1838	**232 841**	**296 076**	**343 787**	**400 774**		
3. Areas added to the city, 1891:						
Harborne	2 350	3 617	5 105	N/A	7 935	10 113
Balsall Heath	N/A	N/A	N/A	N/A	30 581	38 827
Saltley & Ward End	1 451	3 247	4 670	7 267	10 429	25 012
Total for city as constituted in 1891					**478 113**	**522 204**

Source: Elrington and Tillott, 1964

The city takes shape

In this section we consider those remaining elements which went to provide the important features of Birmingham at the end of the century. The basic elements we have already reviewed: industry, housing, territorial spread and measures of town improvement carried out by an energetic local Council. The popular image of the city at the end of Victoria's reign was conveyed by impressions as to how its inhabitants earned their living, and the goods they produced, how they were housed, the size of the city and what it looked like, its political leaders and their reputation for embarking on big schemes and getting things done; above all of a city which was powerful, thrusting, unlovely perhaps, but part of the country's imperial might. These pictures augment those marshalled by Dyos and Wolff (1973) in their monumental review of the images and realities of the Victorian city in general.

To complete the perspective we give further consideration to three matters: the city's transport system, the consolidation of the central area as Birmingham's hub, and the question of parks and open space.

Birmingham was a late and uncertain developer with regard to that late 19th century form of transport, the tram. The Public Works Committee was responsible for tramway policy until a Tramways Committee was formed in 1900 (Macmorran, 1973). The situation was bedevilled by protracted disputes over forms of power and the rivalry between different companies. The Tramways Act 1870 enabled councils to construct tramways by a provisional order, and in 1872 the first (horse-drawn) fixed-track tram ran between Monmouth Street (now Colmore Row) and Hockley. In 1876 a second tramway was opened from Monmouth Street to the Borough boundary in Bristol Road at Selly Oak. Steam traction was applied to the Birmingham and Aston Tramway Co. in 1882. The cable system was then investigated and in 1888 the tramway between Hockley and Colmore Row operated with cable traction. Thereafter the competing claims of overhead and underground power supply fuelled an ongoing debate in which, because of prevarications, the loser was the travelling public of Birmingham. The end of the century came with the situation ripe for change. The Birmingham Central Tramways Co., supplemented by the Birmingham and Midland and Birmingham and Aston Companies, provided a network of routes along the main radials from the city centre: to Smethwick, Handsworth and Aston, and along the Coventry, Stratford, Alcester and Bristol Roads, but two extensive areas were not tapped – Harborne and Edgbaston to the west and Saltley and Little Bromwich to the east.

As far as the filling in of the central area was concerned, the completion of the Council House in 1879 and the progressive opening of Corporation Street did much to provide a scale and a dignity to match the bustle of two railway stations. But in fact from the middle of the century central Birmingham had been subject to the gradual removal of old properties, which paved the way for a variety of commercial projects. Birmingham took its time in shedding a dowdy, provincial image, but by the end of the century a rather more impressive central area was the result. The shopping centre, centred on Bull Street, was always small and not until the 1870s did a few large shops with imposing facades appear.

The first agent of change was the railway and from the 1850s the North Western and Midland lines transformed the district around New Street and Suffolk Street and the Great Western reshaped Monmouth Street, Livery Street and Snow Hill. New Street station, as we have seen, opened in 1854; boasting the largest single-span roof in the world at that time, operations had taken seven years to complete. Snow Hill station opened in 1852, beginning life as a temporary wooden structure; rebuilt in 1870 it was transformed into 'a light and elegant building worthy of the Great Western Company', as Dent (1880, p. 616) describes it. After further rebuilding it assumed its final form in 1914. This longer line came into Birmingham over an iron bridge across Sandy Lane and a viaduct of brick arches at Bordesley, finally through a tunnel, constructed as open cut, but later covered.

Some of the great landowners engaged in clearance and rebuilding. The falling in of the Colmore leases from the 1860s led to changes in Colmore Row, Edmund Street, Newhall Street and the surrounding area. The shoddy tenements on the other side of New Street, in an area known as the 'Inkleys', belonging to Col Vyse, were swept away. Crooked Lane, where John Cadbury began his business in 1831, and Union Street were rebuilt. Houses and workshops were destroyed to create John Bright Street. The Birmingham historian Bunce (1885) was full of praise for the cutting of Corporation Street and John Bright Street which:

> swept away a series of narrow streets, close courts, and confined passages, shut out from fresh air, imperfectly lighted, fetid with dirt, ill-supplied with water, and so inhabited that at one time – in the flourishing days of the Inkleys and Green's Village and the like – the police could not venture into them single-handed; while no family could dwell there without destruction to the sense of decency, or peril to health and life. (p. xxiv)

The old gardens of the central area finally went as building development became more intensive. The landlords leased out their land to others to engage in speculative enterprises, sometimes other individuals, firms or syndicates. In a drive to build new shops in the 1870s the Great Western Arcade was developed by a syndicate over the line of the underground railway from Snow Hill to Moor Street.

During the last two decades of the century a number of important public buildings were added. The decaying St Martin's in the Bull Ring was demolished in November 1872; the rebuilt church was consecrated in July 1875. With Birmingham obtaining its own Assizes a site was reserved in Corporation Street for the Law Courts. The foundation was laid by Queen Victoria in 1887 and the Victoria Law Courts were opened by the Prince of Wales four years later; by Aston Webb and Ingress Bell, the building's harsh red terracotta external finish, compensated by the creamy pink or yellowish brown of the delicately detailed interior, gave Birmingham a distinctive new building, judged by Little (1971) in his review of the city's architecture as a 'brilliant success'. The Central Library Buildings had been completed in 1865 (and restored in 1882 following a fire). An Art Gallery followed in 1885, on a site behind the Council House, interestingly enough built above the offices of, and on the profits from the Gas Department; municipal pride saw no conflict between a public utility and art. (Later, in 1911, when the Council House Extension was built, an imposing new Gas Rates Hall was incorporated where the public went to settle their accounts. That same Hall, now a Grade 2 listed building, was reopened in 1993 as Birmingham's new Exhibition Gallery.)

Compared with the appearance of central Birmingham 50 years before, all this was impressive, but apart from a very few individual buildings the whole ensemble was scarcely memorable. No urban landscape of quality had been created. The city was of course hostage to geography as well as history: it had no water space as in Bristol, Liverpool or Glasgow, and its site, while hilly, lacked drama. But the builders of the city rather let it down; it lacked a dominant unifying hand through a diffusion of ownerships and leases. At the close of an energetic building period the central area lacked any sense of singular style; it was a city of bits and pieces (Figure 4.6). Architecturally the most one can say is that Birmingham became a city of terra cotta, which became 'the architectural symbol of the civic gospel' (Stratton, 1989, p. 21).

Finally, the city acquired a University (Vincent and Hinton, 1947). Josiah Mason, whom we have already noted as a prosperous manufacturer of steel pen nibs, founded a scientific college suited to the requirements of local industries: Mason College opened in 1880, a flamboyant gothic building in bright red brick in Edmund Street. Nearby was Queen's College which offered a variety of courses, including medicine. By 1892 Mason College had absorbed them all, except theology. Mason died in 1881 and the idea of a University for the Midlands simmered uncertainly for some years. Joseph Chamberlain, a trustee, urged a bold resolution: a University of Birmingham. The College became a University College in 1898 and in October 1900 the University, having received its royal charter in May, admitted its first students. Chamberlain now Chancellor, secured a large site at Edgbaston from Lord Calthorpe, and Aston Webb and Ingress Bell were employed to build Britain's first redbrick university, its huge clock tower, Great Hall and semicircle of buildings punctuating the fields on rising ground overlooking Selly Oak.

The sixth Lord Calthorpe proved much more tactful in dealing with the Corporation than his predecessor had been, providing land for the University in 1900 and 1907. It marked an increasing willingness to play a new and more public role in municipal affairs. As Cannadine (1990) has observed in his study of the decline and fall of the British aristocracy, deliberate attempts were made in a number of cities to project a more favourable public image. Late 19th century urban (and rural) landlords

Figure 4.6 Central Birmingham, late 19th century. Council House, Chamberlain Memorial and Town Hall.

87

were increasingly beleaguered, with no little hostility shown to nearby notables. In Birmingham the 1880 General Election, when Joseph Chamberlain defeated Augustus Calthorpe, brother of the owner of Edgbaston, was a particularly vitriolic campaign.

Although not as densely built up as some northern towns, Birmingham lacked open space within its urban area; no common land had been protected from development. In the second half of the 19th century the provision of public parks and recreation grounds came to the town's rescue, an Act of 1854 permitting councils to accept gifts of land and provide for their maintenance. The national picture of the provision of 'people's parks' at this time is well sketched by Conway (1991); Birmingham fell into the pattern for big cities generally. Lord Norton gave a ten-acre site to create Adderley Park and Lord Calthorpe offered 30 acres at a nominal rent to create Calthorpe Park. Aston Hall and Park was acquired by a private company for entertainments and exhibitions but, after financial difficulties, was purchased by the Corporation. Cannon Hill Park was the result of a gift of 47 acres by Miss Ryland of Barford who also gave 43 acres at Small Heath to create Victoria Park. Highgate Park and Summerfield Park were open spaces rescued from the builder and paid for out of public funds. Finally Birmingham's acquisitions extended to the Lickey Hills, thanks to the generosity of various donors.

5
At the Turn of the Century

Important developments with regard to housing and town planning took place in Birmingham in the quarter of a century between 1890 and 1914: let us say during the last decade of Victoria's reign, through the Edwardian years and the immediate aftermath up to the outbreak of the Great War. Birmingham took a lead nationally in a new approach to social and environmental problems where the key issue was the provision of satisfactory housing for the working classes at rents they could afford. Towards the end of the period extensive boundary changes dramatically increased the territorial size of the city. In due time this would mean that the solution to Birmingham's housing problem would increasingly lie outside the old 19th century city, and in the rural areas beyond. We explore these matters in this chapter.

But first we sketch the Birmingham of around the year 1900, a city on the brink of considerable change in both shape and form.

Context for change

We look first at the geographical structure of Birmingham – the composition of its various parts, separate yet linked in a functional whole.

By the end of the century the city centre had its separate quarters which we would recognise today. New Street, Corporation Street, High Street and Bull Street were the main shopping areas; the Bull Ring provided cheaper shopping and markets. The area of Colmore Row, Waterloo Street, Temple Row and Newhall Street was the chief business district. Victoria Square and Chamberlain Square were the focus for city administration and public services. The central area was noisy and smelly, horse-drawn vehicles of all descriptions rattling over the cobbled, granite or wood road surfaces, which were covered with sand or perhaps wood shavings to prevent horses slipping. Footpaths were flagged, but less important streets were paved in vitrified blue bricks. Central area shops were largely owned by individual traders, but department stores had begun to appear, notably with the opening of Rackham's and Lewis's. The streets were punctuated with other buildings now long since gone: Christ Church on the corner of New Street and Victoria Square, the Theatre Royal in New Street, the Exchange Buildings on the corner of New Street and Stephenson Place where merchants and manufacturers met to conduct business, demolished in the 1960s to make way for the new Midland Bank premises, and next to it King Edward VI's School, vacated in 1935 in favour of a move to Edgbaston.

The central area was surrounded by districts of workshops and factories intermingling the closely packed courts and back-to-back houses in a belt stretching from Spring Hill and New Town Row to Nechells in the north, through Lee Bank, Highgate and Deritend to Bordesley in the south. This formed a tight-knit community with impoverished housing conditions, but with immediate access to factories, shops and public houses; it was an intricate social network of suppliers, producers and distributors, the heart of Birmingham's celebrated 1000 trades.

Beyond this area lay the by-law ring of terraced through houses and 'tunnel-backs' (Figure 5.1) dominating the districts of Sparkbrook, Small Heath, Saltley, Winson Green, Rotton Park and parts of Hockley, Lozells and Nechells. Houses here were superior in quality to the back-to-backs; they had four or five rooms, a pantry, their own lavatory and a cellar. Bay windows were a common feature, perhaps overlooking a small patch of front garden, or alternatively the front door opened directly onto the footpath (Figure 5.2). These were the homes of the better-off artisans and lower middle classes, comprising late 19th century suburbs with their own local amenities, higher environmental standards, though with a rigid street layout and monotonous design that later generations came to disparage.

The Birmingham boundary was tightly drawn, particularly to the north, where the independent local government units of Handsworth, Aston Manor and Perry Barr lay beyond the Jewellery Quarter. Hockley, Newtown and Nechells were densely populated, with factories interspersed with back-to-back properties, while within the Jewellery Quarter residences of wealthy entrepreneurs had been converted into factories and workshops. The owners had moved out to Handsworth, Lozells and Birchfield to build their villas in more salubrious surroundings.

Beyond the boundary, Aston boasted an old nucleus of middle-class properties; artisan houses had followed, including some substantial ones for the Freehold Land Society. Industrial areas developed too, accompanied by clusters of working-class accommodation close to well known manufactories such as Ansell's Brewery and HP Sauce, and other industries

Figure 5.1 Tunnel-back houses, Stirchley.

established along the Fazeley Canal. Adjoining Aston, but in Handsworth for local government purposes, lay Witton, scarcely developed yet but already housing Birmingham's Borough Cemetery, while Kynochs (making ammunition and explosives) heralded the development of the area for industrial purposes. Erdington lay further to the north, fast absorbing middle-class villas and tunnel-back terraces. Handsworth was already marked by industrial and residential development.

Formerly east of the city boundary (but absorbed in 1891) Saltley was covered by streets of tunnel-backs, industry having been attracted by the coming of the railways. Further to the east lay Yardley (improbably as it now seems) within Worcestershire; its gas and water supplies came from Birmingham.

To the south, beyond Hay Mills and Tyseley, largely undeveloped countryside spread towards Hall Green. Balsall Heath, swallowed up by its neighbour in 1891, first developed like Aston as a middle-class area, but its middle classes moved on again to Moseley and elsewhere. Moseley itself developed as a suburb somewhat in emulation of Edgbaston for the relatively comfortable of Birmingham's business classes. Further to the south the small middle-class housing area of Selly Park (an interesting well-to-do

Figure 5.2 Better class villas, Bournville Lane.

enclave which never quite 'took off') was part of the administrative area of King's Norton in Worcestershire; so too was artisan Selly Oak, just emerging as an industrial district, helped by the recent opening of the Birmingham Battery and Metal Company factory on the Birmingham and Worcester Canal.

To the west, beyond Edgbaston, lay Harborne, formerly for local government purposes in Staffordshire, but annexed in 1891. The village centre was Harborne High Street, around which further residential development was attracted. In the north west of Birmingham, Ladywood had its congested back-to-backs and courtyards but along Hagley Road were large houses in keeping with adjoining Edgbaston; north of Hagley Road was an area of middle-class terraces on the former Gillot estate. Northward still lay Winson Green and Summerfield; Winson Green was surrounded by industry and before the end of the century accommodated a remarkable collection of institutions: a prison, an asylum (later All Saints' Hospital), a workhouse, a fever and smallpox hospital and an infirmary (later part of Dudley Road Hospital).

By the turn of the century, then, Birmingham, while tangential to the manufacturing heartland of the Black Country, was the centre of a large urban area where local authority boundaries seemed particularly archaic. In 1891 Balsall Heath, Harborne, Saltley and Little Bromwich had been absorbed by Birmingham, but a much greater area still lay tributary to the commercial and retailing power of the central area. Shortly the administrative tentacles of a vigorous Council would reach out for further territorial gain.

The geographical structure of Birmingham at the close of the Victorian period was on the point of change. The precise ways in which developments would unfold were related to attempts to address the housing problem. There was at this time a national groundswell of reformist opinion (largely professional, middle class, Liberal and partly nonconformist) concerning housing and social issues. Birmingham proved active in various reform movements and, amongst local authorities, established a premier position for the new activity, town planning. The city favoured a ring of low density suburbs to absorb its growing population, and territorial annexation of undeveloped land promised to make this possible; town planning would be the method of implementation.

Nationally, the housing question unfolded as follows. During the last two decades of the 19th century increasing concern was expressed about the housing of the working classes: poverty, squalor, and ill-health seemed to prevail amongst the overcrowded slum dwellers of the older, structurally deficient, insanitary houses close to the central cores of the larger towns and cities. Access to improved quality dwellings at rents the working classes could afford made housing the crucial rung in the ladder of social progress.

The latter years were remarkable for the sustained adverse comment on the state of British cities and their disadvantaged population – ironic perhaps because this came at the very time that by-law regulation was promising to usher in a new period for better housing, and local authorities were taking further powers against the unfit and insanitary. Local enquiries, collection of statistics and advocacy for reform went hand in hand; ill-health and poor housing seemed inextricably linked. Following the example of Charles Booth's mammoth survey of London, published in 17 volumes from 1889 onwards, it became popular for local conditions to be ruthlessly investigated. One method was for surveys to be conducted by local journalists. In 1901 the *Birmingham Daily Gazette* sent a special correspondent, J. C. Walters, to report on conditions in the slums; his findings were reprinted in *Scenes in Slumland* (1902).

It was argued that the very nature of big cities was inimical to man, and the future lay in leaving the cities in an organised way. Ebenezer Howard's garden city model, enunciated in his book published in 1899 and reprinted in 1902, and brought into practical application at Letchworth from 1904 onwards, was a clarion call to that end. But that was just one solution among many; there proved to be many ways in which the targets of the housing reformers (space, air and sunlight to defeat the evils of high density, overcrowding and congestion) might be met. The developing housing reform movement, which urged new forms of housing provision, came to be identified with low density layouts and estate design featuring tree-lined streets, landscaping in the romantic tradition and generous open space, both public and private. Garden suburbs were popular creations, with a number of successful co-partnership and other schemes in place in England and Wales by 1914. As we shall see, Birmingham would have its own examples.

Those initiatives were antidotes against the poor housing and general environmental conditions of the late 19th century. They were reactions to poor standards, an insanitary milieu and the bleak design of working-class housing in the late Victorian years. But they were a belated reaction too against the industrial philistinism of much of the century, and we should note the importance of the Arts and Crafts movement, again in which Birmingham would play a part. The movement in Birmingham had its own flavour (Crawford, 1984). It was less intellectual than some members in London, but its vision of the countryside was intense and romantic; crucially, its relationship with local Liberal nonconformist politicians and the Municipal School of Art in Margaret Street was uniquely close. The Birmingham Guild of Handicraft grew out of the Birmingham Kyrle Society, founded in 1880. With its motto 'By Hammer and Hand', it emphasised beauty of design and soundness of workmanship.

Housing

We have already seen that the question of the housing of the working classes was at the very heart of the crisis that afflicted late Victorian cities. It was a rock on which the force of 20th century reform movements would break. The years around the turn of the century were indeed a point of origin for many new 'arrangements' – social, political, economic, land, technological and environmental. The issues, complex and interrelated, embraced the cardinal urban features of the day: low wages, poverty, high rents, poor sanitation, ill-health, structural housing defects, minimum space standards (both public and private), overcrowding and high population densities. Birmingham was by no means the worst housed of British cities, but all these factors applied to the city to some extent.

In the last two decades of the century, the housing of inner London attracted greater national attention than that of the new manufacturing towns – a reversal of half a century earlier when Engels' (1845) survey of 'The Great Towns' included Dublin, Edinburgh, Liverpool, Nottingham, Birmingham, Glasgow, Bradford and, notoriously, Manchester, all to set against London. Political action was increasingly driven to respond to London conditions, and it was here that municipal housing was undertaken on a serious scale as one of the remedies to the lack of sound, rented accommodation. But by the end of the century the London-oriented tide had begun to turn as *national* housing policies, applicable to all cities, took shape in at least two respects: tenure and location of dwellings.

The Housing of the Working Classes Act 1900, extended to provincial boroughs the powers given to London in 1890, the most important of which was the power to establish lodging houses outside their own district (Gauldie, 1974). Importantly, lodging houses had been defined in 1890 to include separate cottages and tenements for the working classes. In effect, therefore, boroughs now had powers to build houses not only on land cleared by town improvement, but on other suitable land. Moreover, the Act was interpreted as giving powers to *build* and not just *rebuild* for those in need, legislation so far having been seen as giving powers only for the rehousing of those displaced by slum clearance. There was now growing support for council house building for the working classes. As we have seen, Birmingham had largely set its face against this form of provision, and, as will be recounted, continued to do so, even in the Corporation Street scheme, where unhealthy properties were cleared, though with no replacement. Birmingham was for some years yet a formidable urban bulwark against the rising tide of the council tenure option in housing provision.

Not that there was much by way of a popular demand for municipal housing; working men were encouraged to turn to building societies rather than the State. The problem for the individual family rested on the question of rents. Obviously, the smaller the income, the higher the proportion devoted to rent; less was available for other outgoings, with 'disposable income' at a very low level. In Edwardian Britain rent could well absorb one third of the income of the very poor.

Another factor was the growth of expenditure by local councils. Between 1890 and 1900 the rateable value of England and Wales increased by nearly 17%, while expenditure rose by 47% (Englander, 1983). In the next decade, the growth of expenditure from the rates was more than twice as fast as the rise in assessable value. Statutory duties imposed on local councils aggravated the plight of local authorities, and a financial situation, which would prove typical for much of the 20th century, began to unfold.

Accordingly rates soared alarmingly and pressure was transferred to ground landlords. Faced with diminishing returns, they sought (with little success) to reduce local expenditure and redistribute at least some of the rate burden away from house property. At a time of declining real wages, attempts to raise rents proved futile. The burden of social and civic reform imposed by central and local government fell on both property owners and the rented classes, but inevitably the latter had the least room for manoeuvre.

What had been astonishing so far in the national housing situation was that housing reform had been feebly assimilated into politics. A political consensus remained largely unbroken until 1914, reliant upon an ethos of voluntaryism. Working people failed to engage in the politics of housing; the silence of the poor in reform movements was deafening. But before the outbreak of the Great War tenancy agitation significantly altered the situation. There was also an accompanying industrial unrest. The West Midlands engineering and metal workers' strikes in 1913 began with spontaneous outbreaks in Birmingham, Smethwick and West Bromwich, and escalated into a district-wide demand for a minimum wage. Militancy over rents in London, Glasgow and other cities was exemplified also in the Birmingham area. Englander (1983) reveals a local but significant story.

In March 1913 the Wolverhampton and District Property Owners' Association resolved to raise weekly rents from the end of the month: by 3d for houses let at 5s a week and for houses at 5s 3d by 6d a week. Local outrage led to the formation of a Tenants' Defence League; a rent strike was called, but it collapsed by May.

In April that year one of the largest landlords in the Erdington area raised the rents on nearly 200 houses by a shilling a week. Rents of 7s 6d which nine months earlier had commanded a substantial house were now advanced to 9s. A quiet, prosperous suburb, much favoured by teachers, clerks, superior artisans, shop assistants and travellers, found this imposition too much, and an Erdington Tenants' Defence League was formed.

The agitation continued, with rents rising right across the city. National rent strikes multiplied in the early war years after 1914, a new grievance being the question of subsidised working-class houses for munitions workers. Again, Birmingham was no exception. At the beginning of October 1915, 130 tenants in Lozells combined to refuse the new rents. They were later joined by tenants in Witton. Another body active in agitation was the Aston and Handsworth Tenants' Association, formed six months earlier, and a rising tide of militancy affected Saltley and Erdington.

The immediate problem was defused by the Rent Restriction Act 1915 which fixed rents at pre-war levels – seemingly temporary legislation, but the objective of which would be pursued for much longer, after hostilities ceased. Rents agitation would prove sufficiently powerful to prevent the lifting of controls at the end of the war, when additionally, the arguments for cost rent municipal housing became even stronger.

Housing policy after 1918 is considered in Chapter 6, but sufficient has already been indicated to suggest that developments in the 1920s, and subsequently, have to be seen against an extensive and colourful backcloth. In the meantime other developments were afoot, which also affected the situation.

During the 19th century an important feature of innovation in British housing centred on the workers' settlement for improved housing, as in various Quaker developments in Ireland, Robert Owen's New Lanark, Titus Salt's Saltaire, Clark's shoe factory village at Street, Lever's Port Sunlight and elsewhere. They were accompanied by various ideal community experiments (Cherry, 1970; Hardy, 1979). A variation on these enterprises came with Cadbury's Bournville. In 1879 George and Richard Cadbury decided to move their cocoa and chocolate works from Bridge Street, off Broad Street in central Birmingham, to a green-field site four miles to the south west. A factory adjoining the Bourn Brook became the centre of a new settlement, called in the interests of French fashion in the confectionery trade, Bournville. Sixteen houses were built to the design of George Gadd to accommodate a few key workers (Figure 5.3).

In 1895 the building of the first three pairs of dwellings on the west side of Mary Vale Road marked the beginning, not just of a factory estate, but of an architectural enterprise which linked environment to housing provision and social purpose (Atkins, 1989). Almshouses and semi-detached dwellings on the east side of Linden Road and Mary Vale Road followed, and other building development progressed rapidly (Figure 5.4). Bournville was an experiment in estate building which was innovative in design by virtue of its emphasis on open space, tree-lined streets, cottage architecture and well stocked gardens; it provided dwellings let at reasonable rents; and, with the founding of the Village Trust in 1900, it had the means to control its future development in ways to ensure a full range of community provision. Of all the initiatives taken around the turn of the century Bournville proved one of the most influential, offering a model that showed low density housing to be an effective antidote to prevailing urban conditions.

Figure 5.3 Cadbury houses for key workers, Bournville Lane. Built 1879, demolished 1914.

Medical evidence from school children locally, compared with those from inner Birmingham, suggested that a combination of sun, space and fresh air gave the village the healthy environmental conditions Victorian Birmingham lacked. Bournville's subsequent expansion would be followed with interest.

By 1900 the estate consisted of 330 acres and contained 313 houses; by 1914 894 houses occupied an estate of 587 acres, when the core of the village was almost complete, with its infant school, church hall, shops and rest house (Figure 5.5). A young Birmingham designer, William Alexander Harvey, was estate architect from 1895 to 1904 (and thereafter consultant); his aesthetic control, and design of individual buildings, had a crucial early impact. He was ideologically committed to the enterprise.

> Desolate row upon row of ugly and cramped villas, ever multiplying to meet the demands of a quickly increasing population, where no open spaces are reserved, where trees and other natural beauties are sacrificed to crowd upon the land as many dwellings as possible, and where gardens cannot be said to exist – such are the suburbs which threaten to engulf our cities. (Harvey, 1906, p. 2)

In their place, Harvey was engaged in a revival of domestic architecture, not for grand country houses but for small cottages, capable of great variety. His crusade was to build homes and gardens, the produce from which would provide an income.

The early houses were for sale, on long leases, and evidence of profitable speculation prompted George Cadbury to revert to rent houses and vest control of the estate in a trust. His aims were clearly expressed in the Trust Deed: 'The Founder is desirous of alleviating the evils which arise from the insufficient and insanitary accommodation supplied to large numbers of the working classes, and of securing to the workers in factories some of the advantages of the outdoor village life.' With rents ranging from 4s 6d to 12s a week, the contribution of the lower working classes was in providing heterogeneity in a socially mixed community.

Bournville was the creation of an enlightened benefactor and entrepreneur. But there were other providers of the new design fashion, sought by the promoters of garden suburbs. In Birmingham Harborne was the setting, the developer a housing association, as we would call it today. The Harborne Society was inaugurated in June 1907, to promote the erection, cooperative ownership and management of houses; 54 acres at the Moor Pool Estate were developed by Harborne Tenants Ltd, with 494 dwellings, three shops, a club house, tennis courts, a bowling green and a public hall eventually built after its commencement in 1908. The estate catered for the upper end of the middle-class market but there was a range of rents from 4s 6d to over 9s a week. These were scarcely cheap houses for the working class poor (any more than Bournville provided) but we should recall that a large proportion of the dwellings in the congested parts of

Figure 5.4 Linden Road, Bournville. Built 1899–1900. Photo early 1900s.

Birmingham would then command rents of more than 4s 6d. In any event, the low density model of layout had once again been endorsed.

A third, distinctive housing colony was developed in the eastern side of the city, at Bordesley Green. The land had been purchased by the city council with the intention of building workmen's dwellings there, but various proposals were rejected on cost grounds. In 1908 the Council accepted a plan submitted by the Ideal Benefit Society for a 'workmen's garden colony'. The main function of the society was to provide sickness benefit to members of the artisan and professional classes in times of illness, and to pay capital sums to members on retirement from full employment. The society invested surplus funds into housing projects. On open fields on land leased from Birmingham Corporation and the Yardley Charities Estate, a garden suburb was laid out in the triangle between Bordesley Green, Belchers Lane and Drummond Road. The pivot of the internal layout was a 'market square' (which never came to anything); a small park was provided and densities were kept down to no more than 22 dwellings to the acre (Wise, 1982). The so-called Ideal Village did not have the romantic layout provided at Bournville or Harborne; but its long blocks of houses were enlivened by a variety of house design and generous tree planting. An estate of 225 houses and shops became engulfed in municipal house building in the 1920s and the open country setting was destroyed.

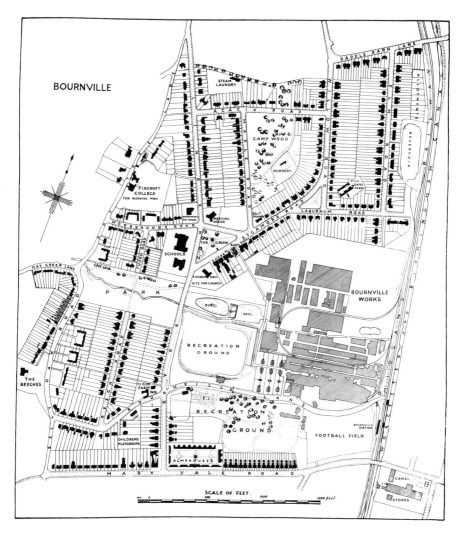

Figure 5.5 Plan of Bournville, 1907.

Bournville, Moor Pool and Bordesley Green, interesting and important in themselves, contributed only a fraction of the houses built in Birmingham between 1900 and 1914. The City Council was not a provider and the new housing stock came entirely from a variety of small private builders. Undoubtedly there was an incremental improvement in the quality of the stock at this time. Edgbaston's supply of grand houses was still increasing (though the boom years had passed), Moseley's reputation for solid respectability was enhanced, and throughout the city local authority regulations ensured control over building standards. The major problem of

101

course was the inheritance from the past, and it was to this that the City Council turned in 1913.

In July of that year a committee was appointed to investigate the housing conditions of the poor in Birmingham and to review past policies in administering the Housing Acts. The chairman was Councillor Neville Chamberlain, son of Joseph. Their report, presented to Council in 1914 made doleful reading: 'The evidence received by the Committee fully establishes the fact that a large proportion of the poor in Birmingham are living under conditions of housing detrimental both to their health and morals' (*Report of the Special Housing Inquiry Committee, 1914*). There were more than 43 000 back-to-back dwellings, and 27 500 dwellings in courtyards; 42 000 had no water supply inside the dwelling and 58 000 had no separate wc. Shared toilet facilities attracted much objection to the 'degrading and disgusting conditions of their outbuildings'.

To counteract such conditions, the committee urged a 'gradual reconstruction of the old City on better lines', undertaken to a 'pre-arranged and carefully thought out plan'. Such a plan of a reconstructed City:

'would not only show amended street lines, but would also differentiate the quarters which should be allotted to various classes of buildings and should make proper provision for the requisite open spaces . . . it would serve as a guide to the Council in many of the problems of transit, street widening, provision of public buildings and other matters with which they now have to deal separately and without regard to the City as a whole . . . The Committee accordingly attach considerable importance to the preparation of a Town Plan to include the whole built-up area of the City, and they recommend the Council to give instructions to the Town Planning Committee to put the work in hand immediately'. (*op cit*, 1914)

This was the voice of confidence, vision and no little sagacity. It was a Council sure of itself, with authority, and prepared to embark on new waters. Town planning was a new field of activity and a comprehensive approach such as that recommended put it in the forefront of local authority enterprise. In the space of a few years how had Birmingham achieved such a command of the situation? At least part of the reason lay in the force of advocacy of a Birmingham Councillor, J. S. Nettlefold.

The wider view

John Sutton Nettlefold was born in London, in 1866. He came to Birmingham at the age of 12 and later entered the Broad Street offices of Nettlefold and Co. A Unitarian, his local connections were further secured on marriage to Margaret, daughter of Arthur Chamberlain. He was elected to the City Council for Edgbaston Ward in 1898, was chairman of the Housing Committee from its inception in 1901, and also chaired the

Committee for the Extension of City Boundaries between 1908 and 1911. He was a strong supporter of the Garden Cities Association and became chairman of the Town Planning Committee of the Association of Municipal Councils. For ten years between 1901 and 1911 (when he failed to be re-elected to the City Council) his personality, forthright views, commanding authority locally, and his national influence combined to make him a crucial figure in policy matters regarding housing and town planning.

In 1901 the Council established a separate Housing Committee (though only just, with a vote of 32 to 30), housing matters previously having been dealt with by the Health Committee and Estates Committee. Nettlefold was appointed chairman. It was timely for a new approach to the housing question. The sanitary debate, extended over half a century, had largely run its course. Sanitary imperfections had been, or could be overcome. The quality of the wider housing environment was now crucial, particularly for the poor.

There was a readily apparent need to increase the supply of good, cheap houses in the city, but the precise means to achieve this objective remained elusive. Bournville was in its infancy and there seemed to be little likelihood of either rapid development or emulation elsewhere. Meanwhile there was no great warmth for municipal building. The Ryder Street, Lawrence Street and Milk Street projects had been embroiled in controversy, and Nettlefold himself took a decided stance against the very principle of municipal house building.

The solution appeared to lie in the making available of tracts of land in the suburbs, which could be laid out with a sufficient number of broad streets and a sufficiency of open space and playgrounds. For Nettlefold cheap suburban land for cheaper housing was the promise which fitted well with a prevailing ethos in housing circles at the time: decentralise to benefit from open space and healthier living conditions, provide low density housing layouts and build to a vernacular cottage tradition. Ebenezer Howard's garden city ideal as proposed in his book *Tomorrow: a Peaceful Path to Real Reform* (1898), reprinted with the title *Garden Cities of Tomorrow* (1902), and propagated by the Garden Cities Association, was one way forward, but Letchworth was the only practical example built before 1914. Garden suburbs represented a variant and before the Great War there were over a hundred examples nationally; the nearest was at Wolverhampton at Fallings Park.

Nettlefold was attracted to the lessons provided by Germany where town expansion planning was a well established practice in the larger cities. He avidly seized on the work of a Manchester reformer, Thomas Horsfall, who had published a book in 1904, *The Example of Germany*; his argument was that if town councils obtained powers to incorporate and purchase large suburban tracts, adopt good building plans and establish a zoning system, situations could be created whereby healthy, soundly constructed dwellings could be provided for the working classes, and the dwellings would not be spoiled by their surroundings (Harrison, 1991). In 1905 Nettlefold proposed that a small deputation be sent to some of the principal German towns and to report on their inspection. The visit was made to Berlin, Ulm, Stuttgart, Mannheim, Frankfurt, Cologne and Dusseldorf in August and a Report went to Housing Committee in October, and to Council in June 1906.

A plea for a 'consistent policy for dealing with the housing conditions in Birmingham', it was based on 'the encouragement of, and assistance in, the provision of healthy, cheerful houses on the outskirts of the city'. The Report (Housing Committee, 1901–7) called for a general plan to guide the development of all 'uncovered' land within the city boundaries. Specifically, it advocated a 'policy of the Municipality creating ground rents, and directing the development of building land on sound, sanitary and cheerful lines', one which has worked successfully in Germany without putting a charge on the rates. The Report concluded that:

> Your Committee are of opinion that a Corporation cannot own too much land, provided that it is judiciously purchased. Municipal land could be laid out with open spaces and all other essentials to a healthy, happy community, with the additional advantage that any future rise in the value of land would directly or indirectly go to the ratepayers. The Corporation could then assist private individuals and Public Utility Building Societies, with whose *bona fides* they were satisfied, to erect at the lowest possible rate healthy, cheerful houses for people with small incomes. The policy of buying land and encouraging other people to build the houses would enable the Corporation to give a great stimulus to the supply of good, cheap houses on the outskirts of the city, and would thereby benefit a very large number of people.

A coherent policy was in the making, well honed to the tradition of a strong, Birmingham municipality. The council would prepare a general zoning plan, assemble land for development, lease it for housing of a particular kind, and ensure that open space and social facilities were provided. The freedom and energies of local people were safeguarded; there would be no municipal landlord. In a memorable passage, the Report continued: 'The Garden City idea, the Garden Suburb idea, have taken hold of the minds of Englishmen. We cannot hope to make Birmingham into a Garden City, although something can be done towards that end, but we can, if we will, create Garden Suburbs around Birmingham.'

This future geography of the city would, of course, require legislation. With Council approval, Nettlefold took his ideas to a conference of local authorities at Manchester and the AMC prepared a scheme for a draft Town Planning Bill. A deputation met the Prime Minister and the President of the Local Government Board who in an emollient response promised that the matter would receive earnest and sympathetic attention.

In the meantime Nettlefold was chairman of the Harborne Society and prime mover in the Harborne Tenants' Association project; Mrs Nettlefold cut the first sod for the development in 1907. As a vigorous propagandist he lost no opportunity in his public life to advance his cause: that the home of the individual, the prosperity of the nation and the strength of the Empire depended on putting an end to overcrowded cities and jerry-built suburbs, and securing efficient, healthy houses in a 'town planned' city. He was active in the setting up of a Birmingham Playgrounds, Open Spaces and Playing Fields Society, founded in 1906, which in 1908 amalgamated with the Birmingham Housing Reform Association. His lively views on housing and town planning policy were given in his book *Practical Housing* (1908), a volume curiously neglected in later years, though in its power and influence might be matched with the works of Ebenezer Howard (earlier 1902) and Raymond Unwin about the same time (1909).

Planning and the suburbs

Nettlefold's precise ideas did not materialise, though a good deal of subsequent development in the city was clearly derivative. But in the years up to the Great War, Birmingham was foremost amongst British local authorities in advancing the cause of town planning and making use of the first available legislation, the Housing, Town Planning etc. Act 1909.

The target of housing concern had long been the overcrowded central parts of the city. But change could already be detected. Between 1896 and 1911 the number of occupied houses in the twelve innermost wards of Birmingham fell by 9½% while the number in the six outer wards rose by nearly 30%. The market processes of decongestion and decentralisation, observable in London since the 1870s, were now apparent in the heart of the West Midlands. Strategically there was great need to control the direction of this outward expansion, and Nettlefold's dream of a ring of garden suburbs, with the municipality the ground landlord, would at least partly answer this. But there were two other issues: transport and local authority boundaries, and they both fell into place at this time.

As we have seen, improvements in Birmingham's tram network came with the phasing out of horse and steam trams and the introduction of overhead electric wires, first on Bristol Road (1901), then the Dudley Road routes (1902) and Coventry Road (1904). Private companies were taken over and a full municipal service was available by 1911. Hagley Road succumbed after long opposition, in 1913. Old lines were reconstructed and more double-decker trams provided; by 1914 cheap fares and an increased carrying capacity gave greater public transport penetration to the outer edges of the city than ever before. Just before the war, in 1913, the first Corporation petrol buses ran from Selly Oak to Rednal and Rubery, and the Birmingham and Midland Co. ran from the Ivy Bush to Quinton,

Handsworth and Moseley. To all this should be added the advent of the private car. Outer Birmingham had never been so accessible.

We have also seen that Birmingham as a unit of local government historically was spatially constrained. In 1891 Saltley, Balsall Heath and Little Bromwich were added to the city in the east, and Edgbaston amalgamated with Harborne in the west. In 1909 and, massively in 1911, other urban and rural districts were added.

In 1907 Halesowen RDC introduced a scheme for the disposal of the sewage of one of its parts, Quinton. The Quinton Parish Council protested on cost grounds and resolved in favour of incorporation with Birmingham. In July 1908 the general purposes committee of the City Council advised the Council to reject unification, but in full Council an amendment proposed by Nettlefold was carried convincingly (44 votes to 18); typically he urged expansion as a means of securing housing areas and planning future suburban growth. A special boundaries committee was set up (with Nettlefold as chairman), entrusted to make representations to the Local Government Board; Quinton was duly incorporated in 1909, adding 838 acres and a population of 1100 to the city.

But much more was to come. In a report to Council in 1909 the boundaries committee proposed massive extensions. The Local Government Board's inquiry into Birmingham's claims opened in December; the inspector reported favourably and in May 1910 the Board issued a provisional order following the city's scheme in almost every respect. As a Bill went through Parliament earlier resistance to Birmingham's proposals crumbled. First, Erdington Urban District Council declared its wish to join Birmingham; it had always relied heavily on the services provided by its neighbours. The populous Aston Manor, which had become a municipal borough in 1903 (following rebuffs in 1876 and 1888 because of Birmingham's opposition) then agreed. King's Norton and Northfield UDC followed in October 1910, Yardley RDC in November, and Handsworth UDC, after spirited resistance, finally capitulated in March 1911. When the Bill went through the Lords in May, Birmingham gained control of a city area three times the size of Glasgow, and twice that of either Manchester or Liverpool. The city held sway over an area which tripled its former size; a city with an area of 13 478 acres was granted annexations to the extent of an additional 30 123 acres in November 1911:

Handsworth UD, Staffordshire	3 667
Aston Manor, Borough, Warwickshire	960
Erdington UD, Warwickshire	4 630
Yardley RD, Worcestershire	7 590
King's Norton and Northfield UD (part) Worcestershire	13 276
	30 123 acres

The city's population increased to around 840 000. Rich pickings came from Aston Manor, with a population of 82 000 (1908); King's Norton and Northfield, 78 000; Handsworth, 68 000; Yardley, 60 000; and Erdington, 29 000.

Nettlefold's town planning dream had now the context of available rural land on the fringes of the city; 55% of the total area of the city was undeveloped. Unfortunately the housing and planning legislation of 1909 had received rough treatment from the Lords during the passage of the Bill on grounds of compensation and betterment (Cherry, 1982) and a cumbersome, enabling measure was as much as could be retrieved. It simply permitted local authorities to prepare town planning schemes in respect of land about to be developed or in course of development. But it was enough, if the political will was there.

In February 1910 a town planning sub-committee of the general purposes committee was set up; it became a committee in its own right in November 1911, with Neville Chamberlain as chairman. Son of Joseph, born in 1869, his first business involvement was to direct a sisal-growing experiment in the Bahamas. This failed and he returned to Birmingham, becoming chairman of Elliotts, manufacturers of copper, brass and yellow metal at Selly Oak, and joining Hoskins, a manufacturer of cabin berths in Bordesley. In 1911 he was elected to serve as second of three councillors for All Saints Ward. He was quickly plunged into weighty matters, and, as things turned out, town planning questions would concern him for much of the rest of his life (Cherry, 1980).

He was presented with a major report from the Town Clerk, E. V. Hiley, on two town planning schemes which were then in course of preparation: for Quinton and Harborne, and for East Birmingham. The first, covering 2320 acres and comprising the parish of Quinton and parts of the parishes of Harborne, Edgbaston and Northfield, became the first town planning scheme in the country to be approved by the Local Government Board, in May 1913 (not the first to be submitted; that distinction lies with Ruislip–Northwood UDC in respect of land in that urban district and the Parish of Rickmansworth in Watford RDC). The area, ripe for development as soon as drainage improvements were carried out, was situated between two populated areas, to the north at Smethwick and Oldbury, and to the south at Selly Oak and Northfield. The scheme aimed to provide communication between these two centres, and two main arterial roads were proposed. The proposed land use was entirely residential, apart from four acres set aside for parks and open spaces. The average number of dwellings to the acre would be twelve, with a maximum number of twenty on any one acre (Cherry, 1974).

The East Birmingham Scheme, approved in August 1913, covered 1442 acres in the Washwood Heath, Saltley, Small Heath and Sparkbrook wards of the city. This was an area which had developed rapidly in recent years:

12 miles of new streets had been laid out and 10 000 houses erected in the Saltley and Little Bromwich districts since 1891. Once again, the scheme provided for improved communications, a control of land use, and lower densities.

Town planning progress was clear. Three sub-committees were appointed: for the two schemes (George Cadbury Jnr was chairman for Quinton and Harborne) and a general survey sub-committee. The latter recommended early schemes for Yardley and King's Norton and Northfield and proceeded to recommend coverage for the whole of the extended city, 'to outline a scheme which should include a general settled policy with regard to Open Spaces, Radial Roads and Ring Roads and the division of districts into residential, business and factory areas. This would necessitate the preparation of a skeleton plan for the whole area.' (General Survey Sub-Committee, 1911). This was December 1911, when the City Surveyor could report a staff of 17 engaged in town planning work. In 1914 three schemes were being prepared: East Birmingham (1673 acres), North Yardley (3164 acres) and South Birmingham (8400 acres).

Birmingham's progress in planning matters was remarkable, but there was good reason for optimism not to exceed reality. As Neville Chamberlain explained to the British Association's meeting in the city in 1913:

> We cannot expect to achieve all at once the perfection of a garden city. The community does not own the land, and it does not propose to carry on the business of a land surveyor or of a builder. All that can be done at first is to see that the main lines of communication, both radial and circumferential, are correctly laid out as to direction and width, that some limit is imposed on the number of houses to the acre, that open spaces are reserved for parks, recreation grounds or playing fields, and that factory and residential areas are duly separated and confined to the situations most suitable to their respective needs'. (Chamberlain, 1913, pp. 177)

The planning principles were sound enough, but it was many years before they could be applied effectively to the processes of land use change.

However, Birmingham was clearly in the forefront of national town planning; statutory provisions seemed suited to an efficient local government administration like Birmingham, and its political will had been fired by Nettlefold's drive, ably continued by Neville Chamberlain. Nettlefold continued to proselytise, but no longer on the City Council he became increasingly maverick and disenchanted with what the city was doing; indeed, he was an objector to the Quinton and Harborne Town Planning Scheme, on certain technical aspects. His book *Practical Town Planning* published in 1914 degenerated into a tirade against those against whom he was most critical – the drafters of the Birmingham town planning schemes and the Local Government Board.

But there were other important figures to make the running, not least a generation of some highly effective chief officers: the Medical Officer of

Health John Robertson, and the City Engineer Henry Stilgoe. George Cadbury Jnr was a member of the town planning committee and his book *Town Planning with special reference to the Birmingham Schemes* (1915) was a useful outline of the city approach for other authorities to follow. Meanwhile, between 1912 and 1914 the city had a luminary as part-time lecturer at the University: Raymond Unwin was engaged to give two lectures a week on town planning matters, 'Civic Design and Town Planning' and 'Social Origins and Economic Bases of Towns' for the Department of Civil Engineering.

What would have happened had not war intervened must be a matter of conjecture, but certainly housing and town planning policy had made enormous strides in the city up to 1914. The geography of Birmingham would be recast.

6
Between the Wars

Joseph Chamberlain died in July 1914; for Birmingham it was the end of an era. The onset of the Great War came within a month and over the next four years the city directed its industrial energies to the war effort. The businessman's motto was soon changed into 'busier than usual' (Brazier and Sandford, 1921). Awesome statistics testify to the vast quantities of rifles, cartridges, military ornaments, saddlery, tinplate goods, shells, and mechanical transport including armoured cars, tanks and aeroplanes produced from the city's factories. New plant of abnormal capacity, such as the Vickers' off-shoot at Drews Lane, Ward End, sprang up with astonishing rapidity, and existing works like those of the Birmingham Small Arms Co, Kynochs, and Longbridge underwent very large extensions. Birmingham became a veritable arsenal. The National Shell Factory was established at Washwood Heath. The Mills' hand grenade was invented in the city. Kynochs were contracted to manufacture 25 million rifle cartridges a week. The BSA made 10 000 rifles and 2 000 Lewis guns a week. As many as 4 500 aero engines were built and 700 complete aeroplanes were turned out by Wolseley Motors. Adderley Park made firing gear and sight mechanisms for naval guns. All branches of industry thrived.

Other changes followed in the wake of this war effort. Some were of short duration, such as the take-over of academic space at the University (the Great Hall) for hospital purposes. Of longer-term significance was the stimulation of the allotment movement, responding to the need for home-grown produce. More significant still was the recruitment of women labour for city factories; altogether 15 000 women were brought to Birmingham from all parts of Britain, with a resultant housing problem in the city.

Not until the Second Battle of the Marne in July 1918 was it suggested that military ascendancy had conclusively shifted to the allies, and that the end of the Great War was drawing near. Even so, the announcement of the Armistice on Monday 11 November came with a certain suddenness. The country had lost 745 000 of its younger men and was left to count the cost. The pre-1914 world had gone and a new one was in the making: 'out went gold sovereigns, chaperons, muffin men and the divine right of private enterprise; in came State control, summer time, a new prosperity and a new self-confidence for families long submerged below the poverty line, and in the aftermath, a biting scepticism and challenge to established authorities' (Marwick, 1965, p. 7). In this context much would change in Birmingham too, and this chapter looks at the factors which, during the 1920s and 1930s, helped to shape a rather different city from the one remembered by those who had marched from its recruiting offices in the summer of 1914. A total of 150 000 men and women of Birmingham served in the forces during the war. Altogether 13 000 did not return to the city to enjoy what would have been the fruits of their loyal service.

We turn first to housing and planning, because it was in this area that the city had already begun to establish some very clear objectives before 1914; in seeing what happened to them we shall conclude that there were some very different outcomes indeed from what had been earlier envisaged. From housing we turn to industry and the local economy, where we note the changes wrought by the introduction of new manufacturing concerns, beneficial enough to deflect the colder chills of economic recession. We turn finally to other areas where the city was shrugging off the past and adjusting to a new future.

During this period the City Council was increasingly an agent in securing progressive change; noteworthy were its activities with regard to housing, roads and traffic, and central area projects. This may suggest a continuation of the heroic era of Chamberlain. But there was a major difference: government policy now took the lead, not municipal enterprise. Whereas before 1914 action emanated from the Council House, after 1918 the Council largely took its line from national legislation. Moreover, local politics had changed. In 1919 the Birmingham Liberal Unionist Association and the Birmingham Conservative Association amalgamated. The Unionists (as they became known) found that their main opposition came from Labour, which in 1926 held 30 out of the 120 places on Council; their number declined, then rose to 32 (out of 136) in 1935 and fell again to 27 in 1938. The private, voluntary philanthropic face of the Birmingham community remained active, promoting schemes and taking initiatives which had a bearing on the city of the future.

Housing

Wartime circumstances had already conspired to affect the post-war situation. As we have seen, the Rent and Mortgage Restriction Act 1915, which fixed rents at the levels obtaining in 1914, became politically impossible to repeal. But the whole question of housing after the war took on a new light as it became apparent that there was no returning to a *status quo* position and that new initiatives for post-war reconstruction were required. Lloyd George's Reconstruction Committee, set up in February 1917, gave strong support for a Ministry of Health (responsible for housing) and an extensive housing programme for the working classes. A severe national housing shortage, variously estimated at between 400 000 and 600 000 dwellings, had to be addressed, and there were profound doubts as to whether the private building industry had the capacity to meet the challenge.

Action was also called for in matters of housing quality. The Local Government Board set up a committee to consider the whole question of the provision of dwellings for the working classes, including the technicalities of building construction. It was chaired by Sir John Tudor Walters, an MP and Director of the Hampstead Garden Suburb Trust, and the Report when published in 1918 bears his name (Tudor Walters, 1918). However, in fact the contents of the Tudor Walters Report owed much to the contribution of a committee member, Raymond Unwin, advocate for many years of low density layouts and cottage-style architecture in vernacular style (Miller, 1992). New standards were set for the working-class house: enhanced room space, wc approached under cover and bathroom provision on the first floor, a larder and a coal store, access to sunlight and a private garden. Densities were not to exceed 12 houses to the acre and design elements would incorporate the *cul-de-sac*, courtyard and green. The Government's *Housing manual*, published in 1919, adopted these recommendations and a particular housing style was set for many years.

These provisions were not all that novel for Birmingham, of course. Bournville and Moor Pool Estate had established low density, cottage-style architecture many years previously, and the city's early town planning schemes similarly aimed at low density housing, as advocated by Nettlefold in his dream of a ring of garden suburbs. But the real significance of the Tudor Walters Report came with housing legislation in 1919. The Housing and Town Planning Act made it obligatory for local authorities to prepare surveys of their housing needs, to draw up plans to deal with them, and to carry out their schemes. That was in July, but the Minister, Christopher Addison, was soon persuaded to go further; in order to speed up housing production, direct subsidies (as opposed to the Exchequer simply meeting any losses incurred by local authorities) would have to be granted. A

Housing (Additional Powers) Act was rushed through by December, which provided for subsidies for local authority dwellings.

Lloyd George's election promise to the voters of Wolverhampton in November 1918 that returning soldiers should have 'homes fit for heroes', was being met at a pace and scale which few could have anticipated. But there was a price to pay. At a time of rapidly rising prices the housing programme met with escalating costs. In April 1921 Addison fell from office and the housing scheme was halted. But in 1923 Neville Chamberlain, elected to Parliament in 1919 at the age of 50 and now Minister of Health, introduced another subsidy scheme, of a kind that resulted in smaller houses, let at lower rents and with the express intent of stimulating private development. This programme was extended in 1924 by John Wheatley, Minister in the first Labour Government, who gave higher subsidies, promised a long-term housing programme, and confirmed local authorities in their role as house builders. The Wheatley provisions remained in force until 1933 (though with a reduced subsidy), and the effect of the various arrangements was that in England and Wales 31% of the 2.5 million dwellings constructed between 1919 and 1934 were built by local authorities; moreover, a quarter of the remainder (built by private enterprise) were also subsidised. Other subsidy arrangements, continuing during the thirties, meant that by 1939, of the four million dwellings built in Britain between the wars one in four was local authority provided.

Precisely why Britain embarked on such a massive shift in housing tenure has attracted vigorous debate (Orbach 1977; Swenarton 1981; Daunton 1987). We can be cynical ('buying off the working class to forestall revolution') or circumstantial ('the pieces of the jigsaw simply fell into place') but the fact is that a radical departure took place in national housing policy. Deep rooted political prejudice against municipal housing was overturned, and for 60 years the council house held an ever-increasing share in national tenure options.

Birmingham's housing performance between the wars has to be seen against this background. Remarkably the Unionist City Council, with a history of sustained antipathy to municipal involvement in housing provision, and with an ethos of individualism established by Nettlefold, proceeded to build more council houses before the Second World War than any other local authority in the country: 30 000 by 1930, 40 000 by 1933 and 50 000 by 1939. The social geography of Birmingham was dramatically altered as the suburban fringe was developed for both public and private housing; suburban estates were both working class and middle class.

Birmingham ended the war with a pressing housing shortage, exacerbated by a population increase boosted by a war-time influx of workers; a backlog was estimated at over 12 000 dwellings. The City Council did not find it immediately easy to respond to the challenge posed by the 1919 legislation. It first set up a Housing and Estates Department, with a regular sub-committee and a new Housing Director. The first houses were built in Alum Rock and others followed at Billesley Farm, Pineapple Farm (King's Heath), Stonehouse Farm (California) and elsewhere. Over 3200 houses were built under the Addison provisions, woefully behind an intended target of 10 000. But worse would be revealed: the escalating cost of building construction led to the houses being built for between £900 and £1000, four times the pre-war level, and as we have seen, the Addison subsidy programme was terminated.

Locally there was mounting dissatisfaction with the housing and town planning committee (two bodies fused in 1917) and, after a special committee of inquiry, institutional changes were made. A newly-named public works and town planning committee became responsible for building council houses and a housing and estates committee assumed responsibility for the management of corporation estates and for dealing with housing allocations to applicants.

Chamberlain's Act of 1923 successfully stimulated private house building, annual construction rates rising from 382 in 1922 to 1201 in 1924. The city even enhanced the government subsidy, increasing the lump sum grant from £75 to £100. Moreover, there was a scheme to assist corporation tenants to buy their own property. But in spite of the support and encouragement, and the fall in house prices, home buying remained a distant dream for most working-class families.

The public works and town planning committee proved more productive than its predecessor, and was suitably poised to take advantage of the provisions of the Wheatley Act. In 1924, the year of the Act, the city erected 1663 houses; it nearly doubled to 3066 in 1925, when at the Batchelor's Farm Estate, Bordesley Green, an average of six houses per hour were being completed. Green-field sites were being used up quickly and it required a further boundary extension to release land in the north at Perry Barr, where the Perry Hall Estate was purchased from the Gough-Calthorpe family (the Hall was demolished in 1929), and Kettlehouse Farm at Kingstanding in 1930.

By the end of the 1930s vast municipal estates ringed the city periphery in the north, east and south, no less than fifteen individual estates each having more than 1000 houses. Manzoni (1939) chronicled the City Council's achievements in a publication to mark the building of 50 000 municipal houses. Kingstanding was the largest municipal estate in England, outside the London area, while Fox Hollies and Lea Hall were still dauntingly large.

A new design element was introduced into the morphology of the city. A complex geometric pattern of straight roads intersected by circles and crescents made for a loose, open layout, often wasteful of land, and, with poor landscaping, bleak and lacking in intimacy. All houses had front and

Table 6.1 Principal municipal estates 1919–39.

	houses
Kingstanding	4802
Fox Hollies & Gospel Farm, Hall Green	3762
Lea Hall, Stechford	3486
Weoley Castle, Selly Oak	2718
Billesley Farm, Yardley Wood	2442
Marlborough House & Fast Pits, Yardley	2171
Allen's Cross, Northfield	2161
Kettlehouse, Perry Barr	1500
Witton Lodge Farm, Perry Barr	1374
Batchelor's Farm & Norton Boys' Home	1360
Tyseley Farm & Spring Road	1350
Pype Hayes, Erdington	1344
Kent's Moat	1227
Dad's Lane, King's Heath	1114
Heybarn Farm, Small Heath	1041

Source: Developing Birmingham, 1989.

back gardens, and an overall density of 12 to the acre followed conventional norms. Major roads were tree lined, but the free flowing layouts envisaged by the pioneer planning advocates were reduced to mechanistic interpretations of space and mass, often the most achieved being some variety in appearance by breaking up frontages of terrace blocks.

As for the dwellings themselves, they represented a marked improvement on most privately rented property then available (Chinn, 1991). They were all fitted with dressers and cupboards and, after 1923, electric lighting superseded gas. Each had a gas range and gas heating for a washing copper. Parlour-type homes (a minority) had a hot water circulating system. A typical house design would provide a hall, large living room, scullery, bathroom, three bedrooms, toilet, larder and coal shed. All houses had gardens (for the first time for the working classes) and gardening became a new household leisure pursuit. In many ways circumstances were in place for an alternative working-class life-style to emerge. A sociological as well as a geographical shift was unfolding in the development of these estates.

The provision of community facilities lagged behind other aspects of estate development and unfortunate comparisons were made with the wealth of provision and the social cohesion of older districts left behind. School places were often insufficient at first and shops and libraries were poorly provided; the first Council community centre was not opened until November 1936 (at Billesley Farm Estate). Local employment was slow to build up and lengthy and costly journeys to work became a new feature of daily life. Dearer food in local shops was also a new factor for family budgets. But the biggest strain came from house rents. In 1933 the average weekly rent for a municipal parlour house was 15s 6d a week, for a non-parlour house 11s 4d and for smaller, non-parlour houses between 8s 6d and 10s. This compared with private rents in the central wards being largely under 10s a week. As Chinn (1991) observes, 'superior housing and a better environment remained out of the reach of the poor'. Even so, poverty and ill-health remained no stranger to the new estates and in 1939 a survey of Kingstanding suggested a lack of nutrition there at a time of relative plenty elsewhere. The Birmingham Social Survey Committee (1942) found that 31% of the families were below the minimum standard of sufficiency (the minimum standard of spending on food necessary to maintain adequate health, using the BMA minimum diet scale of 1933). Clearly, new housing alone was not the answer to sub-standard living accommodation.

The local authority estate was just one novel feature of suburban Birmingham. Another and more extensive innovation was the take-up of land for private building. A total of 54 500 houses was built by private enterprise between 1919 and 1939. The growth in houses for owner occupation marked the second departure from the 19th century emphasis on private building for rent. The 20th century tenure shift had gone full course when by the last quarter of the century the trend away from private renting was almost complete, owner occupation had become the norm for the majority and council renting had clearly peaked as a second option.

The post-war period started with an interesting development at Hawkesley Mill, Longbridge. During the war Austin's factory witnessed a rapid growth in production, which required a major increase in the size of the workforce. There was a pressing problem to find accommodation for workers and Austin embarked on a scheme to build a local estate. 120 acres of farmland were purchased and, for a first phase on a third of it, he ordered 200 'Readicut' red cedar bungalows in 1916 from a company in Bay City, Michigan. Within a year this development had been completed, but the intention to complete the whole site was thwarted, first by the increase in U-boat activity, and finally by the end of the war and the reduction in the workforce. One of the timber bungalows was destroyed by fire during construction; the rest were erected alongside 50 brick-built houses, regularly interspersed as fire breaks. They were located in a pleasant, landscaped estate; there were sports facilities and a village hall; and the houses were well planned with an inside toilet, bathroom and central heating. The external appearances of these bungalows on the whole remain in their original condition and the entire estate is now a potential conservation area.

Around the Birmingham ring, Hall Green, to the south beyond Sparkhill, emerged as a favoured district for private building. The tramway was extended along Stratford Road to the city boundary at Shirley, and the

Robin Hood Lane area became the centre of middle-class housing with semi-detached properties costing between £550 and £600. In the south west, Northfield, Rednal and Rubery proved attractive; in the north Birchfield and Perry Barr were opened up; in the west, Quinton; and in the east, Sheldon (once brought into the city after 1931).

Beyond the city boundary rail access to favoured environments made Sutton Coldfield and Solihull increasingly popular for the better off. The railway was a modest agent of change, however. The North Warwickshire line (a late development, opening in 1908) had local stations at Hall Green, Yardley Wood and nearby Shirley, and the GWR encouraged living out of the city. Their quarterly publication of a property register for 'Birmingham and its Beautiful Borderlands' advised in 1914 that 'within 15 minutes of leaving Snow Hill, the busy toiler either in his brains or in his hands can alight among the fields of Shirley, Solihull or Knowle.' But Greater Birmingham was no Metroland.

Rural land readily came onto the market at low prices; agriculture was in depression and large estates were being broken up, the victim of death duties and higher taxation. Owner occupation as a tenure option became socially desirable and 'modernity' in house design appealing to the upwardly mobile; Home Exhibitions (Bingley Hall a frequented venue) vied to improve on consumer gadgets, labour-saving devices, window designs and house heating installations. Building societies underwent a sustained expansion, with the 1930s in particular an era of cheap money; interest rates were low and small initial deposits available. There was no great rise in salaries or wages, but employment in professional and administrative services was expanding. For those with a well-paid job, and likely to keep it, owner occupation was increasingly attractive. So for a modest semi-detached house in a suburban location at £450 (as it might cost in the mid-1930s), purchase could be made for a deposit of £25 and repayments over 20 years would not exceed 13s a week.

Speculative building boomed in these conditions, especially in the 1930s; in the 1920s the number of municipal dwellings built exceeded the number of private houses by more than two to one in the period 1924–31, whereas this ratio was reversed after 1932.

Advertisements from the period reveal the number of small private building companies then active, and the way they targetted their product for a widening market. A local booklet of 'useful knowledge for health and home' (Green and Wolff, 1933) indicated that Stanley J. Smith and Co. of Halesowen was building the Lyndon Barn Estate at Acock's Green: three-bed houses at £435 and two-bed at £385. C. F. Price, a builder of Alum Rock advertised houses at Castle Bromwich with the message 'Regain your health and happiness!!! Why live in unhealthy cities? When sunshine and country breezes can be yours for £395?'. N. Thomas and Son of Edgbaston was building locally and at Shirley; T. Newbury and Sons of

Handsworth specialised locally; and H. Greaves and Sons of Moseley was building in Hall Green. R. & H. Fletcher Ltd offered 'Ideal Houses' in a 'Garden Village' at Victoria Park Estate, King's Norton, from £435; also in King's Norton, houses on the Dell Road Estate, built by Stanton G. Marsh of South Yardley, from £390. More expensive properties were provided by D. W. Hubbock of Northfield, building near the Lickeys from £650, while E. L. Howell of King's Norton advertised houses 'to purchasers' own requirements' for £750. Hodgkinson of Shirley invited purchasers to 'Live in the gorgeous fresh air at Olton in one of Hodgkinson's Wonder Houses', for £550 including a brick garage. E. Wilkinson advertised 'Villa Residences of Distinction' on the Perry Barr Estate; more modestly the Midland Building Co. of Yardley were building 'modern homes' in Wagon Lane, Sheldon. William Vaughan's 'Goodrest Croft' Estate at Yardley Wood boasted houses with a brick-built garage and a separate tradesman's entrance. This snap-shot catalogue summarises much of inter-war private house building: small estates built by small builders, low-cost housing in real terms, the lure of fresh air and countryside, the marketing ploy of 'modernity' and the appeal to social distinction.

Without great architectural or layout flair, a multiplicity of builders created as distinctive a suburban environment as that of the council estate. Private building in inter-war Birmingham reflected all the national characteristics of the time (Oliver, Davis and Bentley, 1981; Edwards, 1981). The three bedroomed 'semi', red roofed, perhaps with mock exposed timbers, bay windows, porches, a distinctive front door design, side garages, garden gates, privet hedges, flower beds and lawns were the components of a landscaped estate where increasingly private, individual family lives were led. At their worst the housing areas degenerated into ribbon developments piercing the countryside along rural lanes, and they attracted criticism on aesthetic grounds, the mean, anonymous architecture derided by informed critics. But the seeds of a very different residential architecture and estate layout to come had been sown. Only in a few areas, like the carefully managed expansion of Bournville, were residential environments of quality actually achieved (Figure 6.1). On the Garden Village Estate special societies and housing cooperatives provided both houses for sale on 99-year leases, and also for rent, in addition to ordinary housing built by the Trust (Bournville Village Trust, 1955).

But each suburb is worthy of individual exploration, each phase of development leaving its record. Kennedy's (1993) study of South Birmingham is a case in point. Hall Green had its railway by 1908. Small-scale building operations followed, focusing on the station and fronting Stratford Road. A parade of eleven shops was built in 1913. After the war a pre-urban landscape was submerged, though old rights of way remained, as roads and field boundaries dictated garden shapes and street layouts. Stratford Road was progressively dualled to cope with increasing traffic.

Figure 6.1 Houses for sale, Hawthorne Road, Bournville, 1933.

The Hall, Hall Green and the adjoining Hall Farm were demolished in 1934 to make way for a sea of private housing. H. Dare and Son Ltd built houses and shops between 1933 and 1936 along School and Miall Roads; in 1988 it became a conservation area in view of the quality of its untouched suburban architecture. A house style of semis with bay windows and twin gables, often half-timbered, predominated along Stratford Road, but a rare incursion of three-storey flats can be seen in Springfield Court. Industrial development was relatively close: Robin Hood Works, owned by Newey, made pins and safety pins, Priory Engineering Works were at Shirley Heath and Cranmore Farm Industrial Estate at Shirley was designed by Solihull UDC under a 1935 town planning scheme. Indeed the boundary between Birmingham and Solihull marked two very different local authorities. There were allegations of jerry building on the Shirley Manor Estate, developed after 1936, and the Shirley Residents' Association, critical of its council, explored the possibility of annexation to Birmingham.

More might have been expected from the fact that Birmingham embarked on much greater planning activity than elsewhere, but quality improvements in design and layout did not necessarily accompany scheme preparation. We have already noted the initiatives taken before the Great War in the preparation of town planning schemes, under the 1909 Act. After the war the preparation of schemes was made obligatory for urban authorities over 20 000 population in respect of land in course of development or about to be developed – i.e. suburban land, to all intents and purposes. But the legislation of 1919 had little chance of being enforced as weakly-resourced councils, a shortage of professional staff and political ambivalence combined to render progress in scheme preparation very slow. The Town and Country Planning Act 1932 widened the possible area of scheme preparation, but reverted to a permissive power (Cherry, 1974).

Nonetheless throughout the inter-war period Birmingham maintained steadfastly its programme of covering its suburban areas with schemes for guidance of development. The first scheme after the war covered 3000 acres in North Yardley and Stechford (1921). The South Birmingham scheme (1925) later covered 8000 acres in Acock's Green, Moseley, King's Heath, Yardley Wood and parts of King's Norton. There were also City Council resolutions to prepare schemes for North Birmingham (7000 acres), Perry Barr (3000), Sheldon (3400) and South West Birmingham (10 000), though they never reached the stage of ministerial approval. By 1939, therefore, four authorised schemes were in force, covering 15 000 acres and the rest were in course of preparation, covering a further 23 000 acres. This ambitious programme had the effect of imposing a uniform hand of standard development over the city's inter-war suburbs, particularly those covering public sector estates: pre-determined road widths, densities of 12 houses to the acre and little more, avoidance of mixed land use development through precise zoning and provision for open space were the principal features.

Birmingham's commitment to town planning took it into wider territory. Throughout the 1920s regional planning schemes were encouraged by the Ministry of Health, and in 1923 a Midland Joint Town Planning Advisory Council was set up covering an area of about 15 miles radius from Birmingham and embracing 73 local authorities, with a population of 2.5 million. It was the largest of the conurbation-based town planning regions then created. The council, chaired by a Birmingham councillor and with Birmingham officials as its officers, sought to advise on the promotion and coordination of town planning schemes within the region.

Such professional aggrandisement went alongside the search for territorial expansions; Birmingham's inter-war housing demanded *lebensraum*. A proposal by West Bromwich in 1921 to extend its boundaries past Aston to Perry Barr and beyond was strongly opposed by Birmingham and in 1926 Perry Barr UDC resolved in favour of its incorporation within Birmingham. The city owned Perry Park and reservoir and two hospitals; city trams went to the boundary at Birchfield; there were strong links with gas and water supplies; and Birmingham was a commercial centre of gravity for the district. The boundary change became effective in 1928. The Birmingham Extension Act 1927 provided for the central part of Perry Barr UDC to be added to the city, and West Bromwich and Sutton Coldfield also secured territory. In 1931 another boundary extension (and the last for nearly 40 years) absorbed large parts of Castle Bromwich and Sheldon where land for both public and private houses soon became available. The Birmingham Race Course at Bromford Bridge, the British Industries Fair complex and Castle Bromwich airfield were brought within the city boundaries.

By the 1930s, then, much had already been achieved. Nettlefold's enthusiasm for town planning had been translated into action. Birmingham had acquired vast tracts of land to form suburban estates, and a variant of his low density garden suburb ring was in place. But it was a variant with a difference as municipal house ownership was unexpectedly favoured. However, a quarter of a century, if not more, of a headlong rush to build houses on the city outskirts, as a solution to its housing problem, was coming to an end. Certainly the worst excesses of overcrowding and congestion had been relieved, and in some cases dilapidations removed; population levels had fallen sharply both in the central wards with their courts and back-to-backs, and in the middle ring wards of by-law housing (by 22.5% and 24.1% respectively between 1921 and 1938), the migratory trend of course to sharply boost the outer wards (by 90.8%). But the housing market was in need of adjustment; a problem which had received scant attention for decades now took an increased political significance – slum clearance.

Birmingham fell into line with national trends. London and all the major cities could demonstrate that migration to the suburbs left behind the very low paid, especially the casually employed, and they inhabited the oldest and worst of the housing stock. It made sense for public policy to phase out financial support for a house building programme such as the one that had dominated the 1920s, in favour of steps to tackle the slum conditions.

Neville Chamberlain, Minister of Health, favoured a policy of reconditioning the older housing stock. But, as Yelling (1992) has described, Labour's return in 1929 gave Arthur Greenwood a chance to change tack, and his 1930 Housing Act made provisions for rehousing subsidies and the declaration of improvement areas. This signalled a move towards encouraging slum clearance and rebuilding on cleared sites; interestingly, it also provided a special subsidy for flats. Local authorities were given extra subsidies related to the numbers of people displaced and the higher price of central area land. Subsidies of other dwellings were cancelled in 1933, but the major effect came with the Housing Act 1935.

A national slum campaign was vigorously conducted between 1933 and 1935; it was also a time of Labour Party recovery, marked by Rev. Charles

Jenkinson's radical housing policies in Leeds and by the capture of the London County Council in 1934 with the slogan 'Up with the houses, down with the slums'. The Housing Act 1935 repealed the improvement area procedure, instituting redevelopment areas which could be declared where one-third of the dwellings were unfit or overcrowded. Slum clearance progress had so far disappointed, and new forms of subsidy were introduced to stimulate the rehousing of overcrowded families. Between September 1934 and March 1939 a quarter of a million houses were demolished and a million persons displaced, a programme which dwarfed all previous attacks on unfit housing. Much still depended, however, on the particular drive shown by local authorities, and an official calculation of the number of slum dwellings in England and Wales in 1939 was, at 472 000, dauntingly high.

Birmingham was not the blackspot that Manchester was, for example (which had one third of its houses classed as unfit), but the city undeniably had a substantial clearance programme to tackle and it responded to changed national sentiment by once more considering flats in its housing policy (Sutcliffe, 1974). In spite of a long reluctance by the City Council to accept flats as an answer to the housing problem, nonetheless, due to the promptings of the City Surveyor, Herbert Humphreys (overcoming the opposition of the Medical Officer of Health, Dr Robertson), the public works and town planning committee had been persuaded to erect four three-storey blocks of flats on a former clay pit in Garrison Lane, near to St Andrews Football Ground, in 1927 (Figure 6.2). In external appearance their mansard roof style was very distinctive. With a bath, gas boiler and other amenities including refuse chutes they let at rents up to 8s 10d a week, but even then the Corporation experienced a financial loss.

The national anti-slum campaign prompted a delegation from the public works and town planning, and estates committees to visit cities in Germany, and Prague and Vienna, where innovative flat design in modern movement style was beginning to enjoy an architectural and social vogue. Their subsequent report still favoured the single or self-contained house with a garden as the best system of housing. But it acknowledged that flat or tenement building could provide perfectly satisfactory and healthy living conditions, provided that necessary amenities were also provided in the scheme and that the colony of flats was large enough to make these amenities viable. The delegation recommended a five-year programme of 1000 flats for slum housing.

But in effect the city was prevaricating. It had nowhere near the political or professional will for flats such as displayed in Liverpool and Manchester (as two northern examples); neither had it a revolutionary scheme such as that at Quarry Hill, Leeds, to arouse passions. Till now, only 355 new dwellings had been built in the central areas since 1918, and although five clearance areas had been declared, the most that could be realistically

Figure 6.2 Garrison Lane municipal flats, Bordesley. Built 1928. Inner courtyard with later attempts at play space provision.

hoped for was the policy of patching and improvement declared by Nettlefold 30 years earlier.

Yet some progress was made. In 1933 180 maisonettes were built on the site of the former Cavalry Barracks, Great Brook Street, Duddeston to rehouse people displaced from the New Summer Street area near Summer Lane; two- and three-bedroomed flats with a large living room, scullery and bathroom formed the Ashcroft Estate, six sections each surrounded by an asphalt area for playing and drying. This was followed by the Emily Street scheme in Highgate, a design for 267 flats with balcony access built in four-storey blocks around courtyards, opened by the Queen in March 1939. They were erected on a five-acre site close to the city centre, bounded by Angelina, Dymoke, Leopold and Vaughan Streets, crossed by Emily Street. Declared a clearance area in 1934, nearly 1300 people were displaced. As an alternative to a traditional brick construction, an experimentation with concrete was carried out. Drying rooms were provided and there were plans for playgrounds, gardens and a bowling green. The only other scheme before 1939 was a project for 98 maisonettes in Kingston Road, Bordesley, built in 1937. But overall, rebuilding was not keeping pace with clearance: between 1930 and 1939 8000 dwellings were declared unfit and most were demolished.

In the meantime the Housing Act 1935 gave local authorities more encouragement as well as opportunity to engage in clearance and rebuilding. It used the term 'Redevelopment Areas' for the first time: districts which contained more than 50 working-class houses, of which one third were unfit for human habitation and where land use arrangements made comprehensive redevelopment expedient. The year 1935 also coincided with the retirement of the City Engineer and Surveyor, Herbert Humphries, suitably knighted in the centenary year of local government, and his succession by a vigorous, young deputy, Herbert Manzoni. A new determination to engage in redevelopment was apparent and the situation changed abruptly; Manzoni's scheme for 267 acres at Duddeston and Nechells (by far and away the largest such project in the country) was approved in November 1937. Later details outlined the planning principles which would govern the redevelopment: careful zoning would end the intermixture of residential and industrial uses, and of the population affected 30% would be rehoused elsewhere. Properties were acquired in other run-down areas of the city, notably Gooch Street, Summer Lane and Ladywood, but the outbreak of war in 1939 put a stop to the redevelopment schemes. Astonishingly, however, a city council, long opposed to flats, was on the point of reversing its hostility to this form of development, just as 20 years earlier it had reversed its opposition to municipal housing. There was a refreshing pragmatism to it all.

Economy and industry

The 19th century had seen Birmingham enjoy sustained economic growth. Its manufacturing industry gave the city wealth, power and prestige. Science and technology applied to local skill, and entrepreneurship had triumphed. Overseas, Britain's imperial might ensured dominance over world markets. Confidence was high; downturns in one industry were more than matched by innovation and expansion elsewhere.

But an economically prosperous future was not assured. Britain had already learned to share its European lead with Germany and by the end of the century it was apparent that competition from the USA was increasing. Until 1914 the signals of economic change were not strong enough to shake a general confidence that industrial strengths would be maintained. Within five years, however, sentiments would be radically revised as Britain experienced the reality of its post-war position.

Between 1914 and 1918 Birmingham was at the forefront of the war effort, as we have seen; it was a prosperous city. From a national point of view, Britain emerged from the Great War in a healthier economic position than many of her European neighbours (Aldcroft, 1986). There had been shipping losses and sales of overseas assets, but there had been neither great internal disruption nor dislocation. Yet Britain had a poor record of economic achievement in the 1920s. A short economic boom was followed by a sharp downturn and the early and middle twenties saw historically high unemployment rates and labour unrest. Modest recovery was only followed by another depression, less severe but longer in duration, which extended into the 1930s. From 1932 a long slow recovery set in, though unemployment remained high.

Within Britain certain regions, and certain industries, were hard hit. The highest rates of unemployment were concentrated in areas of heavy industry, including coal mining, heavy engineering, ship building, textiles and iron and steel manufacture. On the other hand London, the South East and parts of the Midlands were relatively protected, and some districts experienced comparatively boom conditions, particularly where new industries were flourishing.

The relative fortunes of Birmingham and the West Midlands in this period reflect this national picture. The region's employment structure was not over-reliant on any of the staple trades where downturn had been most marked. The exception was South Staffordshire with its coal mining, heavy engineering and iron and steel production. Here, the demand for iron had revived during the war, but recovery was short-lived. Furnaces, put out during the coal lock-out of 1926, were not relit. Belgian and German imports were cheaper. The blast furnaces of Bilston and the Round Oak steel works were exceptions; basically the Black Country turned from iron and steel manufacture to metal working.

But difficulties in such an area were compensated by a broad economic base regionally (admittedly with metal working at its core) where a wide range of industries was represented. Moreover the West Midlands and particularly the heartland conurbation was able to share in some of the growth industries of the time, particularly those related to car manufacture and automotive engineering. The buoyancy of the local housing market should be noted; its relevance to an expanding demand for industries well represented in the conurbation was considerable. Builders' and plumbers' hardware, kitchen hollow-ware and brassware establishments flourished.

So the region had a mixed experience in the inter-war period. Parts of the Black Country had to withstand recession for a long time, but other districts not so reliant on hard-hit industries did reasonably well, and recovered earlier. Birmingham itself, much more insulated and indeed able to share in new prosperity, did quite well. Unemployment peaked in the city in August 1931, with a total of 76 000 out of work. The average rate for the year was 17.7%, against 20.7% for England, 27.4% for Scotland and 33.5% for Wales. Over 20 000 people in the city were receiving poor relief – but this was only one-fifth of the number in Glasgow. There was a strong recovery over the next five years; by 1936 the number of unemployed had fallen to less than 16 000 and there were indications of a labour shortage in certain sectors. There was strong growth in building and construction trades, and in the consumer industries; upward trends in real incomes encouraged a buoyant housing market. The prosperity evident, for example, in the private suburbia of South Birmingham in the 1930s was more akin to parts of outer London than the comparable suburbs of the northern industrial cities.

In more detail the picture was as follows. In 1930s Birmingham and the Black Country, and particularly the central conurbation, a strong inward tide of migration, 'which by then might have begun to equal the influx into Greater London and the Home Counties' (Walker, 1950) was in evidence. The natural increase of population came to exceed that of any conurbation in the country. Birmingham itself gained more, if anything, than did the conurbation as a whole.

The demographic buoyancy during the 1930s, suggested by population growth and an inward migration of a disproportionate number of people in their early working lives, is confirmed by the region's unemployment record at that time. Data indicates that the Black Country recovered earlier than Great Britain as a whole, and the conurbation performed even better. Nonetheless there is no doubting the depth of the recession in the Black Country at the beginning of the 1930s. The worst hit areas in 1931 were Dudley (40% unemployed), Cradley (36%), Wednesbury (35%) and Bilston (30%). Birmingham, Smethwick and Oldbury suffered least and revived the fastest; in 1937 unemployment was 4.3%, 3.7% and 3.8% respectively.

Table 6.2 Percentage unemployment 1931–39.

	Conurbation	Black Country	Great Britain
1931	22.9	32.4	22.0
1932	21.5	30.4	22.7
1933	16.6	23.5	19.7
1934	10.9	15.2	17.0
1935	9.4	14.5	15.7
1936	6.9	10.2	13.1
1937	4.7	6.7	10.1
1938	10.7	14.5	12.8
1939	4.7	6.4	8.1

Source: Walker (1950), p. 253

Birmingham may be said to have led the national revival in employment after 1931.

The region was experiencing economic change as prosperity declined in some industries and growth came to others. The metal trades in various guises were still predominant in the Birmingham district; in 1931 37% of all those engaged in industry, trade and commerce in Birmingham were concerned with metal in some capacity (nationally the figure was 10.5%). In the smelting and refining processes there were iron and steel manufacturers, brass foundries, tube manufacturers, iron founders, drop forgers and stampers and piercers; machining embraced the sheet-metal workers; treating included the electrogilders, enamellers and engravers. In the metal products trade there were those manufacturing components like bolts, nuts, springs and washers. The sub-assembly category accounted for cycle accessories, electrical fittings, and motor car accessories. The assembly trades included bedstead makers, and the manufacture of hearth furniture, hollow-ware, locks and guns. When it came to general finishing there were the chain makers, electroplate manufacturers and jewellers. And these trades supported a range of services, advisers and middlemen.

Some industries had already peaked in terms of their employment. The jewellery trade for example employed 28 000 people (6% of the total employment in the city) at its height in 1914; by 1927 it was down to 19 000, and falling. But the inter-war period showed expansion elsewhere (Tilson, 1989). For example, Birmingham overtook Coventry as the major centre for cycle manufacture and expanded as the product reached a mass market; the Halford Cycle Co. had begun trading as early as 1890 (though under another name). The motorcycle became a Birmingham and District product through a number of companies: Ariel Motors in Bournbrook, Triumph in Coventry, the AJS (later the AMC) in Wolverhampton, the Royal Enfield at Redditch, and the BSA in Birmingham which acquired a number of companies.

But perhaps it was development in the motor car industry that was most dramatic. The Austin Motor Co. was formed in 1905 and a factory at Longbridge was expanded for car construction. The launching of the Austin Seven in 1922 set the pattern for the European small car at low cost. English cars sold well both in the home market and in the Empire, which regularly took more than 85% of British exported cars. In 1938 Britain was second only to the United States in both total production and exports.

Companies spawned, based on the car industry, making components, accessories, electrical equipment, tyres and body trims. One such enterprise was Lucas: Joseph Lucas had begun as a one-man business making lanterns and lamps in 1860; cycle lamps were patented in 1880; and there was an easy transference to the automobile later. The expansion began in the 1920s and by 1932 had moved into the manufacture of aviation equipment. Another company was Fisher and Ludlow which switched from making kettles and pans to car bodies.

A range of other companies did extremely well. The Dunlop Co had a complex background, but before the Great War Birmingham had come to house its early factories. In 1915 a 206-acre site at Castle Bromwich became 'Fort Dunlop' and an expanding range of rubber products from tennis balls to flooring and tyres featured in the 1920s and 1930s. Another new industry was plastics, developing out of the local chemical industry, and bakelite, very much an inter-war product, was produced first at Greet, and later Tyseley; in 1933 30 Birmingham firms produced plastics, most of them starting during the previous decade. Electrical trades prospered throughout the inter-war years, never experiencing any serious recession.

Much had happened, then by the close of the inter-war period (Thoms, 1989). The Midlands now contained a number of large business concerns with control exercised in London or elsewhere, rather than within the region. The increased size of manufacturing concerns was evident, the average size of plant (in terms of numbers of workers) increasing in every trade, except those which were in decline (such as jewellery and guns). The Great War had speeded up the process of mass production and standardisation and many Birmingham establishments now employed several thousand workers. But smaller concerns, run on traditional lines, were still predominant. About 4500 firms employed less than 50 people, the vast majority located in the Birmingham area, and another 1500 firms employed between 50 and 500 people. Modern methods of management and production were not widely applied and professionally managed businesses, skilled in factory organisation, were to be found only among the larger concerns. This was a regional limitation which the next few years would test to the full.

As in any period of change it was a question of seeing the new, cheek by jowl with the old. At the close of the 1930s Birmingham's industrial location map showed features akin to 50 or 70 years previously. The jewellery quarter was still concentrated within the triangular area of about 100 acres bounded by Vyse Street to the west, the vicinity of St Paul's Church to the south and Great Hampton Street to the east (Wise, 1951). The core area around Vyse Street exhibited a high degree of specialisation and sub-division; in the south around Warstone Lane larger factories were characteristic; and around Great Hampton Street factories built after 1918 were engaged in the gilt and cheap jewellery trades. The gun trade only just extended beyond the limits of Steelhouse Lane, Lawley Street, Lancaster Street, Tower Street, Livery Street and Caroline Street; a quadrilateral sector had contracted sharply due to the inroads of public works schemes and extensions to the General Hospital. The brass foundry complex could still be seen in Ladywood and Deritend. There were concentrated pockets of industry in the east and north: Nechells, Saltley, Bordesley, Small Heath, Greet, Balsall Heath and Aston (where local wells still provided ideal water for the brewing industry). Late 19th century developments at Selly Oak, Bournville and Longbridge had prospered.

But a shift was in evidence. As large factories became the norm, most new plant was increasingly sited at a distance from the old industrial districts, where cramped conditions were experienced. In the 19th century the tract of the Birmingham and Fazeley Canal had been a particular concentration of factories, warehouses and depots; in the inter-war years it was the generally flatter land of the Tame Valley (from Perry Barr to Bromford and Castle Bromwich) which became built up with industrial plant, the location determinant no longer the canal but the main roads.

From past to future

In 1918 Birmingham was still a 19th century city; in 1939 it undeniably belonged to the 20th century. Between the close of one world war and the onset of another the city struggled to shrug off the past. A local architect, William Haywood, who followed Raymond Unwin as lecturer in Town Planning at the University (in the Department of Civil Engineering) laid out his plans for the improvement of the city in an essay published in 1918. His starting point was that:

> In no city of its size is there more need for civic improvement than in Birmingham, which in its present condition is little more than a huge collection of people and buildings, with no evidence of proper control, and little of the convenience which so large a community should possess. (p. 17)

He went on to propose a vast People's Hall at the end of Corporation Street, beyond the Law Courts; pleasure grounds and zoological gardens at Rotton Park Reservoir, Ladywood; improvements to New Street station with a vast new booking hall; improvements to the station area; future municipal buildings, including a tower block; and a new road plan for the central area with embellishments to goods yards, wharfage and other key spaces. In an introduction Neville Chamberlain generously wrote of 'lofty and inspiring conceptions', but the future was not going to be guided by such set-piece architecture.

The search for 'modernity' had already been articulated in its new housing arrangements, the broad swathe of post-1918 houses giving the city a very different stamp from the past. New industries, particularly associated with automobile manufacture, gave an expanding workforce a new prosperity, while the products invaded the streets in a tangible sign of a new age. The pattern of life was changing, albeit in selected areas: there were new buildings for new uses, with new designs (cinemas and the jazz architecture of the 1930s for example, provided by the architectural practice of Harry Weedon for Oscar Deutsch and the Odeon chain), new leisure pursuits (the introduction of the greyhound racing track, ballroom dancing, the wireless and home activities, such as gardening), and new attitudes, including concerns about the appearance of town and country. Respected observers of national culture detected and proclaimed a disenchantment with the past and a restlessness for change; the old and the ugly would no longer do and we should strive to sweep away the relics of the past.

Louis Macneice's poem *Birmingham* (1934) conjured up a rather tawdry image of the city: train smoke, traffic policemen, slums, thrusting suburbs, an alien anonymity, industrial chimneys and the factory gate:

Smoke from the train-gulf hid by hoardings blunders upward, the brakes of cars
Pipe as the policeman pivoting round raises his flat hand, bars
With his figure of monolith Pharaoh the queue of fidgety machines
(Chromium dogs on the bonnet, faces behind the triplex screens)
Behind him the streets run away between the proud glass of shops
Cubical scent-bottles artificial legs arctic foxes and electric mops
But beyond this centre the slumward vista thins like a diagram:
There, unvisited, are Vulcan's forges who doesn't care a tinker's damn.

Splayed outwards through the suburbs houses, houses for rest
Seducingly rigged by the builder, half timbered houses with lips pressed
So tightly and eyes staring at the traffic through bleary haws
And only a six-inch grip of the racing earth in their concrete claws;
In these houses men as in a dream pursue the Platonic Forms
With wireless and cairn terriers and gadgets approximating to the fickle norms
And endeavour to find God and score one over the neighbour
By climbing tentatively upward on jerry-built beauty and sweated labour.

On shining lines the trams like vast sarcophagi move
Into the sky, plum after sunset, merging to duck's egg, barred with mauve
Zeppelin clouds, and pentecost-like the cars' headlights bud
Out from sideroads and the traffic signals, Creme de menthe or bull's blood,
Tell one to stop, the engine gently breathing, or to go on
To where like black pipes of organs in the frayed and fading zone
Of the West the factory chimneys on sullen sentry will all night wait
To call, in the harsh morning, sleep-striped faces through the daily gate.

Louis Macneice *Birmingham* (1934)

The unappealing city was described by J. B. Priestley (1934) in his account of a journey through England during the autumn of 1933. He took a bus from Coventry to Birmingham and, having entered the city past houses, shops and factories, asked 'Did all this look like the entrance into the second city in England? It did. It looked a dirty muddle'. In the city centre he caught a tram for 'one of the most depressing little journeys I ever remember making'.

> In two minutes, its civic dignity, its metropolitan airs, had vanished; and all it offered me, mile after mile, was a parade of mean dinginess . . . I only know that during the half hour or so I sat staring through the top windows of that tram, I saw nothing, not one single tiny thing, that could possibly raise a man's spirits. Possibly what I was seeing was not Birmingham but our urban and industrial civilisation. The fact remains that it was beastly. It was so many miles of ugliness, squalor, and the wrong kind of vulgarity, the decayed anaemic kind . . . This was, I suppose, the common stuff out of which most of our big industrial towns are made. (Chapter 4)

Macneice and Priestley were not alone in portraying the 19th century industrial city and inter-war society in such unflattering terms; it was fashionable among the writers of this period from T. S. Eliot to W. H. Auden (another of Birmingham stock). But a balance of judgment has to be struck, on the evidence available. As Hopkins (1990) has pointed out, by the close of the inter-war years a substantial majority of Birmingham's working classes 'profited from steady employment, a shorter working day, an improved working environment, better housing conditions, better health and a wider range of leisure activities' (p. 146). On the other hand the central wards of the city remained a black-spot, where malnutrition was most prevalent, death rates highest, and unemployment likely to be heaviest among the unskilled and low-waged. Urban Britain was making a painful and uncertain transition from the pre-1914 era, in a period in which the depression years were particularly difficult. Birmingham was no exception, though it had ridden out, and recovered from economic downturn better than most. By the end of the 1930s a number of new urban features were in place and Birmingham's record was more enterprising than most in this respect.

Attention to the traffic problem absorbed City Council energies throughout the period. As early as 1911 an outer ring road had been defined and the route was subsequently incorporated into various town planning schemes. The question of the future width of main arterial roads was addressed in 1917–18; dual carriageways, a central reservation for trams and extra space for tree planting were approved for eight arterial roads which approached the city centre, where 'a kind of loop' of streets would be widened to circumnavigate the central area. This loop later became the Inner Ring Road. Pebble Mill Road became the first dual carriageway, opened in 1920, an example for others to follow: Bristol Road, Tyburn

Road and parts of the outer ring road. As part of an unemployment relief scheme, Birmingham contributed to the construction of the Wolverhampton New Road opened in 1927.

There were innovations in traffic control. Island refuges were introduced in 1920. The traffic roundabout, first to be seen at Six Ways, Erdington, was widely followed elsewhere. Automatic traffic signals were first installed in 1929 (after a much earlier experiment at Wolverhampton) at the Bristol Road/Priory Road and Pershore Road/Priory Road junctions. Pedestrian crossings made their appearance in 1934: 'Belisha crossings', after the then Minister of Transport, Hore-Belisha. A one-way traffic system was installed in the central area in 1933, with changes and extensions in 1936. A High Street bypass, at Erdington, was begun in 1937, taking the A38 traffic and tram tracks away from the congested shopping area.

Suburban spread required public transport extensions. The Transport Department became one of the city's major trading undertakings and the country's largest municipal service. It was the first to introduce a double-decker, top-covered trolley omnibus (in 1922). Trams gained extended routes to Acock's Green, Alum Rock, Hall Green and Cotteridge (for the Lickeys); Birmingham began to run the tram services of West Bromwich in 1924 and four years later took over the services in Smethwick, Oldbury and Dudley. Buses were widely introduced to all parts of the city; in 1927 the bus route mileage was 63 miles and that for tramways 77, but in 1938 the mileage was 153 and 65 respectively.

The City Council was a crucial agent for change in Birmingham's modernisation programme. This ranged from school provision in suburban housing areas to the acquisition of a large site at Gosta Green for a new Technical College, College of Art and College of Commerce. It also included improvements in the central area to realise a long-held dream for a new Civic Centre. In 1925 properties along the north side of Broad Street were demolished and the road itself widened. The Hall of Memory was erected as a memorial to the fallen in the Great War. Baskerville House, begun in 1936 and completed in 1939, was designed for local government departments. On the south side the Municipal Bank was begun in 1933. In the central shopping area, Bull Street was widened, followed by a widening between Temple Row and Colmore Row; Lewis's rebuilt part of their premises in the area. A new central Fire Station was opened in 1935 at Lancaster Circus. At the beginning of the 1930s it had been hoped to acquire a site at Shirley for an aerodrome, but negotiations were held up. In December 1933 the Council approved a site at Elmdon instead and in 1939 the Airport was opened, the terminal designed on the lines of Tempelhof, Berlin; flights to Weston super Mare and the Isle of Man were available.

Meanwhile the leaders of the Birmingham community also strove to give the city a more acceptable and modern image. The Birmingham Civic Society was involved in such matters as parks, playing fields, the preservation of amenity areas (as at Northfield), buildings (such as the Old Crown Inn, Deritend) and the design of street furniture. The Birmingham and Midland Institute, founded in 1854, sought to diffuse culture, though from a membership of 2400 in 1922 its numbers fell steadily and its influence waned (Waterhouse, 1954). The City of Birmingham Symphony Orchestra was founded in 1920. The University successfully established itself, its early growing pains past (Vincent and Hinton, 1947). The teaching hospitals and the University Medical School came together in the new Birmingham Hospitals Centre opened in July 1938 by the Duke of Gloucester; in March 1939 it was named the Queen Elizabeth Hospital. Also at the University, the Barber Institute of Fine Arts was opened in 1939.

Philanthropic gestures were not absent. In the depression years of the early 1920s the objectives of improved housing were taken up by a body known as COPEC, taking its initials from a Conference of Christian Churches on Christian Politics, Economics and Citizenship in 1925. The preservation of the countryside continued to attract support, the area of the Lickey Hills prominent in private generosity for the common good. The Birmingham Association for the Preservation of Open Spaces succeeded in purchasing Rednal Hill in 1889, and handing it over to the Corporation. There were subsequent purchases and gifts, including those by Edward and George Cadbury Jnr. In 1935 Cadbury Brothers created a charitable trust to permit the purchase of land on the perimeter of the city which could be preserved as a green belt. Within one year four estates were purchased by the Company and Bournville Village Trust (Weatheroak, Forhill, Groveley and Moundsley Hall). The freehold of the first three was vested in the Trust, and the freehold of Moundsley Hall was transferred to the City of Birmingham.

This wider, strategic view was adopted more generally by Bournville Village Trust when it inaugurated a programme of research into the conditions of living and working in the city. Its subsequent report, *When We Build Again* (1941) had a title which somehow conjured up the spirit of the age, and it is to how this was realised that we must now turn.

133

7
The Forties

A brief wireless announcement was made to the nation at 11:15 a.m. on Sunday 3 September 1939 by the Prime Minister, Neville Chamberlain. He announced the declaration of war on Germany, for the second time in a quarter of a century. For his city it heralded the end of an era, eight decades 'in which the Chamberlains and their friends had guided Birmingham through an age of unprecedented growth, prosperity and good government' (Sutcliffe and Smith, 1974, p. 14). Much would now change; Chamberlain's name would soon disappear from the community's affairs, and the war years would have an unprecedented impact on the fabric and social life of the city. After six years both the appearance and the mood of Birmingham would be very different and its agenda for the future transformed.

In this chapter we focus initially on the years 1939–45 from the point of view of enemy action: the nature of the war economy and the shift in manufacturing production, and the physical damage caused by air raids. Then we turn to the aftermath and consider first the sustained commitment to redevelopment, particularly in housing and road improvements. Finally we examine the various plans and policy statements for the future that were drawn up during the decade, all of which lay an important groundwork for the post-war development of Birmingham in its regional setting.

The war economy

The First World War enabled the motor industry to demonstrate its technical versatility. Several leading firms became involved in different aspects of aircraft manufacture, giving clear evidence of the engineering links between the motor vehicle and aircraft industries. Birmingham had not produced aircraft in peacetime, but once again the city could hardly be excluded from national, war production plans (Sutcliffe and Smith, 1974). Proximity to aero-engine works at Coventry and Derby made the decision obvious when, in 1935, the Government embarked on the expansion of the military aircraft industry. 'Shadow factories', specially constructed to build engines and airframes, were managed by existing motor concerns in Birmingham and Coventry. In the city work started in October 1936 on the Rover shadow factory at Acock's Green, for aero-engine parts, and Rover built another shadow factory at Solihull for aero-engines and airframe parts. Austin's built their equivalent adjoining their motor works at Cofton Hackett, the first aircraft completed there in 1938. The third and largest scheme for Birmingham was provided by the Nuffield Organisation, makers of Morris cars, which in 1938 bought a large site from the City Council at Castle Bromwich; managed by Vickers from May 1940, it was a factory occupying between 12 and 15 000 people.

The implementation of the state-led shadow engine and airframe programmes left a permanent imprint on the industrial landscape (Thoms, 1989). Rover's factory in Solihull absorbed 60 acres of farmland and the company acquired another 200 acres of land adjoining. Austin's works, also built on agricultural land, eventually included engine shops, an airframe factory, flight shed and airfield facilities. Castle Bromwich finally came to house 52 acres of buildings on a site of 345 acres.

This massive injection of resources for the war effort had a significant impact on the economic structure of the city and its region. As we have seen, the Midlands already had an enviable reputation for its light engineering industries and multiplicity of small metal wares. Austin, Lucas and GEC were already among the country's largest employers, but there were many hundreds of small engineering concerns, all of which enjoyed a high specialist reputation. The sudden flood of new industry led to five million square feet of factory space being constructed between 1938 and the end of 1944 – equivalent to almost four Castle Bromwich plants. The total effect was to give the Midlands a key role in the British war economy. It is remarkable that only a quarter of a century later industrial recession would begin to erode much of this prosperity.

The region was responsible for about 16% of all aircraft manufactured in Britain during the war, together with a huge number of parts, including aero-engines. Coventry (in particular) and Wolverhampton were important centres, but Birmingham excelled in the production of Spitfires at Castle Bromwich, with a total output of almost 13 000 by the end of the war, three quarters of the national total. Three hundred Lancaster bombers were also produced there. Austin manufactured the Fairey Battle medium bomber, significant numbers of Lancasters and Stirlings, and around 300 Hurricane fighters.

The Midlands was even more important for the manufacture of aero-engines, contributing perhaps 40% of the British total. Rover's Acock's Green factory figured prominently; so too did the Austin works. The region was also a notable supplier of components, its history of expertise in forgings and castings being so valuable. Light engineering, geared to the motor vehicle industry, quickly adapted to the manufacture of aircraft components – none more important than the carburettor; SU of Birmingham, bombed out and relocated in Shirley, was a major producer. Lucas and other firms manufactured technical gadgetry from injection pumps to dynamos, transformers and generators. Birmingham's watchmakers and jewellers found employment in the manufacture of instruments, radio parts and other equipment. Light reconnaissance vehicles, heavier armoured vehicles, tanks, weapons, and steel helmets added to the range of wartime products from the region. The Birmingham Railway Carriage and Wagon Co. engaged in the manufacture of tanks; the Nuffield Organisation specialised in armoured carriers and tanks; and the Birmingham Small Arms Co. supplied rifles, machine guns, barrels and ammunition. By the end of 1944 around 470 firms in the Midlands were engaged on work related to the aircraft and motor vehicle industries, about half of which employed fewer than 50 workers. No wonder there was a labour shortage, despite constant appeals for more women workers; Irish migrants and Italian prisoners of war were brought in to supplement the workforce.

And so over five years the Midlands increased its importance as a centre of the engineering industry; additional factory space, plant and labour were testimony to this. Some firms, the ailing Singer Motors for example, was rescued by wartime contracts. New products and new systems of manufacture were developed. Employment boomed and incomes rose. As the war drew to a close, the relationship with government changed, and more normal market functions were restored; but in many ways economic circumstances, social life and labour relations (trade union membership soared) would not be the same again. The tragedy was that opportunities were lost and a business complacency set in.

War damage

The Birmingham blitz began at lunch time on 9 August 1940 when a lone German bomber jettisoned its bombs over Erdington; one man died and six people were wounded in a quiet suburban street (Sutcliffe and Smith, 1974). That was the prelude to a period of nearly three years of enemy action during which Birmingham became one of the most heavily bombed cities in provincial Britain.

Minor attacks continued throughout August on targets in the east of the city, after which the tactics changed. On the night of 25–26 August the city centre was raided and the Market Hall was burned down. In September and October daylight raids were carried out against industrial targets, but they were a relative lull before the storm. The Coventry blitz occurred during the night of 14 November, resulting in heavy casualties and widespread physical destruction. Birmingham was next: on the night of 19 November a force of 350 bombers dropped large quantities of incendiary and high explosive bombs, affecting most parts of the city and inflicting the heaviest casualties of the war, with some 400 deaths. BSA's Small Heath factory was badly hit. The *Luftwaffe* returned on the night of 22 November with a smaller force but succeeded in inflicting more dislocation and damage, Tyseley and Saltley being particularly badly hit. Further small-scale attacks followed in late November and early December, but after a short respite the city was attacked by 200 bombers in a 13-hour raid on the night of 11 December.

The enemy offensive was then switched to British ports, and Birmingham remained almost unmolested until April 1941. On the night of the 9th the city was attacked by a 250-bomber force in what proved to be the last really heavy raid of the war. Both industrial areas and the city centre (in particular) suffered damage, and there were heavy casualties. A fire at the corner of New Street and High Street got out of control and many buildings were destroyed. (The site was later used for exhibitions and entertainments which took place inside a large marquee; it became known as the Big Top site.) Numerous buildings on the east side of the Bull Ring were also destroyed and the Prince of Wales Theatre in Broad Street was burnt down.

For over a year Birmingham remained free from attack but, on the night of 27 July 1942, a force of between 60 and 70 aircraft bombed the city (Figure 7.1). A few lighter raids followed, but with heavy losses in aircraft, the enemy air offensive was on the wane. Birmingham was not visited again until a short hit-and-run raid on 23 April 1943, and this proved the last occasion for an air attack.

Over a period of nearly three years, 63 separate raids were made. But most of them were relatively small-scale: only four raids destroyed more than a hundred houses and only three demolished more than ten factories. Out of 87 serious fires, only eleven developed into major conflagrations. Damage to factories led to 99 factory premises being totally destroyed and a further 184 being so seriously damaged that demolition was necessary, but loss in manufacturing production was never significant.

Estimates of damage to residential property varied: an officially quoted figure of nearly 12 400 so seriously damaged that they could be considered a total loss, has to be set against a figure of 4600 reported to the City Emergency Committee. But out of a city total of 275 000 dwellings, figures in this range meant that the percentage destroyed was low. Even in an area like Duddeston and Nechells, which adjoined industrial targets, only 170 buildings were destroyed by bombing out of a total of 6800 houses and

Figure 7.1 War damage, July 1942 Bridge Street, West Newton.

other properties in the area; such relatively small-scale destruction meant that war damage played little part in subsequent reconstruction plans for the district.

Yet Birmingham was a heavily bombed city in the British context: in England and Wales there were 23 towns and 18 London Boroughs which experienced losses of more than 1000 totally destroyed houses, and outside the London area the total of 5065 for Birmingham was only exceeded by that for Liverpool (see Table 7.1 below).

As with housing, damage to industrial plant was not heavy. Factories were already geographically dispersed and the important firms further dispersed production to other units. The Austin premises at Longbridge and Cofton Hackett were bombed only once during the whole war, in a

Table 7.1 Totally destroyed houses in the Second World War.

England and Wales		
LCC	47 314	(18 metropolitan boroughs)
West Ham	9 254	
East Ham	1 498	Greater London: 60 339
Croydon	1 194	
Willesden	1 079	
Liverpool	5 487	
Bootle	2 006	
Birkenhead	1 899	Merseyside: 10 542
Wallasey	1 150	
Manchester	1 951	
Salford	1 934	Greater Manchester: 3 885
Portsmouth	4 393	
Hull	4 184	
Southampton	4 136	
Plymouth	3 593	Ports: 21 975
Bristol	2 909	
Yarmouth	1 636	
Swansea	1 124	
Norwich	1 780	
Exeter	1 700	Cathedral towns: 4 694
Bath	1 214	
Birmingham	5 065	
Coventry	4 185	Inland industrial towns: 12 156
Sheffield	2 906	
Grand total	113 591	

Source: E.V. Marmaras (1992)

single, abortive daylight raid. Fort Dunlop was bombed on several occasions, but damage was repaired almost immediately. Only Fisher and Ludlow suffered badly, losing 40% of its million square feet during bombing in 1940.

For such a vulnerable target, therefore, Birmingham escaped lightly, especially compared with cities on mainland Europe where systematic destruction approached 'biblical annihilation' (Diefendorf, 1990). It was fortunate that for most of the war the *Luftwaffe's* heaviest land bomber was the Heinkel He 111, which had only two engines, and whose long-range bomb load was little more than one ton. While the British Bomber Command was built up as a long-distance strategic bombing force, the German *Luftwaffe* was developed as a tactical support arm for the army, with a stress on light aircraft, both fighter bombers and bombers. Even so, the *Luftwaffe's* tactics were marred by inconsistency: first to aim at the industrial concentration in the east of the city, then to engage into a more general attack on industry in order to damage civilian morale, and later to secure city centre conflagrations. Furthermore, raids were not pressed home; other cities, including those targetted in the 'Baedecker' raids on historic towns, became alternative centres to attack and Birmingham, in spite of its economic vulnerability, escaped.

Yet Birmingham's civilian casualties were not inconsiderable: well over 2200 people lost their lives in the city and 3000 were seriously injured. Such personal tragedy and disruption did not end there, damage and threat to life setting in train a series of social consequences. The city's slum problem was partially eased in that conscription and the evacuation of school children made it easier for wives and mothers to live with friends and relatives elsewhere. Some families moved to avoid the bombing and by the end of the war some 4400 back-to-back houses had been abandoned and were classed as void. Civilian movement across the city on a daily journey to work basis was increased through the dispersal of industrial units, and there was some permanent migration of households to the suburbs.

The aftermath: redevelopment resumed

Overall, as Sutcliffe and Smith (1974) observe, 'the war caused more inconvenience than injury, more decay than destruction' (p. 56). Moreover it failed to deflect the City Council from pursuing policies regarding its housing stock and its road network which had been agreed upon in the late 1930s; indeed it helped to realise them all the quicker, and certainly with greater public support. The consensus was that the renewal and redevelopment of central Birmingham and the inner ring of outmoded premises should be pursued as soon as conditions permitted; the war was a hiatus, not a disruption, and there was no cause for any reconsideration of objectives.

Birmingham in the immediate post-war years maintained a continuity both in its redevelopment policies, and in preserving the lead role of its chief officers – which was not necessarily the case in other war-damaged cities (Hasegawa, 1992). In Coventry there was conflict between architect/planner and engineer, the former reigning supreme; Southampton showed the same conflict amongst professional officers, but planning was downgraded; in Bristol a scheme for appropriate road layouts dictated proposals for shopping relocation and hostility from the architects came later. In Birmingham a city council consensus on public works and slum clearance enabled a powerful Chief Officer, City Engineer Herbert Manzoni, to engage on schemes to which he had been dedicated for almost a decade. Even local political change made no difference to policy in these fields; Labour surged in the municipal elections of November 1945, and took full control in 1946, only to lose it again in 1949, but the consensus was unbroken.

The powerful public works committee would be the main agent for post-war redevelopment schemes. A rival contender was soon brushed aside. A new Lord Mayor, Norman Tiptaft, considered that all post-war planning should be placed under a single direction, and persuaded Council to set up a reconstruction committee; he became its chairman. Political in-fighting by other committees which resented its interference in their own plans led to the public works committee mounting a successful campaign to limit its scope, and in fact it was wound up in 1945.

The city's long-standing concerns with housing and slum clearance were resumed. The local situation had deteriorated sharply. Fifty thousand municipal houses built in Birmingham between the wars had largely eradicated the city's overall housing deficiency and in 1939 the number of applicants on the housing register was as low as 7000. But by 1945 a housing shortage had built up again thanks to the complete building standstill during the war, the loss of housing stock due to enemy action, and the effect of higher marriage and birth rates. Moreover the condition of the older dwellings in the city had continued to deteriorate, the general quality being far removed from the level anticipated for post-war housing (Figures 7.2, 7.3). A Public Health Department survey in 1946 revealed 81 000 houses without baths, 35 000 without separate wcs and 29 000 built back-to-back. The central parts of the city were the worst: here over half the houses were built back-to-back, nearly two thirds had no separate wcs and more than one in ten lacked internal water supplies. In these areas overcrowding was high (though falling), residential density was still excessive, and houses were intermixed with factories, workshops and warehouses (Figure 7.4). The targets of the housing reformers were still present, and in abundance.

Figure 7.2 Model by-law houses, Whitehall Road, 1941.

Slum clearance remained the way forward, as it had been in the 1930s. In December 1937 267 acres in Duddeston and Nechells had been proposed as a redevelopment area under section 34 of the Housing Act 1936, and other areas in the Summer Lane, Gooch Street and Ladywood districts were regarded as suitable for similar treatment. War interrupted progress but did not halt it entirely. In 1943 Bath Row was designated a redevelopment area (between Ladywood and the Gooch Street area, it had experienced considerable bomb damage) and in the same year a revised scheme, incorporating different design elements, was approved for the Duddeston and Nechells scheme.

Yet the actual mechanics for dealing with the redevelopment of areas as large as those which Birmingham envisaged faced not only complexity, but slow and cumbersome procedures of implementation. Manzoni, speaking at a Conference of the Town and Country Planning Association in 1941 catalogued the contents of a 300-acre site (no doubt taken from Birmingham):

> nearly 11 miles of existing streets, mostly narrow and badly planned; 6800 individual dwellings, the density varying locally up to 80 to the acre; 5400 of these dwellings, classified as slums to be condemned; 15 major industrial premises or factories; several of them comparatively recent in date; 105 minor factories, storage buildings, workshops, industrial yards, laundries, etc.; 778 shops, many of them hucksters' premises; 7 schools; 18 churches

Figure 7.3 Older housing, Coleman Street, 1944.

and chapels; 51 licensed premises. Many miles of public service mains, water, gas and electricity, including over a mile of 42-inch trunk water main, nearly all laid under carriageways and consequently in the wrong place for good planning. Add to these a railway viaduct, a canal, a railway goods yard and a gas works, and you have a beautiful problem in redevelopment. (Uthwatt, p. 6.)

This 'beautiful problem' (Figures 7.5, 7.6, 7.7) could only be tackled by using the due procedures of the day. Had a detailed plan for the proposed redevelopment area been approved, first by the City Council and then by the Minister of Health, notices would have been served individually on owners, lessees and occupiers. The Minister would then hold a public inquiry to hear objections. Any person still aggrieved had recourse to the High Court, a move which could lead to the suspension or quashing of the Minister's approval. Six weeks after the approval the plan would become operative, when the Council was required to purchase the whole of the land within the area, except where arrangements could be made with the owners themselves to carry out the requirements of the scheme. Purchase had to be made within six months in respect of land for residential use, and within two years for other purposes. Compulsory purchase orders could be made, but the procedures were aggravated by the difficult issue of compensation and betterment and hence a local authority would

Figure 7.4 Courtyard housing. View from the roof of the Lucas factory, Great King Street.

be anxious to purchase sites as they came on the market.

One of the first tasks of the newly-established Ministry of Town and Country Planning (1943) was to consider how adequate powers could be provided for local councils to acquire large bomb-damaged areas, expeditiously. A draft Town and Country Planning (Reconstruction) Bill had been prepared as early as November 1941 and government committees were at work. The Uthwatt Committee (the Expert Committee on Compensation and Betterment) had reported in September 1942, recommending a rapid procedure for the acquisition of land in reconstruction areas. This would enable the whole of an area required for redevelopment to be vested in the acquiring authority as a single operation, thereby dispensing with the need to ascertain ownership and to negotiate separately for the acquisition of their interests before a start could be made on the work.

Some very complex financial, and sensitive political issues were at stake, as Cullingworth (1975) has described, but for our purposes we might simply note the provisions of the Town and Country Planning Act 1944. This legislation dealt with the redevelopment of both blitzed and blighted areas (hence it became dubbed the Blitz and Blight Act); what began as a concern for the reconstruction of bomb-damaged city centres, typically Plymouth and Coventry, grew into legislation which also addressed the

Figure 7.5 Jewellery Quarter. Lees and Sanders premises, 1944/5.

problems of rebuilding slum areas. Manzoni's appointment to an advisory panel considering this problem served to widen the spectrum of opportunity and in fact the measures that Birmingham wanted were incorporated in the 1944 Act. The city was well placed to take advantage of the new powers.

The new legislation enacted that after a compulsory purchase order had been authorised, a new, expedited procedure for transfer of ownership could be exercised, whereby the vesting of land *preceded* the assessment and payment of compensation instead of following it. A local authority could give notice of its intention to enter on land and take possession after 14 days. It was argued that these remarkable measures were required because of the exceptional circumstances of the time. The Act permitted a local authority to become the owners of property contained within the boundaries of a redevelopment area very speedily, and as a consequence would be able to manage, repair or demolish property without delay in accordance with its redevelopment programme.

In December 1945 Birmingham City Council rescinded the declaration of the Duddeston and Nechells Redevelopment Area, made in 1937. Instead it proposed compulsory purchase orders for the acquisition of properties required in the redevelopment of the Duddeston and Nechells,

Figure 7.6 Jewellery Quarter. Houses converted into workshops. Early 1940s.

Summer Lane, Ladywood, Bath Row and Gooch Street areas. These five central redevelopment areas contained some 30 000 houses, accommodating over 100 000 people, and some 2650 shops and 2300 commercial and industrial premises.

The public inquiry into the Birmingham (Central Redevelopment) CPO 1946, the first to be held under the 1944 Act, took place in July (Ryan, 1976). There were 325 objections; the majority involved business premises, only seven being primarily concerned with residential disturbance. Twelve objections were lodged by breweries (no less than 147 licensed premises were owned by Mitchell and Butler alone), but negotiations conducted during but outside the inquiry proceedings led to an agreement amongst the brewery companies. Overall there was a remarkably small number of dissenting voices to compulsory acquisition and the CPO was substantially approved in June 1947.

Birmingham Corporation became a slum landlord virtually overnight. But its demolition work was slow; no slums were pulled down until the summer of 1948 and only 270 had been demolished by March 1949. The prevailing housing shortage and resultant overcrowding meant that greater attention had to be paid not only to the repair of slums and their modernisation through the provision of water supplies and WCs, but also to

Figure 7.7 Canalscape, early 1940s. Cambrian Wharf at the top of Farmer Bridge Locks.

the provision of new housing, when such building was authorised by the Ministry of Health. But even then house construction rates were retarded, and the programme, such as it was, ground to a halt in the severe winter of 1947.

Meanwhile the city accepted a big allocation of Government-built temporary (prefabricated) houses, although with reluctance on account of their alleged inferior accommodation. The Council agreed to take 2500 'prefabs' as soon as they were available and to erect them on council-owned sites; a further 2000 were earmarked for private plots. They were erected on the road frontages of parks and open spaces, and not on sites identified for permanent housing (Figure 7.8). Altogether over 4600 prefabs were put up, including 550 made in America and obtained under lend-lease. Although given a ten-year life, their removal was slow, and to this day 17 are still tenanted in Wake Green Road, Moseley (Chinn, 1991).

Delays in slum clearance and rebuilding had the effect of concentrating architectural and planning considerations on the design of municipal housing estates – the concern of ten years previous. War-time thinking nationally had emphasised the importance of the neighbourhood unit and the better planning of community facilities, and mixed layouts of flats and houses were increasingly advocated as against the sterile, monotonous

147

Figure 7.8 Pre-fabricated Houses, c. 1946. The Square, Weoley Castle.

designs of the inter-war years. As to accommodation, a committee under the chairmanship of Lord Dudley (1944) laid down space and equipment standards for post-war housing; these were accepted by Government and published in the *Housing Manual 1944* (Ministry of Health, Ministry of Works, 1944). The flats *versus* houses debate had barely been engaged in Birmingham; neither had the question of the architecture of the post-war city been seriously addressed. These were issues which would be picked up with increasing liveliness in the 1950s.

Meanwhile attention was also being given to Birmingham's other long-standing pre-occupations: roads and traffic. Bomb damage provided new opportunities to build the inner ring road and the public works committee approved the scheme in principle in July 1943, the route hardly changed from that envisaged in 1917. There were new elements, however: a new street across the ring from Snow Hill to Moor Street, a widening of Colmore Row and a decision to acquire even more land for the scheme (in order to lease back to developers). Details were approved by the City Council in July 1944. A Corporation Bill, drawn up so that special powers could be obtained to carry out the scheme, met with almost unanimous local support and was little modified by either the Commons or the Lords in its passage through Parliament. As with slum housing, the times were propitious for private property rights to be infringed in the common interest to a remarkable extent. Also as with slum housing, the conferment of powers did not lead to any immediate action because of restrictions on the use of materials and labour, when other schemes nationally had to be given priority. But the agenda for the 1950s had been set, the power and authority of the public works committee and its chief officer Manzoni virtually unassailable for a critical period in Birmingham's planning history.

The forward look

Wartime literature was replete with visions of a post-war Britain where town and country were reconstructed in a common task of boldness and adventure. Pleasant homes in beautiful towns and noble cities, urban settings of dignity, an end to decay, a protected countryside and a recovery in economic fortunes: these were the recurrent themes offered by professionals and propagandists alike, harnessed to all political creeds. From the planning of the home to the planning of the nation, the conscious application of rational thought to complex situations, garnished by visions of a new future for people and country, would attend all our post-war deliberations. Planning was raised to a new level of expectation.

Wartime experiences had certainly helped to mould this sense of anticipation. But even before 1939 a new national mood was already in evidence, readily apparent in Birmingham where we can trace endeavours extending over a decade, from the late 1930s to the late 1940s, whereby far-sighted strategies were put to the city to set against its shorter-term realities.

We can begin with the decision of the Bournville Village Trust in 1935 to set up a research committee consisting of two trustees, two members of staff and two outside experts. The research would ascertain the nature of the city's housing conditions and the effects of post-1919 suburban developments, and consider whether new policy directions should be followed. The idea of the inquiry grew out of the then new science of market research which stressed the need for measured assessments of market size and availability rather than the pooled knowledge and hunches of directors, staff and salesmen. The research findings were published in 1941, suitably titled *When We Build Again* (Bournville Village Trust, 1941).

To complement data available from the 1931 Census and the annual reports of the city's Medical Officer of Health a survey of 7000 house-to-house interviews was carried out, equivalent to one in 35 working-class houses, to give a detailed picture of Birmingham housing. A second part of the survey was the preparation of a land-use map of the built-up part of the region, from Stourport to Kenilworth in the south and from Newport (Salop) to Ashby-de-la-Zouch in the north. Data analysis enabled a portrait of the city to be prepared: its people, its houses, journey to work, open spaces including gardens, social conditions in three contrasting areas of the city (the central wards, middle ring and outer ring) and a commentary on life on a housing estate.

So informed, its authors offered some important principles for the rebuilding of the city. There should be greater control of the use of land in the public interest, unrestricted by existing administrative boundaries. The existing city area should not further expand but should be restricted by an agricultural or green belt. Satellite towns should be built to relieve city pressure. Factory centres, including 'flatted' factories should be provided, with the necessary rehousing around them. Areas around factories which must remain in their present location should be redeveloped. Central ward population should be rehoused in flats, maisonettes and terraced houses. Parkway-style roads, ring roads and a new traffic layout for the city centre were necessary. Housing estates should be made into living communities through the provision of communal and social centres. The total package of planning policies was replicated in a glossy, well illustrated booklet *Our Birmingham* (1943) published by Cadbury Bros. No authorship was ascribed, but we may assume the hand of Paul Cadbury.

Before the publication of *When We Build Again* another planning initiative, offering guidance for the future, was already underway. The West Midland Group on Post-War Reconstruction and Planning came into being following the publication of the Report of the Royal Commission on the Distribution of the Industrial Population (1940). The chairman of the Commission, Sir Montagu Barlow, visited Birmingham that year and when he came to Bournville he was shown a draft of *When We Build Again*. The first meetings of the group were held early in 1941, the original members being Dr Raymond Priestley (Vice-Chancellor, University of Birmingham), Professor Thomas Bodkin (Professor of Fine Arts, University of Birmingham and Chairman of the Birmingham Civic Society), George Cadbury, Paul Cadbury (Vice-Chairman, Cadbury Bros and member of Birmingham City Council), Herbert Manzoni, Professor Sargant Florence (Dean of the Faculty of Commerce, University of Birmingham) and A. C. Bunch (County Architect, Warwickshire). C. B. Parkes, Chief Architect of Bournville Village Trust was seconded by the Trust as Chief of Staff; from the outset the office was in the estate office at Bournville and the cost of administration was paid for by the Trust. Over its ten years of active work the group was enlarged by additional members and employed a wide range of experts.

Whereas *When We Build Again* dealt mainly with the problems of redevelopment in Birmingham, the West Midland Group had wider interests, concerned with the planning of land use in both urban and rural areas. It published four main reports: *English County: a planning survey of Herefordshire* (1946); *Land Classification in the West Midland Region*

(1947), a reconnaissance of regional land use; *Conurbation: a planning survey of Birmingham and the Black Country* (1948) and, after the field work of the group had come to an end, *Local Government and Central Control* (1956), a review of studies of the local government situation in the region.

The West Midland Group's networks ensured a strong local influence in the University, among industrialists and (through the Unionist Alderman Sir Wilfred Martineau and the City Engineer) in local government circles. Certain of the Group's basic assumptions became conventional wisdom, particularly the premise that the conurbation was already large enough and that redevelopment of the older housing areas should have a high priority after the war. The difficult questions for Birmingham, namely the possibility of further boundary extensions and the likelihood of government control over industrial location were left for another day.

Conurbation, a classic in planning literature, offered strategic guidance of great vision for the future development of Birmingham and the Black Country. A model for the future shape and structure of big cities had already been provided: Patrick Abercrombie's *Greater London Plan 1944* (1945) outlined a decentralist strategy which had met with great acclaim. The proposed structure for the metropolis would take the form of concentric rings: an inner ring of older property which would shed population in a programme of redevelopment, a suburban ring broadly equivalent to inter-war spread, a green-belt ring, and an outer country ring which would be the chief reception area for London overspill, some of which would go to new towns. *Conurbation* endorsed some of the underlying principles of Abercrombie's approach to the planning of big cities, but addressed the needs of a very distinctive region, 'a gigantic sprawl of factories, houses, cities, towns and villages', where 'hundreds of acres of derelict land (lay) awaiting the reviving hand of the imaginative planner to restore them to fruitful use' (p. 16). The Group took the view that:

> by the reclamation of waste land, by the preservation of unspoiled land, and by the restoration of misused land, the Conurbation could become a more attractive and more efficient place. There is room in the area for its present industries to expand naturally; there is room for its inhabitants to be decently housed; and there is room for the preservation of those natural amenities so necessary to a population closely occupied in industry (p. 27).

Birmingham took its place in this regional scheme of things.

The total population of the conurbation had already passed the 2 000 000 mark, half of which was resident in Birmingham. For the future, the Group's starting point was that sufficient accommodation could be provided within the conurbation for such population increase as was likely to occur through natural increase, but any population increase greater than this would imply the growth of an area already large enough. To restrict population growth to that accruing from the excess of births over deaths would require the control of industrial growth to prevent a net immigration increase such as occurred particularly in the second half of the 1930s. The issue, then, was clear: the conurbation could house 2 000 000 people at a reasonable density, with a good measure of open space and undeveloped land retained; if the population were to rise much higher, there would be encroachment on the surrounding agricultural areas and other open land.

Concerning the economic future of the region, the Group concluded that there was no need to introduce new industries into the conurbation. The need was to re-distribute industries within the area, in order to assist districts of relative decline, rather than seek an overall expansion through new firms. Areas of unstable employment (Dudley, Bilston, Cradley Heath, Wednesbury, Brierley Hill, etc.) should be diversified by the introduction of less vulnerable industries and by bringing in industries from more prosperous areas, such as Birmingham and Smethwick.

The Group followed Abercrombie's decentralist model for urban redevelopment, but added its own distinctive perspective. Their vision was of a green city. The replanning of the conurbation was essentially a tidying-up process, the looseness of the existing urban structure making it possible to regroup the development areas within it. The morphology envisaged was that of an archipelago of urban settlements each 'isolated from its neighbours and set in green open land, from which all development other than for agriculture or amenity is rigidly excluded' (p. 200). The redevelopment pattern was therefore a system of green strips or wedges running uninterruptedly through the conurbation, each township surrounded by a green border. Birmingham was but the largest part of this pattern: in the Black Country the problem was to develop a continuous network of strips of open land, while in Birmingham the need was to split the central core of continuous urban development and introduce open space. Future urban development would take the form of planned extensions of existing centres. A 'limit of development line' would be drawn around each centre, and the resultant green setting for the whole built-up area would rectify the mal-distribution of open space, central and inner Birmingham being particularly deficient.

It is necessary to emphasise that the Group thought that the rehousing of all excess population could be accommodated within the conurbation. There was no call for dispersal beyond, so there was no green belt and no attention given to the distribution of surplus population over a wider region. There was a crucial difference between *Conurbation* and the *Greater London Plan* in this regard. Nonetheless, the imagery of a green setting and the sharp demarcation between town and country proved as powerful as Abercrombie's concentric rings for the metropolis.

But the Group's recommendations on the future housing needs of Birmingham and the Black Country were not the last word; indeed they were overtaken from another source. Abercrombie was commissioned by the Minister of Town and Country Planning to prepare a plan for the region. Since his work on Greater London he had been in high demand, preparing a regional strategy for the Clyde Valley and publishing plans for Edinburgh and Kingston upon Hull, from all of which there was a remarkable consistency to his planning approach: redevelopment of the old, reduction of densities, and dispersal of population to a wider regional setting. Working with Herbert Jackson, a local consultant, he submitted the *West Midlands Plan* to the Minister in mimeo form in 1948; it was never published (Abercrombie and Jackson, 1948). Only in one aspect was there material difference between *Conurbation* and the *West Midlands Plan*. But it was a vital one: the West Midland Group had considered that sufficient room existed in the conurbation for some 2 000 000 people and there would be no excess to be housed, whereas Abercrombie and Jackson worked to a target figure of 2 200 000, which obliged them to consider where the excess would go. The issue became where, and in what settlement form, would the surplus population be accommodated. It was a question which would bedevil planning and politics in the region for the next quarter of a century, setting local authority against local authority and Birmingham against virtually every other local authority in the West Midlands.

Abercrombie and Jackson argued that the urban heartland of the region had a finite capacity in terms of population. Once those numbers had been accommodated the options for future settlement were: development at a distance from the conurbation, peripheral spread around the existing built-up areas, or higher densities within them. The authors adduced powerful arguments against the two latter, and urged the former. The recommended policy therefore was that Birmingham and the Black Country should not continue to extend into the countryside other than by consolidation or filling in. A general peripheral spread would create transport difficulties, further perpetuate obsolescence in the centre and isolate city dwellers from the open country.

Over the next fourteen years or so (1948–62) large numbers of people would have to be accommodated, many well away from the conurbation and a figure of some 220 000 from Birmingham alone, as the major generator of housing requirements, was estimated. No new towns were proposed, rather a general scatter of population amongst towns of various types: Stafford, Worcester, Burton, Rugby, Nuneaton, Uttoxeter, Coventry, Kidderminster, Redditch, Tamworth, Lichfield, Warwick, Leamington, Stratford, Droitwich, Stourport, Malvern, other country towns, selected villages and a development in the Cannock Coalfield. Meanwhile the existing built-up area of the urban heartland would be given a clear edge between town and country; an envelope was envisaged outside which the land uses would be those involving little in the way of resident population. A green belt was recommended, but of a temporary nature, until the effectiveness of an urban limitation policy could be determined.

The battle lines were set: the future distribution of population and location of industry in the region, and the very form and nature of urban settlement would shortly become the issues of major planning contests. For the moment Birmingham accepted the Minister's recommendation that the *West Midlands Plan* should guide the drawing up of the city's development plan. However, officers might well remember the city's response to the Royal Commission on the Distribution of Industrial Population, given in May 1938: it would 'view with alarm any measures which had for its object the diversion from Birmingham of industries which by their nature would seek a location in that area' (Minutes of Evidence, quoted in Hall, 1973 p. 509). Over the years the city would never willingly accept the logic of national control over the city's economic interests, but for now it let sleeping dogs lie. As to housing dispersal, this again was something for the future, but strained relations with the county authorities were looming.

The visionary enthusiasm of the 1940s would soon pass. The title of the book of the former Birmingham Lord Mayor, Norman Tiptaft, *I Saw a City* (1945), could scarcely belong to any other period. But major planning statements had been made, and, with the Town and Country Planning Act 1947, a powerful national planning system was in place. Birmingham in particular was in an ideal position to take advantage of the new opportunities presented; it had, after all, helped to make them come about. Thus, although the idealism may have waned in the cold light of harsh reality, there could be some confidence about the future. As Paul Cadbury (1952) wrote from the Bournville Village Trust, anticipating Birmingham 50 years on: 'Central planning and control have come to stay; we may change the pattern of the wallpaper, but Town and Country Planning has fixed the foundations, walls and roofs of our cities for a century. Today the plans are on the drawing board, but in fifty years they will have taken shape' (p. 2). We must now turn to see how far this confidence in the future would fare and consider the twists and turns Birmingham would have to make in order to adjust to changing circumstances.

8
The Post-War Economy

We now turn to four chapters on post-war Birmingham, essentially post-1950, dealing with the economy, housing, planning (including roads) and city centre developments. They are best taken separately because over the four decades they emerged with very distinctive themes, evolving within their own particular time scales.

With regard to the economy the account breaks down into two quite different halves on either side of the mid-1960s. The first period was one of sustained prosperity, the underlying changes to the city economy being easily contained. The second period has been quite the reverse and years of adjustment are not yet worked out: disinvestment, unemployment rates at above the national average, deep recession dominating most of the last 15-year spell, collapse of much manufacturing industry in the traditional sectors and the emergence of economic hardship in the inner wards of the city to rival anything that the depressed regions of the 1930s could muster.

To the mid-1960s

For perhaps 20 years, let us say from the mid-1940s to the mid-1960s, there was not all that much detectable change in the Birmingham economy. The city remained an engineering and metal-working centre, an increase in size in the large concerns failing to disguise the profusion of small work-shops. They were buoyant years and Birmingham was a prosperous city (Sutcliffe and Smith, 1974).

Birmingham, together with its immediate appendages of Smethwick and Solihull, maintained the distinction from the Black Country which had been a feature of the previous century and more. Figures showing the number of persons registered at the city's six labour exchanges (which included part of Solihull) in 1951 indicated that vehicle manufacture employed 16% of the city labour force, the majority with the actual manufacture of motor vehicles and bicycles, but significant numbers also producing accessories. Engineering employed a further 13% of the labour force and 12% manufactured other metal goods. More than two in five of the city's workforce were engaged in these three categories. Other industries, long associated with Birmingham, now actually employed small numbers – the jewellery trade, iron and steel tube manufacture, the hollow-ware trade to name some. But the metal-working, engineering and ancillary trades were complemented by other sizeable manufacturing categories, as the following list shows.

Table 8.1 Birmingham employment area 1951, insured employees in manufacturing.

	Number in labour force	Percentage of labour force
Vehicles	98 703	16.2
Engineering, shipbuilding & electrical goods	81 355	13.3
Metal goods not specified elsewhere	72 698	11.9
Metal manufacture	29 245	4.8
Food, drink, tobacco	28 972	4.7
Precision instruments, jewellery	12 983	2.1
Paper, printing	12 315	2.0
Chemical & allied trades	12 175	2.0
Manufacture of wood & cork	9 230	1.5
Clothing	6 987	1.1
Textiles	4 865	0.8
Leather, leather goods, fur	1 931	0.3
Other manufacturing industries	19 847	3.3
	391 306	64.0

Source: Sutcliffe and Smith (1974), p. 156.

While nearly two thirds (64%) of Birmingham's workforce was engaged in manufacture, just over one third (35%) was in service employment. To all intents and purposes we can ignore the numbers engaged in the primary sector of agriculture, mining and treatment of non-metalliferous mining products. There was a broad spread, but the city was essentially under-endowed with service occupations.

In spite of the heavy dominance of motor manufacture (and this would continue throughout the 1950s, when perhaps between a fifth and a quarter of the city's capital and labour was involved in it, directly or indirectly) Birmingham's industry was still broadly based and reasonably resilient to change. Its small workshops were able to adapt to changing circumstances and they contributed to evening out the fluctuating economic

Table 8.2 Birmingham employment area 1951, insured employees in services.

	Number in labour force	Percentage of labour force
Distributive trades	54 113	8.9
Professional services	35 612	5.8
Transport, communications	27 857	4.6
Building & contracting	27 834	4.6
Public administration & defence	17 282	2.8
Insurance, banking, finance	10 534	1.7
Gas, electricity & water supply	9 980	1.6
Miscellaneous services	30 316	5.0
	213 528	35.0

Source: Sutcliffe and Smith (1974), p. 156.

fortunes of the time. However, over the years their obsolescence, particularly where located in the redevelopment areas, proved a visible and rather embarrassing legacy of a past industrial era. In fact the old-core industrial area of Birmingham lost 42% of its plant between 1956 and 1966, a quarter by disappearing from the records, presumably going out of business (Smith, 1977). The City Council, however, did make land available (for example at Garrett's Green) for rebuilding, and for smaller firms flatted factories were provided: the first in 1957 was Nechells House at Dartmouth Street and the second, the following year, was Lee Bank House, Holloway Head. The city's real liveliness, though, lay with the big firms, particularly those on the periphery, of which the Austin Motor Works at Longbridge, was the most extensive. Its assembly shop gave trade to a host of smaller firms which supplied it with components. During the buoyant 1950s expansion in this industry protected Birmingham against any passing down-turn in increasingly 'boom and bust' years of the national economy, and perhaps lulled the city into a position of false security as regards the future.

In fact, a long-term secular trend was already being worked out. Between 1951 and 1966 there was a decline in the absolute and proportionate size of the labour force in most of the manufacturing sectors, overall by 10%. On the other hand there was an increase of nearly a quarter (24%) in the service sector. This addition more than offset the losses in manufacturing employment so that there was a rise in the total number of jobs overall. This movement (a contraction in manufacturing and a rise in the service sector) was not of course confined to Birmingham; these post-war trends have affected all cities to mirror a national shift in occupational structure.

By 1966 the proportion of the city's labour force engaged in manufacture had fallen to 52%; the proportion in services, chasing it hard, had risen to nearly 45%. In manufacturing the numbers engaged in chemical and allied industry had increased, and also (marginally) in paper, printing and publishing. Otherwise, widespread losses had been recorded, including a fall of 18% in vehicles; proportionately the losses in some of the smaller industries such as clothing and footwear (-66%), and timber and furniture (-45%) were strikingly high. However, the broad base of engineering, electrical and metal goods remained largely unscathed.

By contrast, gains in the service sector had been recorded virtually across the board. Those employed in transport and communications just about held their own, and the numbers engaged in public administration and defence actually fell, but otherwise most occupational groups recorded impressive gains. Professional and scientific services leapt by more than half, so too did insurance, banking and finance, manifest in the office development in the city centre and along Hagley Road on the Calthorpe Estate. The proportion for construction was not far behind, a reflection of the building boom of the period.

Birmingham was economically buoyant throughout the 1950s and well into the 1960s, the decline in manufacture not yet a source of real anxiety. Adaptation and innovation would surely remain cushions of protection, and government policy regarding industrial location was unlikely to be a serious threat. Certainly some Birmingham firms such as BMC and Fisher and Ludlow were persuaded to establish plants in South Wales, Scotland and Merseyside by government financial incentives and the application of industrial development certificate (IDC) control, but by and large Birmingham firms experienced no great difficulty in obtaining permission to build new factory floorspace within the city.

However, the question of government regulation of industrial location in a way that might or would be detrimental to Birmingham's interests was potentially damaging, and a new enthusiasm for regional planning in the 1960s, signalled in the last years of the Conservative Government, and strongly reinforced by Harold Wilson's Administrations 1964–70, heightened the concern. The average number of jobs created each year outside the region by West Midlands firms was merely 2000 between 1952 and 1959; during the period 1960–65 it rose to 5800, falling somewhat to 4000 between 1966 and 1971 (Crompton and Penketh, 1977). Perhaps it was a conurbation problem rather than one for the city, but there were, nonetheless, implications for Birmingham. Many firms decided that if they could not move or expand over a short distance, because of Board of Trade restrictions, they would not move at all (Wood, 1976). There was therefore an inhibiting factor in the dynamism of the regional economy, and given the inter-linkages in the metal-based industries on which Birmingham depended, it was clearly something that the city could not ignore, quite apart from the Council's concern over rateable value and civic strength.

With the expansion of the motor car industry Birmingham became the centre of an exporting region of national significance. This was a change of fortune, because in their 19th century heyday Birmingham and the Black Country had largely serviced an expanding domestic market. But the dynamism of the Austin Motor Company put a new complexion on the importance of Birmingham to the national economy. In 1947 Austin unveiled the first British car of completely post-war design (the A40 Devon saloon); export successes in the 1950s were continued in the 1960s with the Mini. Post-war reorganisation at Longbridge had led to changes in the factory and a completely new car assembly plant took shape by 1950. The troubles afflicting the car industry in the 1970s and later were still some time off.

Birmingham's economic strength saw the growth of financial institutions in the city; London merchant bankers established premises and London banks followed. Birmingham grew as a regional banking centre and by the mid-1960s many features of an enhanced commercial centrality were in place. The London–Birmingham motorway foreshadowed additional links to other cities; rail connections to London were now electrified and city centre railway termini rationalised (though not terribly successfully with the abandonment of Snow Hill and an imposed anonymity given to New Street); and Elmdon Airport services were being extended.

But there was one black spot: labour relations. A strong trade union organisation had developed during the late 1930s and had further strengthened during the war years. The motor industry in particular provided the opportunities for shop steward militancy in the pursuit of higher wages. From the early 1950s the size and duration of disputes increased rapidly, and the strike at Austin from February to May 1953 was the biggest in Birmingham since the war. Engineering disputes remained infrequent, but stoppages multiplied in the motor and associated industries which became as strike-prone as the traditionally vulnerable areas of mining, ship building and the docks elsewhere in the country. Official and unofficial disputes over pay and conditions were serious portents of the more disruptive years to come.

Overall, however, the chief impression of Birmingham at this time was of a prosperous city. Industry was buoyant, there was a shortage of labour and earnings were high, particularly of male manual workers, high basic wages rates boosted by long hours of overtime. More women entered the labour market in the city compared with the national average. Unemployment rates were low, amazingly so compared with figures recorded in the 1970s, 1980s and 1990s. Between 1948 and 1966 only in one year (1962) did the unemployment rate in the Birmingham employment area reach 2.0%, and in most years it was under 1%. These of course were years of minimal unemployment nationally, but even so Birmingham's record was enviable. Britain had a series of low troughs interspersed with peaks: booms in 1951, 1955, 1960 and 1965; depressions in 1953, 1958, 1962 and 1967. Basically, when the country prospered, Birmingham did even better; in years of depression the Birmingham economy was less seriously affected.

The West Midlands as a whole had benefited from the post-war boom, with solid representation in two of the three major growth sectors of UK industry (motor vehicle and electrical equipment industries, but not chemicals). Until 1960 the UK was the second largest national producer of cars after the USA; Japanese and European competition had not yet been seriously mounted and there were Commonwealth trading preferences. The West Midlands economy had surged: Birmingham and Coventry were second and third only to London in the growth of new jobs between 1951 and 1961.

From the mid-1960s

But there were different times ahead. The July squeeze of 1966 and the labour 'shake out', the effects of which were felt almost immediately in the conurbation with the British Motor Corporation making over 5000 workers redundant, were a portent of difficulties to come. The cut-backs soon spread to the component manufacturers and from this time there was a clear acceleration of a fall in manufacturing employment.

The city's (and indeed the region's) industrial structure, with its heavy dependence on engineering and metal manufacture, and especially the car industry, finally demonstrated a deep-seated vulnerability. Chickens were coming home to roost. New firms had not been established; wartime engineering had proved a temporary feature in Birmingham's economy; and new science-based industries had failed to gain a foothold. The city, as a regional capital for service provision, was still a relatively weak provincial centre.

The next quarter of a century marked a protracted crisis in the industrial heartland (Spencer *et al*, 1986), which Birmingham is still experiencing. A new era of heightened competition in world markets exposed industries which for years had been comfortably protected. From the mid-1960s there was the reduction of tariffs on industrial goods with the Kennedy round of GATT talks (General Agreement on Tariffs and Trade), the reduction and final elimination of Commonwealth preferences, exposure to free trade consequent upon entry to the EEC, and the remorseless economic advance of the newly industrialising countries. The economic fortunes of the West Midlands and of Birmingham were poised to change markedly.

After the dramatic rises in world oil prices in 1973 vast trade surpluses were built up by the OPEC countries. Deficits occurred elsewhere, affecting most non-OPEC countries, Britain (at that time) amongst them. Oil importing countries were obliged to reduce public sector expenditure, leading to a sharp recession in 1974 and 1975. For various reasons the

West Midlands' relatively favoured regional economic position deteriorated sharply and the 1970s proved to be a chastening decade.

Between 1971 and 1981 the workforce of the city declined by 200 000
to half a million (of whom 450 000 were resident in Birmingham); the
losses were concentrated on manufacturing industry, the service sector
registering a small increase. Manufacturing investment was halved and output shrank by more than a third. The change reflected the unfavourable
position of the region as a whole. Between 1970 and 1983 relative earnings in the West Midlands fell from being the highest of any region in
Britain to being the lowest of any region. The region also fared badly with
regard to unemployment; in 1976 it was above the national rate for the
first time since the war. The post-war hierarchy of regional strength was
profoundly altered as the West Midlands joined those regions where contraction in coal, textiles, iron and steel, heavy engineering and ship building had long kept them in difficulties. Unemployment in the city soared, the
city average masking the particularly adverse positions of the inner districts
of Deritend, Sparkbrook, Soho and Aston.

In a traumatic ten years or so the economic landscape of the industrial
heartland of the West Midlands was fundamentally altered and Birmingham, with its own dependence on the metal industries, could not remain
immune from change. There was widespread labour shedding in all the key
sectors: vehicles, metal goods, metal manufacture, mechanical engineering
and electrical engineering. Rationalisation in the car industry left only one
major car manufacturer not in foreign ownership and placed the fortunes
of this key industry largely in the hands of one company, British Leyland.
The West Midlands remained an over-specialised economy dependent on a
much smaller number of very large firms. Birmingham's own manufacturing base was being starved of new investment and its economy was increasingly concentrated on a single, vulnerable product – the motor vehicle.

The reasons for the economic downturn are many and varied. Spencer
et al (1986) place the greatest responsibility with entrepreneurship; the
failure to generate new ideas and to translate them into production and
sales, and the reluctance to grow by expansion. But there were other
factors, all of which had a part to play. The unattractive land in the region
available for new development did not help. There was also the question
of ineffectual labour skills. Labour militancy and high wages were blamed.
Under-investment of capital locally (while investment proceeded elsewhere,
often abroad, by Midland-based companies in new corporate strategies),
was a factor. A longstanding regional policy was alleged to deter development and hinder diversification. Businesses were lost in the process of comprehensive redevelopment; small-scale metal goods firms were vulnerable,
and foundry and plating firms, while crucial in industrial linkage chains,
proved unpleasant neighbours for new housing. Poor management was
held responsible, and the consequences of organisational restructuring were

criticised when local control (i.e. from Birmingham) was relinquished in favour of control from elsewhere, typically London or abroad.

There was also the secular trend of urban-rural shifts in location, typical of any regional city in the second half of the 20th century, whereby the peripheral 'outer' districts proved more attractive to new, green-field site development than the older, congested, environmentally unattractive 'inner' districts, because of motorway building and other highway improvements and because of the effect of the on-going revolution in telecommunications. A dispersing factor, which leaves the inner parts of the 19th century industrial city at a severe disadvantage, has certainly operated in Birmingham, as we shall see, but it has been much more a question of the closure and demise of plants rather than their relocation which has been a factor in job loss.

A further factor relates to technological change whereby modernisation of processes leads to labour shedding. Automated production processes at Longbridge cut a workforce of 19 400 in 1977 to 11 000 by 1982, while output increased from 158 000 cars to around 255 000 during the same period. Lucas introduced new flexible working practices in 1984; 700 jobs were lost and two plants in Solihull were closed. Cadbury-Schweppes modernised its chocolate and confectionery division in 1980 with the loss of 3000 jobs, the majority at Bournville.

By the mid-1980s the growth and prosperity which had characterised the local economy up to the 1960s, and which had sustained Birmingham post-war as Britain's most buoyant city outside London, had gone, replaced by unemployment and decline.

> Although the character of the manufacturing base of the area remained essentially dominated by the metal-using and engineering industries, many of the traditional activities of the local economy – steel making, motor cycles, foundries, fasteners, machine tools – had been drastically run down. Furthermore, the decline of the vehicle industry had brought into question its centrality in the industrial nexus of the West Midlands economy. (Spencer *et al*, 1986, p. 109).

In this vivid period of disinvestment and rationalisation, when key industries and companies were restructured, there were some spectacular developments. For example, BL's Rover plant at Solihull was only five years old at the time of its closure in 1981.

But perhaps we may best cite the collapse of the motorcycle industry, the speed and extent of which somehow encapsulated Birmingham's decline, and the complex reasons for it: was it murder by the Japanese, suicide by neglect, accident before final demise, or an unhelpful British government? (Smith, 1989). The number of motorcycles in Britain peaked in 1960 with nearly 1.8 million machines; during the 1960s licences halved, with some recovery in the late 1970s before another fall. British producers neglected the new demand expressed during the 1950s and 1960s for small capacity machines (Italian scooters, French mopeds and small motorcycles from Germany and, after 1962, Japan), preferring instead to concentrate on the over-500 c.c. 'superbikes', mainly for export to the USA. Meanwhile the geography of world production shifted markedly; in 1953 Europe claimed three quarters of world production; by 1973 its share was one third, with another third in Japan and the remainder in Eastern Europe and Asia. At its peak, BSA produced 50 000 machines a year – 43 000 at Small Heath and the rest at Triumph at Meriden. But this was still a relatively small number, and it contrasted sharply with the mass production of the Japanese. All in all, the collapse of the industry was a sorry story; of BSA, it stemmed from 'weak and divided management, complacent that British motorcyles would sell without undue effort, investment or change and diverted by internecine arguments and difficulties in other product fields' (*op cit*, p. 183). Small Heath went into receivership in 1973, though its closure was postponed until 1975. The BSA name on new motorcyles effectively disappeared and the Small Heath factory was demolished. The Meriden Cooperative (a union and worker buy-out) limped along to finally expire in 1983. Internal company failings, an unsuitable product and foreign competition had rendered a great Birmingham industry extinct.

However, it was not all gloom and doom. The City Council took an important initiative which had implications both for the economic base of the city and the economic geography of Birmingham. In 1968 the Birmingham Chamber of Industry and Commerce had submitted evidence to a House of Commons Committee on Export Promotion which referred to the city's poor facilities for industrial and business promotion and its restrictive effect on the export trade (City Development Department, 1989). It was suggested that the West Midlands might be considered as an alternative location to London for a national exhibition centre. The City Council pursued the idea. Warren Farm at Bickenhill came on the market and the city campaigned intensively for the project. In January 1970 government approval was given to the use of the site. A new company, NEC Ltd, was formed, financed almost entirely by funds raised by the Council. Work began in 1973, the first sod symbolically cut by Prime Minister Edward Heath. The first six halls were opened by the Queen in 1976 and there has been considerable expansion since, including the building of the International Arena. The site area has expanded from 310 acres to 580 acres (1993) and the NEC share of the UK exhibition market rose from 25% in 1978 to 42% in 1990. The NEC is now the largest exhibition facility in the UK and the tenth largest in Europe. In the same year British Rail inaugurated a new railway station adjoining the site, which together with the airport and (ultimately) a motorway intersection, considerably reinforced the strategic importance of this part of eastern Birmingham.

Elsewhere in the city a demand for new factory premises was building up, in spite of worsening economic conditions. Over one million square metres of new factory floor space were built between 1974 and 1979. New sites for industrial expansion were provided at Woodgate Valley and at Minworth (brought into the city after local government reorganisation in 1974). Derelict land was reclaimed at the former Yardley Sewage Disposal Works and land for private development was released across the city.

But into the 1980s the state of the local economy was still worrying. Unemployment was still increasing faster than in other parts of the country, job losses remained concentrated in the manufacturing sector, and the inner city exhibited all the classical features of urban decline. After marginal improvement between 1976 and 1979 unemployment rates soared over the next three years and in 1982 the city jobless rate touched 19.4%. However by the mid-1980s a recovery set in and unemployment fell steadily, though rates for Birmingham (carrying the heavy weight of depressed inner wards such as Sparkbrook, Aston, Soho, Nechells and Ladywood) remained far in excess of the national average – 13.9% in 1988 against 7.3%.

During this time there was no shortage of local enterprise to stimulate a local economy undergoing painful transition. A Conservative City Council elected in 1977 administered a business and employment scheme to provide loans and grants; an incoming Labour Council in 1979 established an economic development committee; on their return in 1982 the Conservatives set up a development and promotion unit under the Chief Executive, and made money available to buy up and demolish old factories and prepare sites for development. The newly-established (and shortly to disappear) West Midlands County Council (1974–86) had its own economic regeneration strategy and set up a West Midlands Enterprise Board. In Birmingham, Labour, returned to office in 1984, ensured that its economic development committee followed policy directions similar to those of the WMCC, and transferred its development and promotion unit to a new unit responsible to the City Planning Officer.

Meanwhile the city was recycling industrial land and bringing forward new land on large sites to an impressive extent and was committed to considerable expenditure on economic projects. Business parks were developed at Witton, Small Heath, Winson Green and Woodgate Valley (release of land here being bitterly contested on environmental grounds). The needs of small businesses were met by the opening of New Enterprise Workshops. Some well known premises were acquired for disposal to developers, including the former Ansell's Brewery at Aston Cross, the Talbot Car Works at Small Heath and the Joseph Lucas factory at Hockley. Aston Science Park was established in 1982, jointly developed by the City Council, Aston University and Lloyds Bank; an area of run-down factories provided a location for 50 new companies. Small wonder that the chairman of the Economic Development Committee, Albert Bore, could inform the City Council in June 1987 that since 1980 some 18 990 jobs had been created by the direct action of the Council and another 10 700 preserved by Council intervention; 152 acres had been developed for sale and 69 acres developed for lease (City Development Department, 1989).

The service sector at last began to take off and by the end of the 1980s the city had become one of the fastest growing office and service industry centres in the country. Birmingham, like all industrial cities, was experiencing profound readjustments to its economic structure. Longstanding trends which impacted on the balance between manufacturing and service employment finally worked their way through to a complete reversal of previous positions. In 1971 304 000 people were engaged in manufacturing compared with 277 000 in services; by 1987 the respective figures were 159 000 and 316 000.

During the 1980s the city looked increasingly to Europe and the EC as a potential source of funding for economic regeneration (Martin and Pearce, 1992). Previous international links had been substantially within the Empire and Commonwealth, but these had largely evaporated. Alternative markets were slow to develop, but during the 1980s the City Council took an increasingly active roll in developing new links, particularly European.

The immediate obstacle was that Birmingham did not qualify for assistance from the European Regional Development Fund (ERDF) because it was not designated as an assisted area under the UK's regional policy. This difficulty was removed when the Department of Trade and Industry accorded this designation to the city and parts of the surrounding region, and this unlocked a variety of sources of EC funding. By 1987 the city had received £78 million from the ERDF and in 1988 Birmingham became the first UK local authority to receive approval for a form of funding known as an 'Integrated Operation', the total package amounting to £203 million of assistance up to 1991. This provided support for a range of initiatives, the most prestigious of these being the construction of the new International Convention Centre, which opened the door to developments in international business tourism (see Chapter 11). Meanwhile in 1989 the EC confirmed the West Midlands as a declining region, and this provided access to further financial assistance under the ERDF.

In the meantime the years of recovery in the mid-1980s were followed by another recession just as deep as the one of the early-1980s, and because of the shallow recovery which had taken place in the interim, even more damaging. In February 1993 the city unemployment rate stood at 13.1% (103 150 unemployed); in the West Midland region 11.5% were unemployed, a higher figure than for any region in the country except the North (12.2%) and Northern Ireland (14.6%). There seemed to be no end in sight to the assaults on Birmingham's traditional metal-working industries, engineering, vehicle making and car components. The city, the product of capitalist enterprise in the 19th century, was now the victim of a world system in which labour was being used for different purposes and in different parts of the world. The locus of international capitalism had shifted; Britain and its industrial cities lost out. Quite apart from fierce competition from Europe and the USA, the extraordinary rise of the Pacific Rim countries, notably Japan, and some other newly industrialising nations, combined to put cities like Birmingham under severe pressure.

Allegations as to poor management, trade union militancy, an inhibiting regional policy, inadequate technical skills from lethargic educational programmes, and poor national economic management may all have played their part, but taking a wider perspective there is no disguising the fact that the city is having to live through, and adjust to, a period of profound change. Market competition affecting product, and technological change affecting labour demand, have required economic restructuring to a radical degree. The collapse of the truck-making firm DAF in February 1993 characterised some of the major symptoms. At a time of world over-capacity in truck and lorry making, a Dutch firm with 13 000 jobs world wide, 5500 in the UK and 2000 in Birmingham at Washwood Heath filed for bankruptcy protection, unable to withstand the competition from bigger producers, Daimler Benz and Fiat. Birmingham, in thrall to a world economy, itself in recession, found that decisions on its workforce were taken in places, and in circumstances, over which there could be little local control.

Over the last quarter of a century the economic geography of the city has taken on markedly different features in terms of occupational structures and spatial patterns of employment. There is no telling yet where the new trends are leading. Birmingham's industrial past has always reflected a capacity for innovation and adaptation, proceeding alongside traditional enterprises and practices. One type of manufacture, one technology, followed another. The adjustment from hardware to engineering during the fourth quarter of the 19th century was a case in point. But the present economic crisis does not yet suggest any sequential phase in manufacturing activity; it has been a case of manufacturing loss, not its replacement. The shift whereby the service sector has gained at the expense of manufacturing industry can only be taken so far, and the 1980s demonstrated that the tertiary sector could be equally vulnerable. The fractures of the last 20 years have therefore proved particularly unsettling, and a period of uncertainty remains.

But from early 1993 the country, the region and the city began to pull slowly from recession. The DAF situation at Washwood Heath improved significantly with the success of a management buy-out. The unemployment figures for February, quoted above, represented a peak; in August the regional unemployment rate was down to 11.0% and the city total had fallen below 100 000. In recognition of local employment difficulties the city was upgraded to full Development Area status in July. As a sign both of a recovery of confidence and determination to take initiatives to secure future prosperity, Birmingham is preparing plans for an Expo world trade fair in 2003.

9
Post-War Housing

As we have seen in Chapter 7, wartime legislation in the form of the Town and Country Planning Act 1944 was a considerable spur to Birmingham's objectives in housing redevelopment, the 'blitz and blight' provisions allowing the city to proceed with speed in tackling its legacy of unfit dwellings and obsolete housing arrangements. In fact, for various reasons, the clearance programme was much delayed and the immediate issue was the housing shortage, met in part initially by the supply of prefabricated dwellings. It took some years therefore, certainly into the 1950s, before the post-war housing scene took shape; when it did, the pattern fell into place with a vengeance and would have a major influence on the development of Birmingham over the next two decades. The residential townscape of the city, which Stedman (1958) described was drastically altered over a period of 20 years.

We look first, therefore, at the 1950s and 1960s: not from a strictly chronological point of view, but in terms of the four recurrent themes – clearance and improvements, redevelopment, new housing, and the question of overspill of population to areas beyond the city boundary. Another question assumed major significance in the 1960s and into the 1970s: housing accommodation and race. During the 1970s these themes lost their dominant force and for the last twenty years or so of our period other issues came to the fore, notably rehabilitation, urban renewal and management of housing stock.

Clearance and improvement

Birmingham began the post-war period with 51 000 houses declared unfit; by the end of the 1960s 38 000 had been demolished. The annual clearance rate built up to a peak in the late 1960s: 24 000 were demolished in the period 1951–66, the other 14 000 in that final flourish to 1969. These figures relate to demolitions by the local authority; there were 12 000 other removals effected by private development for a variety of different purposes (Sutcliffe and Smith, 1974). Birmingham in fact had a relatively slow clearance rate up to 1966: over the period 1955–63 the clearance rate was higher than Bristol, Nottingham, Portsmouth and Southampton, but lower than Leeds, Liverpool, Manchester, Newcastle and Wolverhampton (Stedman and Wood, 1965). But it made up lost ground in a remarkable programme of demolition between 1967 and 1969, outstripping its main rivals Manchester, Liverpool and Leeds.

With an initial slow progress on demolition attention focused first on improvement of stock. Between 1947 and 1967 the Corporation improved 42 000 of its dwellings, work ranging from minor repairs to the provision of water supply and toilet facilities. After the Housing Repairs and Rents Act 1954 local authorities were empowered to give improvement grants to private interests, and by 1967 13 000 grants had been made to owner occupiers and 6000 to landlords. Further improvements came about with city compulsion on private landlords to rectify specific faults ranging from blocked drains to leaking roofs.

Overall, a considerable raising of housing quality was effected during these years. Census data show that while in 1951 22% of city houses were without the exclusive use of a w.c., this figure had fallen to 11% by 1966; and while 46% of the houses had no fixed bath in 1951, the proportion was down to 25% in 1966. The core of the unfitness problem was of course in the central wards, and it is salutary to note that in 1966 60% of the dwellings there still lacked an exclusive hot water supply, 66% a fixed bath and 31% a w.c.

A central areas management committee was set up in 1947 to oversee the work of maintenance pending redevelopment (Chinn, 1991). It launched an extensive programme of reconditioning, intended to make decayed dwellings tolerable to live in until they were demolished, improvements effected according to life expectancy. 'Short life' properties, scheduled for demolition within five years of acquisition by the Council, were given water supplies where this was necessary, but otherwise repaired only to a limit which brought them to minimum public health standards. 'Intermediate' properties, with a projected life of five to ten years, were repaired more extensively, by a labour force of 1000 men from about a hundred small building firms at an average cost of £40–50 per house. Those houses, to be demolished after ten years or more, were reconditioned completely, with costs rising to an average of £195 per dwelling; they were then used to accommodate families waiting to be rehoused in more modern accommodation.

All this amounted to a programme (from 1951 the responsibility of the new housing management department) of 'soling and heeling' properties to extend their lives in an attempt to cope with the pressure of demand for new dwellings from a house waiting list stubbornly slow to decline. Even so, clearance of the abjectly unfit could not be delayed and the beginning of the end for Birmingham's back-to-backs was heralded in 1950 with the clearance of the area around Great Francis Street and Bloomsbury Street in Nechells. The city's five redevelopment areas were subdivided into smaller sections for progressive clearance and redevelopment and by 1953 four of these had been cleared. A new phase of rebuilding was about to begin.

Redevelopment

Within a remarkable period of between 15 and 20 years almost all of the originally declared central redevelopment areas had been cleared and rebuilt; it was a scale of activity unparalleled in a British city, particularly impressive as work had also begun on demolishing property outside the five areas concerned. The social geography and the very appearance of the city were transformed.

Perhaps in an early attempt to humanise the redevelopment process and to give a more sympathetic identity to the new districts created, the names of the redevelopment areas were changed, only Ladywood being retained. Nechells had Green added to it, Gooch Street became Highgate, Summer Lane was renamed Newtown and Bath Row was changed to Lee Bank. The early focus of activity was here, but in 1955 a further fifteen areas were defined, covering 1700 acres, so as to virtually encircle the city centre. Around 30 000 people would be affected in Hockley, Lozells, Gosta Green, Winson Green, Bordesley, Aston, Balsall Heath, Balsall Green and Small Heath. No large scale acquisition powers were available, in contrast to the situation in 1946, and general clearance area powers were used in the redevelopment programme.

Between 1950 and 1956 the bulldozer swept through Nechells and into the other four areas. Revised zoning layouts were prepared, but all followed the basic planning principles of the original plan for Nechells. However, important modifications were introduced, particularly with regard to higher densities. Pressure on housing land within the city led to important changes in housing accommodation, particularly in the form of more and higher flats. The first large building was Queen's Tower at the junction of Great Lister Street and Great Francis Street, one of four 12-storey blocks, opened in 1954. But there would be more. Newtown eventually had blocks up to 20 storeys and on the edge of Lee Bank there were two 32-storey blocks. In all, Birmingham's inner city redevelopment, a programme which cleared 40 000 slums and swept away a legacy of unwanted back-to-backs, was achieved in a very different form from that envisaged in earlier years; more than 400 multi-storey blocks gave the city a new skyline and established new housing conditions for the working classes.

The change in orthodoxy, that Birmingham people would not live in flats, was achieved with surprisingly little political disruption. When the Unionists took control of the Council in 1949, their reform of the city's housing machine entailed the abandonment of most of the local building firms. These had fallen behind with their municipal contracts. Instead, a number of big, national concerns were brought in with a capability of building non-traditional houses on a large scale; some of them were already building flats for other local authorities and could offer fully tested blocks 'off the peg' (Sutcliffe and Smith, 1974). When the 12-storey blocks at Nechells proved very expensive, the house building committee resolved to take advantage of the new opportunity; in 1952 the building programme had 20% of the dwellings in flats. The Labour Party did not demur.

Meanwhile encouragement, indeed pressure, to build in this form came from another source. In 1951 the Unionists proposed the setting up of an Architect's Department; transitionally, a new City Architect would work within the public works department. Labour concurred. The sensitivities of the City Surveyor, Herbert Manzoni, were protected and a new appointment was made: A. G. Sheppard Fidler, formerly Architect at Crawley New Town. A separate department was set up in 1954. An advocate of mixed development, Sheppard Fidler nonetheless fuelled the drive towards high-rise accommodation (and not only in the central redevelopment districts), seeing city renewal as a design exercise whereby variety in mass and outline could result from a range of dwelling types.

There were of course other factors to account for the switch in housing provision. Nationally there was the pressure on land supply to cater for demand, and as densities had to rise, it was argued that this could most readily be achieved by building high; the agricultural lobby was particularly strong. There was tacit ministerial approval to local authority initiatives, and higher subsidies were available for building above six stories. It was architecturally fashionable to build in the modernist style; this was further encouraged by the introduction of industrialised building techniques, increased prefabrication promising a reduction in costs, though architectural variety was sacrificed.

The result was a transformed landscape: two-storey terraces, medium-rise flats and tower blocks in a green setting broken up by parking areas, service roads, the occasional play space and a network of roads. The earlier street pattern was largely obliterated and with it the legacy of 19th century housing at its worst (Figures 9.1, 9.2, 9.3). Also swept away was the culturally-rich intermixture of community facilities and services; while many churches and some industrial plant remained, public houses and particularly shops were victims of change. Above all it was a sociological

171

Figure 9.1 Dilapidated housing, Cato Street, 1958

Figure 9.2 Corner shop and housing, Duddeston Mill Road/Cato Street, 1958.

transfusion whereby one community was largely replaced by another in alternative forms of housing accommodation (Figures 9.4, 9.5).

There were early warning shots across the bows of a potentially insensitive local authority renewal machine. In 1952 Charles Madge, Birmingham's Professor of Sociology, submitted a proposal to the Council for a lengthy sociological monitoring of change in the redevelopment areas; it was rejected. This did not stop enquiry, and Norris (1960) examined the housing satisfaction of those rehoused. No one had ever claimed that Birmingham citizens preferred flats to houses, but the housing programme unfolded remorselessly. Canon Norman Power (1965) alleged that 'the forgotten people' had been ignored. Writing from fourteen years of personal experience as Vicar in the redevelopment area of Ladywood, he claimed that while he 'saw a living community torn to pieces by the bulldozers and scattered to the four corners of the city, there was no consultation with the people most affected and concerned' (p. 14). While acknowledging that slums were doomed and that the new accommodation was welcome, he asked 'Must the re-building be accompanied by so much disruption of personal ties? So much that is destructive of community life? So much that degrades streets, schools, districts?' (p. 119).

Figure 9.3 Run-down property, Great Hampton Row, Newtown, 1961.

Figure 9.4 Redevelopment: municipal flats, Lea Bank.

Birmingham of course was not alone in this dilemma. Nationally the slum clearance programme was a physical as well as a social period of disruption. Between 1955 and 1974 1 165 000 houses were demolished or closed in England and Wales, and 3 116 000 persons moved to alternative accommodation as a result of the clearances (Cherry, 1976). It was perhaps the most profound social dislocation in such a relatively short time in the country's urban history, and Birmingham was a prime example with community patterns disrupted and new life styles adopted. People were moved from one inner city estate to another, to suburban estates and beyond. As the dynamics of social change accelerated, old problem areas were obliterated and new ones created. Sociological commentators sounded warning bells: Young and Willmott (1957) were early Cassandras in respect of East London, and they were echoed in Birmingham. The attack on the slums proved much more complex than had ever been realised.

New Housing

At the end of the war the general understanding was that the State would assume responsibility for the quality, quantity and distribution of the

Figure 9.5 Redevelopment: municipal flats, Nechells Green.

nation's housing stock, and that in this task the full weight of the housing programme would rest on the local authorities. A stream of instruction and exhortation to local councils ensued. The *Housing Manual* of 1944 (Ministry of Health, Ministry of Works, 1944) laid primary emphasis on the provision of three-bedroomed, two-storey houses. The *Housing Manual 1949* (Ministry of Health, 1949) gave advice on a wider range of dwelling types, based on a variety of designs for houses, flats and maisonettes. Supplements followed in 1951, 1952 and 1953, while *Flats and Houses 1958* (Ministry of Housing and Local Government, 1958) dealt with questions of design and economy when building at higher densities. Exchequer grants and local authority rate contributions effectively trebled the money value of subsidies compared with 1939. In order to stimulate local authority house building even more, the Conservatives after their return in 1951 gave even more generous subsidies (and also stimulated private building). The subsidies were reduced for general needs in 1954 and two years later totally abolished.

Birmingham's initial progress was slower than most local authorities, a tardy rate investigated by a cross-party group of councillors. New measures and a change of city administration conspired to effect a considerable improvement: the city's building rate increased from 1200 in 1949 to 4700 by 1952. But the shortage of sites within the city meant that the housing programme dropped back again later in the 1950s, to under 2500 in 1958, to only just above the 2000 level over the next three years, with a recovery to around 2500 annually until the mid-1960s. The 350-acre Castle Bromwich airfield was purchased by the city in 1959, the release of which for housing purposes finally boosted the house building programme; in 1965 the building rate exceeded 4000 and in the seven years 1965–71, when further land came 'on stream', over 42 000 dwellings were built in an explosion of building activity. A major contribution to this total was in the out-city estate at Water Orton which became known as Chelmsley Wood, where 1500 acres were finally allocated in 1964 by the Labour government after years of rebuttal by the Conservatives in the city's attempts to obtain building land beyond its boundaries. For a while Birmingham was renewing itself 'faster than any other city in Europe' (Sutcliffe and Smith 1974, p. 232) and the city's housing machine attracted national attention.

Meanwhile private development played a much less prominent role. Most sites in the city were acquired for municipal housing, so land for the private builder was in even shorter supply than for the local authority. Two consequences ensued: first, private development favoured the suburban areas outside the city, typically Solihull and Sutton Coldfield, and second, residential densities were tightened up, particularly through infill. The number of dwellings per unit area of land (acres or hectares) assumed increasing importance in town planning matters, and geographers took note of changing land use patterns in the residential fringe areas of cities. These were the questions which Whitehand (1987) addressed nationally in considering the changing face of cities and which Pompa (1988) studied locally in south Birmingham between 1970 and 1985. Tighter residential densities had led to 'town cramming' as modern infilling took place in areas of formerly low density Victorian and Edwardian villadom.

Certain areas of private building were distinctive if only because of their past associations. Bournville expanded in the Shenley area (Figures 9.6, 9.7) both with houses for sale and with additions for the local authority housing register; the Calthorpe Estate also developed for both the owner occupied and the public rented sectors, the tower blocks around the fringe changing the appearance of Edgbaston considerably. Overall, the private housing stock increased by under 1000 dwellings a year throughout the 1950s; between 1960 and 1967 it was on a rising curve but only between 1968 and 1971 did the annual totals exceed 2000, after which a decline set in. Both the public and private sectors had peaked.

So much for the general picture; we can now look at some of the detailed aspects of a remarkable boom period in which, first, municipal housing in east Birmingham was extended up to and beyond the city boundary, and then the southern fringe of Birmingham received its suburban ring lapping the hillsides beyond Northfield. The design of municipal estates was the first housing consideration after 1945, and the layout of the Tile Cross estate was intended to make a break from the pre-war geometrical road patterns. A more flexible layout with interlocking open spaces was achieved, however, at the cost of very low densities. On other land, partially developed pre-war estates, where layouts could scarcely be altered, were completed with a variety of both permanent and temporary dwellings; indeed the first high-rise flats in the city were built at Tile Cross (1953), the 6-storey blocks pre-dating the larger towers at Nechells.

In 1953 the Kingshurst Hall Estate east of Shard End, crossing the boundary into Warwickshire, was purchased, providing the city with a green-field site for about 7000 people. The River Cole on its southern flank provided an opportunity for framing the estate against an attractive valley setting. By this time the new City Architect was in his post; the acquisition gave Sheppard Fidler an early opportunity to show how his preference for mixed development and an altogether more adventurous approach to design and layout than had so far been the practice. Part of the estate won a Civic Trust award in 1963. Improvements in design standards in the city were long overdue, but quality was sacrificed in the search for quantity, and Birmingham's housing programme won few national plaudits for its architecture. Some layouts may be commended, however, notably the Lyndhurst Estate, Erdington (1958) and the Primrose Hill Estate (1963).

The purchase of the Castle Bromwich airfield in 1959 gave the city another large area for development, the Castle Vale Estate ultimately housing around 20 000 people. This was a valuable site, no more than five miles from the city centre and closely adjoining a number of manufacturing establishments. But its design became a *cause célèbre*, highlighting the thoroughly unsatisfactory planning situation in the city. The public works department drew up the first layout plan in 1960–1; it was heavily criticised by the house building committee, advised by the City Architect; and

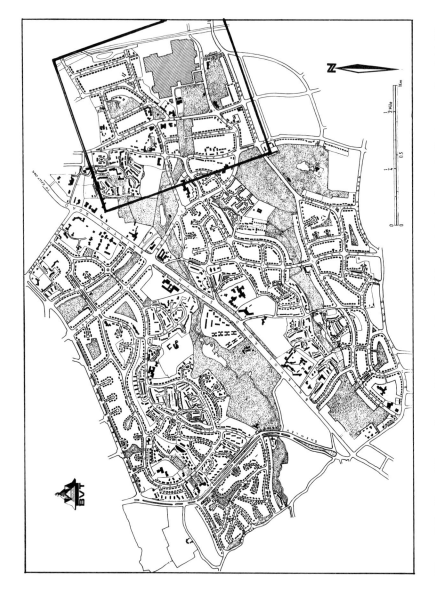

Figure 9.6 Plan of Bournville c. 1983. The original building estate is shown in the box on the right. The grey area denotes open space.

it was not until 1963 that a compromise plan was agreed. The division of planning functions between departments had been starkly exposed. From this unfortunate start perhaps it is not surprising that the estate was soon criticised for everything that was wrong with 1960s building; a third of the population was aged under 14, but 60% of the homes were flats. By the early 1990s the houses and prominent cluster of tower blocks were targeted by the Department of the Environment for refurbishment through the agency of a housing action trust. Certainly the area has an anonymous and forlorn appearance today; an almost flat site did not help, but there is a desperate lack of planting, the tall blocks, all named with airfield connotations, rising from an open, windswept, litter-strewn green sward; the shopping centre is dilapidated, awaiting refurbishment and the whole environment a dreadful testimony to impoverished planning and management.

Sheppard Fidler resigned in 1964 and went into private practice. He was succeeded by J. R. Sheridan Shedden, and when he died in 1966 his deputy, J. A. Maudsley, was appointed. It was he who supervised the building of the Chelmsley Wood Estate. By this time the flats *versus* houses issue had been partly resolved; high-rise building rates had peaked and after 1965 the proportion of flats built fell steadily. The Chelmsley Wood plans, finalised in 1965, provided for only 10–15% of the dwellings in tall blocks. By the early 1970s the city's multi-storey flat building era was approaching its end, reflecting a general situation in the country, professional opinion moving with public anxiety in the aftermath of the Ronan Point disaster in 1968 in the London Borough of Newham. This allowed for experiments with a variety of building methods, materials and house types at Chelmsley Wood in an estate which eventually housed 50 000 people. National commendations were made and for virtually the first time the city's architecture attracted favourable attention. It heightened the irony of Maudsley's departure through allegations of corruption with building contractors. But compared with Castle Vale, Chelmsley Wood 20 years on still works well and provides a liveable environment; now in Solihull by virtue of 1974 boundary changes, its layout and design remain distinctive (Figures 9.8, 9.9). Well landscaped and with a shopping centre cleverly taking advantage of a fall in levels to separate vehicles from pedestrians, as a mini-township its disposition of housing between terrace blocks and occasional towers, while occasionally contrived and lacking real intimacy, today ranks as a good example of the genre of its time.

By the early 1970s, over a period of 20 years, east Birmingham had been extended from its inter-war limits to beyond the city boundary in a sea of municipal building, each phase architecturally distinctive in its own way: Tile Cross, Kingshurst, Castle Vale and Chelmsley Wood, with the more amorphous Bromford Bridge estate helping to link the various elements. The Castle Bromwich race course was swallowed up and housing pressed

Figure 9.7 Bushwood Road Estate, 1965. Mixed development at Shenley.

hard against the elevated section of the M6 running across the flat lands of the Tame Valley at this point. Patches of private housing still ribboned the Chester Road while the old village of Castle Bromwich with its fine Jacobean Hall and enclave of up-market housing remained a relief in what was otherwise a mono-class spread of council-provided housing.

As the east filled up, Birmingham could finally turn its attention to the south and after 1969 Frankley, Rubery and Hawkesley in North Worcestershire were filled in with estates of mixed development. The circumstances for this expansion are traced in the next section.

Overspill

A unifying thread running through Birmingham's post-war housing story is the city's search for housing land on which to build houses both for general need and to accommodate those being relocated from slum clearance projects. In spite of the endowment received from the massive boundary extension of 1911 (and smaller extensions subsequently), such had been the economic vitality of the city, its population growth and household fission and the compelling need to reduce overcrowding rates in the

Figure 9.8 Chelmsley Wood, layout for Districts 1 and 2. Architects Jackson and Edmonds in association with the City Architect.

older parts of the city, that land for residential and ancillary accommodation was simply gobbled up. Birmingham's search for *lebensraum* dominated the planning and housing scene. The demand for land outside the city brought Birmingham on to a collision course with other local authorities.

At this point we should recall that Abercrombie and Jackson had estimated a dispersal of 200 000 population from the conurbation to a variety of locations beyond a temporary green belt in the period 1948–62. No new towns were proposed; instead a multiplicity of additions to existing small towns in the surrounding country ring was envisaged. The Labour government's New Town programme came to an end in 1951 and the Conservatives' Town Development Act 1952 offered another mechanism for population dispersal from big cities: voluntary agreements between exporting and receiving authorities whereby houses would be built for the population of the large cities in the smaller townships. It was financially attractive: cities lost rateable value but made only small contributions to the receiving authority for the housing provided. Birmingham proceeded to negotiate with the surrounding counties (Warwickshire, Worcestershire and Staffordshire) but it was not until 1955 that financial agreements could be made; Warwickshire and Worcestershire were particularly cautious and Staffordshire proved the more cooperative. By 1957

Figure 9.9 Housing, Chelmsley Wood, Area 3 North.

overspill agreements had been entered into with ten receiving authorities, but only 88 houses had become available (Sutcliffe and Smith, 1974). The agreements increased rapidly from then on, but by now it was realised that the provisions of the Town Development Act offered no easy solution to Birmingham's housing problem. The situation was also bedevilled by difficulties over industrial relocation, because of Birmingham's slowness to export jobs at the same rate as population.

Other alternatives were looked at. The purchase of Kingshurst Hall estate in 1953, and its subsequent development as an 'out city' estate in Warwickshire was one option, as we have seen. But further expansion in this area was thwarted by the county's green belt proposals. New Towns were favoured in some quarters and the Midlands New Towns Society was founded in January 1956; its Honorary Secretary, David Eversley, from the Faculty of Commerce and Social Science at the University would prove a sharp thorn to the city over the next few years. In a carefully argued paper Eversley and Keate for the Society (1958) concluded that the West Midlands required two New Towns. They calculated that 80 000 houses would need to be built outside the conurbation over the next 20 years; 18 000 may be negotiated for South Staffordshire under the Town Development Act and a further 16 000 may come from further negotiations with the three counties. This left a shortfall of 46 000 houses, 'too many to be absorbed into the life of the existing small towns of the area' (*op cit*, p. 57), hence two New Towns, not just for Birmingham but for the conurbation were required.

The city's general purposes committee called for a New Town but was rebuffed by Macmillan's successor as Minister of Housing and Local Government, Duncan Sandys, and later by his successor, Henry Brooke. There was only one New Town designated in this period (Cumbernauld, for Glasgow in 1956); the Town Development Act did not apply to Scotland until similar legislation was passed in 1957. Government was determined to pursue its voluntary overspill preference, and when successes in this policy option came with the London County Council negotiating several agreements, the pressure was on Birmingham to comply with the Government's strategy.

With the city's housing and slum clearance programme in jeopardy the solution of a boundary extension was looked at afresh. The Birmingham Labour Party had so far been broadly in favour both of overspill (preferably by New Towns) and of restricting the city's industrial growth to reduce pressure on housing. But frustration with ministerial rejection of a Midlands New Town and the persuasion of a new party leader, Alderman Harry Watton, led Labour to adopt a more expansionist outlook. In March 1959 the City Council approved (by 75 votes to 47) the making of a boundary extension of 2432 acres largely around Wythall, in north Worcestershire in order to develop the land for residential, industrial and ancillary purposes (Sutcliffe and Smith, 1974). A total of 624 acres were in Solihull at Solihull Lodge and Major's Green (510 acres identified for residential and 114 acres for industrial purposes). The remainder, 1808 acres were in Bromsgrove on either side of the Alcester Road at Wythall (1618 acres for residential and 190 for industrial purposes). Both the tactics and the strategy were called into question. The land applied for was too small to meet Birmingham's long-term housing needs, yet its size represented too obvious a break with previous policy. The city scarcely needed the land in the short term because the Castle Bromwich airfield would shortly become available; in the long term it needed much more. Birmingham was accused of expansionism for its own sake and of having abandoned the New Town ideal.

A public inquiry was held in July 1959 (Long, 1961). Eversley effectively demolished the city's case with a penetrating analysis of future overspill requirements, advocating an energetic overspill policy; the irony was that he was an active member of the party which was pressing for the alternative of peripheral expansion. The inspector's conclusions were that:

Such development would be contrary to the firmly expressed policy that there should be no peripheral expansion of Birmingham and the widely held belief that the land in question ought to be preserved as part of Birmingham's green belt. Also, it would offend almost all present residents and it should not be allowed unless there is no clear alternative. The situation is far too uncertain for it to be said either (a) that 14 000 houses at Wythall will solve the problem for the next 20 years and that no further peripheral expansion will be sought; or (b) that as many as 14 000 houses will be needed. (*op cit*)

The Minister rejected the application in April 1960, advised by his inspector that an acceleration of the overspill programme was both desirable and feasible. He called on the city to renew its efforts to decentralise both population and industry. As a concession he indicated that development of part of the area, lying adjacent to the Alcester Road might be favourably considered later.

Within two years there was a surprising turn of events. In August 1961 the Minister gave his blessing in principle to a further application from Birmingham to build on 600 acres at Wythall and to extend the city boundaries to include that area. He also confirmed that a change of heart on New Towns was leading him to consider the Dawley area of Shropshire as a potential candidate. A further public inquiry was held later that year (October–November), the City Council (now with Conservative support because the proposal had emanated from a Conservative minister) ranged against the Midlands New Towns Society and the county and district authorities concerned. The inspector's report was ambivalent in its recommendation, but the critical factor seems to have been that Henry Brooke had by now been replaced by Charles Hill; a new Minister maintained the earlier position that the Wythall area should be preserved as part of the green belt. The application was refused in February 1962 and Birmingham once more urged to accelerate its overspill programme.

By the summer of 1962 only 1500 houses had been built for Birmingham citizens in overspill areas. But the Minister's continual pressure for the local authorities to do more to implement Government policy finally began to pay off. The Housing Act 1961 increased the Exchequer contribution to housing provision and in July 1962 the City Council increased its subsidy to £12 per house per year over fifteen years in the hope that a bigger financial contribution would be an added inducement. Later, it was agreed that additional financial and technical assistance would be provided for town development schemes.

Meanwhile a New Town was designated near Dawley (July 1962) and Charles Hill's successor at Housing and Local Government, Sir Keith Joseph, announced a second at Redditch (February 1963). Demographic data were now suggesting rapidly increasing population projections, and an unpopular government beset with an economic 'stop-start' reputation could not afford to let the big cities fall behind in their slum clearance and housing programmes. A renewed phase of New Town building was now begun in the West Midlands, Merseyside, Tyneside, Scotland and south-central England, and overspill programmes from London and the conurbations were stepped up. For Birmingham, Joseph indicated that if

Birmingham still needed more land for housing it should consult the neighbouring county councils and submit proposals to the Ministry.

The city targetted Warwickshire for 1540 acres at Water Orton and Worcestershire for 420 acres at Kingswood Farm, west of Alcester Road. A formal application in January 1964 was followed by a public inquiry in May–June in conditions less fraught than previously: strong local objection was raised, but opposition from both the counties and the Midlands New Towns Society seemed to be a spent force. A new Minister, now from a Labour government, Richard Crossman ruled (in December) to allow Water Orton but reject Wythall once more. The first site was adjudged suitable for a large-scale programme of industrialised buildings; the latter would prejudice the green belt where it was at its narrowest and most vulnerable adjoining Redditch.

Even this latest tranche of land would not satisfy housing demand. The Department of Economic Affairs' regional report *The West Midlands* (1965) projected an overspill of 500 000 from the conurbation by 1981; the problem would just not go away. Further peripheral developments for Birmingham were inevitable if the necessary sites were to be assembled. This time south west Birmingham was targeted, and rising land on the flanks of the long tongue of housing development extending from Northfield to Longbridge and Rubery fell to the requirements of the housing machine.

In a study of North Worcestershire, authorised by the Minister, agreement was reached between the city and the county authorities for the building of 4000 dwellings at Redditch and a further 11 000 in five areas to the south and south west of the city in the vicinity of Hawkesley, Frankley, and Walker's Heath. For one of them Cadburys withdrew their opposition when more open space was included; they had donated land west of Wythall to the corporation in 1937 for maintenance in perpetuity as open space (Cadbury 1968). Environmentally these areas gave more opportunities for imaginative layout and design than the flatter land in the east, and at Frankley in particular an affinity with the adjoining countryside was introduced to good effect. But the era of council house building was closing and Frankley was the last of the city's large public sector estates.

The overspill programme quickened meantime. By 1966 only 4000 houses for Birmingham had been built in overspill schemes; by 1971 the total had risen to nearly 9000 in fifteen schemes. The chief recipients were Tamworth, Daventry, Droitwich, Lichfield and Aldridge and Brownhills, though the scatter was extensive. But the contribution of overspill schemes to the solution of housing need remained small. A total of 9000 dwellings by 1971 was only equal to one year's housing supply (1967), admittedly the peak year and perhaps exceptional at that. New Town growth at Redditch and Telford quickened later, but for the moment a combination of peripheral growth for municipal housing, a modest private sector programme and 'voluntary' overspill by owner occupiers to favoured locations such as in Solihull, Sutton Coldfield, adjacent areas of Bromsgrove and sites increasingly further afield, kept the city's needs at bay. The Town Development Act programme ran down and agreements were terminated in the later 1970s, but not before nearly 13 600 dwellings had been built and 40 000 people re-housed, totals surpassing those for the whole of Scotland, and much in excess of any other city scheme in England, with the exception of course of London.

Table 9.1 Birmingham schemes in the expanded towns programme

Scheme	Dated scheme	Dwellings built	Population housed (est.)
Aldridge & Brownhills	1960–74	938	2 800
Banbury	1961–66	235	700
Cannock	1957–80	638	1 900
Daventry	1963–76	2 255	7 000
Droitwich	1964–81	1 778	6 200
Lichfield	1957–75	1 039	3 100
Rugely	1957–71	130	400
Stafford	1955–75	421	1 300
Tamworth	1959–81	5 107	13 800
Tutbury	1957–71	49	150
Uttoxeter	1955–65	200	600
Weston-super-Mare	1958–72	802	2 400
		13 592	40 350

NB There was also a Town Development Act scheme between Birmingham and the town of Leek, but no houses were built.

Source: Town and Country Planning, November 1984.

A changed situation

After the heady years of the 1950s, 1960s and into the 1970s when the housing and social geography of Birmingham was transformed, the next 20 or 25 years produced a very different agenda. The slum clearance programme ran its course and wound down; the redevelopment areas assumed their place in the skyline of the city and presented a totally different urban structure to the inner ring; vast public housing estates first in the east and latterly to the south pressed the city against its boundaries, and as before the war, Birmingham's suburbs were working class as well as middle class.

But to begin with, the particularly thorny question of housing accommodation and race dominated socio-political aspects of housing provision.

The influx of increasing numbers of coloured immigrants to the city attracted growing disquiet, not so much because of the impact on employment, but because of the housing situation. By the early 1960s large, old houses in the inner districts (the 'twilight zones' as the literature of the time had it) had become multi-occupied lodging houses as a process of discriminative segregation compelled coloured people to live in certain forms of accommodation and in certain parts of the city.

Racial ill-feeling was exacerbated. John Rex and Robert Moore (1967) observed that:

> The visitor to Birmingham in the early 1960s could not but be struck by the way in which racial problems dominated public discussion. It was hard to imagine, as one scanned the columns of the *Post*, the *Mail and Despatch*, the *Sunday Mercury*, and the *Planet*, that this was a city long famous for its radical and egalitarian tradition. Often the sentiments expressed by those who wrote to these newspapers or those who reported in them, smacked more of the Deep South in the United States, or of settler Africa than of the City of Reform. (p. 19)

Such a conclusion came out of the work they conducted in a study of race and housing in Sparkbrook, then a neighbourhood in course of profound change. Irish immigrants, themselves a heterogeneous group including those from Dublin, from the country (known as 'Culchies' to the Dubliners) and 'tinkers' or travellers, settled with West Indians from a number of islands, Pakistanis from country districts including Mirpur and Campbellpore with the North West Frontier province, and a host of minority groups including Indians (the largest) and Poles, Italians and Greek Cypriots.

The housing problem stemmed from the fact that there was a five-year waiting period before immigrants, from whatever country, or city of origin, could qualify for council accommodation. Birmingham's housing allocation policy, which was centred around this five-year rule, implied that the Council could assist in the housing of only part of its population. The open market was available for the remainder, but for coloured immigrants this posed a major difficulty. The only houses they could buy were the late Victorian and Edwardian terrace houses – which they proceeded to sublet. In a short period of time whole streets went over to multi-occupation.

Birmingham's policy contrasted sharply with that in some other cities where waiting lists were considerably shorter: Bradford for example operated only a six-month waiting period. Rex and Moore criticised corporation policy for forcing upon immigrants a type of housing and a way of life, damaging to the city. The problem was that overcrowding in multi-occupied premises could only be answered by a supply of alternative accommodation – which scarcely existed. In the meantime the problem assumed racist overtones: substandard housing, of the oldest stock, ill-provided with amenities, in an ageing, neglected environment, was the lot of the immigrant in greatest need. The Council used powers to control excesses of overcrowding and to provide basic amenities, but its resources were really concentrated elsewhere: the building of new flats and houses as a permanent contribution and the 'patching' of slums awaiting demolition as a temporary measure. It was a problem only eased with the passage of time, helped by the adoption of new Council procedures for dealing with the waiting list, and the lessening of pressure on housing supply.

This question of access to housing by ethnic minorities simmered on, but from the late 1960s and early 1970s, Birmingham's housing policy increasingly addressed a range of new issues. The driving political question of housing need grew less strident. Population projections (though not so much household forecasts) down-turned almost as speedily as they had risen a decade earlier. When the Government's New Towns programme came to an end and town expansion schemes fizzled out, ministerial concerns about the big cities running short of housing land quickly diminished. Improvement of housing stock through refurbishment of the old, became more important than its clearance for rebuilding. Municipal house building programmes were drastically trimmed, a fall in demand accompanied by calls for reductions in public expenditure. New aspects of demand came to the fore, including homelessness. Sentiment in favour of public housing was sharply reversed and the selling off of council houses was actively promoted by an aggressive right-wing Conservative Government after 1979. Sixty years of encouragement for local authority tenure came to an end.

The period began with a switch of emphasis from quantity to quality of housing. A strategy of stock improvement rather than clearance ensued. Powers for house improvement had long been available, local authorities enabled to improve council housing and give discretionary grants to private owners for the improvement of individual properties. From the later 1960s the emphasis switched from the improvement of single houses to whole areas (Thomas, 1986; Cherry, 1988). The Housing Act 1969 introduced the concept of general improvement areas, later sharpened in the Housing Act 1974 into housing action areas.

The 1970s saw improvement schemes in Birmingham energetically introduced. A total of 68 general improvement areas was designated in 1972 as part of a new urban renewal programme which provided for the retention and improvement of 62 000 houses. Demolition had effectively ceased for the foreseeable future, certainly as far as wholesale clearance was concerned. Later, 15 000 dwellings were included in 28 housing action areas, and the city returned to a policy of reconditioning, first popularised at the beginning of the century under Nettlefold. This time the technique was 'enveloping'; developed by the city's environmental health department, it pioneered an approach to the improvement of whole roads of older houses at no cost to their owners. In the mid-1970s Little Green was chosen as the testing ground for this form of urban renewal and schemes at Small Heath and Havelock, Saltley, followed. Pavements were re-slabbed, roads re-surfaced, waste land cleared, streets pedestrianised and play areas built, while the outsides of houses were improved with new roofs, gutters and windows. Government grants of 90% were available and the City Council agreed to provide the remainder. Grants were also available for internal improvements. Facelifts costing £3000 per house were provided to 500 homes in Moseley, Sparkbrook and Lozells in 1979 (Chinn, 1991).

But the policy switch from clearance to improvement did not resolve the problems faced by those in housing need. With economic downturn during the 1970s, the public sector squeeze on local authority spending on housing sharpened the long-standing questions of affordability and access to housing provision. In a sense the dilemma of the industrial city remained: how to provide housing at rents (or other costs) that could be afforded. Alternative forms of provision always left a large minority of the population in acute need, whether by private renting, model dwellings by private or public action, opening up the suburbs, subsidised council housing, or by encouragement to private ownership. During the late 1970s it became clear that a market system combining housing finance to procure house improvement, a reduced rate of public house building and a basic reliance on private capital for housing production, could scarcely hope to be successful. Paris and Blackaby (1979) in a critique of improvement policies in Birmingham concluded that 'the trend towards improvement has gone too far and that the rate of clearance has fallen far below the level necessary to ensure that the current volume of housing replacement takes place' (p. 189). They advocated a greater level of public-sector resource allocation, with greater public control over the housing market in the interests of social equity.

In another critique Stewart (1981) considered the particular problems of Saltley, namely, in the language of the time, its 'housing struggle'. The district was a leasehold area, with leases created mainly between 1880 and 1910 for a term of 99 years. In the early 1970s they were running out. Although the Leasehold Reform Act 1967 enabled leaseholders to purchase their freeholds, Saltley got caught up in a trap of public sector action beginning with clearance and proceeding to general improvement areas and housing action areas. The politically and economically powerless residents found it hard to cope and the area entered a period of inexorable decline.

The city also embarked on a modernisation programme for 30 000 municipal inter-war houses (Figure 9.10). For an average of £5000 per house (and 60–65p on the rents) roof repairs and rewiring could be carried out, kitchens enlarged and bathrooms moved upstairs. Some houses were converted into two self-contained, one-bedroomed flats to meet the demand for smaller accommodation. Such re-use of stock inevitably

Figure 9.10 St Martin's Flats, Highgate. Refurbished, 1976.

focused on the problem of unwanted flats. In 1979 the 266 flats in St Martin's Highgate, built and opened with royal flourish just 40 years earlier, were demolished. Some of the city's 429 post-war, multi-storey flats, afflicted by the structural defects of industrialised building techniques, awaited their turn. Problems included the loosening of cladding panels, where metal ties had rusted, damp, and defective concrete frames and bases. Four-storey maisonettes had not proved popular and in one scheme in Lozells in 1983 (Bennett Street and Johnstone Street) the top two storeys were lopped off to create two-storey houses. The lively story of urban renewal in Birmingham since the early 1970s has been sketched by Chinn (1993).

By the end of the 1980s a new phase in public housing could readily be detected, local authorities becoming much more aware of aspirations of community-based groups in estate planning and management. This had been some years in the making, the origins perhaps detected in 1974 in the country's first self-help general improvement area, completed at Black Road, Macclesfield (Wates and Knevitt, 1987). Birmingham's housing department showed itself alert to new trends and the Bloomsbury priority estate project, set up in 1985, sought to involve tenant groups living in some 1200 homes to participate in shaping the quality of local housing services. At the Stockfield Estate, Acock's Green, it responded to the local community's election to the demolition of their 477 homes; a partnership with the residents, Bromford Housing Association and the Halifax Building Society to build 425 new dwellings entailed a cost of £24 million.

And so our period ends with circumstances very different from anything experienced before. Birmingham once owned 156 000 properties. A right to buy policy, which brought home ownership within reach of many working class people, ensured that tenure would be dramatically reversed away from council tenancies. The number of local authority dwellings now stands at 112 000. For a Council which for long had set its face against municipal houses, but which had proceeded to build both, between the wars and after 1945, in astonishingly large numbers, there are adjustments still to make with regard to its housing machine. The Government's proposed introduction of compulsory competitive tendering and break-up of arrangements for council management of its housing stock suggests the end of a remarkable era, which has done as much as anything to give an indelible social and physical stamp to the city.

10
The Planning Machine: Land, Roads and People

Much of Birmingham's's post-war change, at least that related to the physical appearance of the city and its land use structure, was guided by a greatly strengthened planning system. We have already seen this in regard to housing (Chapter 9) and we shall see its effects on central area development (Chapter 11). In this chapter we sketch other features which have contributed to the changing scene. We look first at the administrative and organisational aspects of the planning machine established after 1947; we consider the consequences of revised local government boundaries after 1974; and overall we examine shifts in planning policy which affected development in the city. Second we turn to road planning and in particular the construction of the inner ring road. Finally we consider the impact of certain social and economic factors in a rapidly changing Birmingham: first the influx of new immigrants and then the identification of the inner city problem and the raft of measures taken for urban regeneration during the 1980s.

The planning framework

One of the main features of Birmingham's planning has always been its demands for spaciousness; Nettlefold had sought it, the inter-war planners provided it (though on rather different terms) and Manzoni further promised it in his schemes of post-war redevelopment. For many years the assumption was that Birmingham could secure an end to congestion by utilising land within its own boundaries, thanks to the huge extensions it gained in 1911. We know from our account of housing in Chapter 9 that this situation was to change quite markedly when by the middle 1950s a serious land shortage was apparent, but as far as the immediate post-war years were concerned, with the introduction of the new town and country planning system, the land question was not an uppermost consideration.

Notions of an ever-expanding Birmingham had gone from the agenda too, as 'retrenchment replaced expansionism' (Sutcliffe and Smith, p. 120). Up to the early 1930s it was commonplace to argue that sheer size was conducive to the prosperity and good government of Birmingham. But attitudes did change in the 1930s, one symptom being the city's adoption of a green belt policy. By 1939 several thousand acres, mainly in the south and south west of the city were reserved for this purpose, aided and abetted by the generosity and cooperation of Cadburys which gave or sold large areas of land to the city. Another change was the national recognition of the need to assist in the economic regeneration of the depressed regions, by denying further growth in the favoured districts, typically outer, metropolitan London; as we have seen, Birmingham was economically prosperous in the late 1930s too, and nominally at least the city went along with the argument.

So by the time we approach the reconstruction years of the early- and mid-1940s a rather different climate of opinion attended the planning outlook of the city from that which had dominated earlier decades. The argument of the Bournville Village Trust (1941) in *When We Build Again* was for a stop to the spread of suburban Birmingham in favour of satellites beyond a green belt. A few years later the West Midland Group on Post-War Reconstruction (1948) maintained in *Conurbation* that the limits of the built-up area were already large enough and that redevelopment could be achieved within by making more effective use of land. There was another view too: demographers held that the days of city growth were over because birth rates would return to the low levels of the 1930s.

The Town and Country Planning Act 1947 required all local planning authorities (counties and county boroughs) to prepare development plans which would show planning intentions over a 20-year time horizon. Birmingham proceeded to prepare its own plan with little perturbation; the shoals of future disagreements over priorities were still largely hidden. The fears of government control over Birmingham's factories in its industrial location policies were thought to be largely unfounded, and anxieties over Abercrombie and Jackson's population forecasts did not yet amount to real fears about distribution of overspill.

So the development plan was fairly non-contentious. Working on a target population of nearly 1.1 million it arranged the city population in two density-rings: an inner zone with 75–120 persons to the acre and an outer one with 50 persons to the acre, Edgbaston remaining a low-density enclave with 30 to the acre. Overspill was not expected to be a factor until

1962. As to industry, the area zoned for industrial use would be nearly 5500 acres, an increase of nearly a quarter over the existing figure; the additional land was required not for new firms entering the city but to allow for the expansion of existing firms and the relocation of those dispersed from the redevelopment areas. Open space allocation was admittedly a problem, and there was no way in which the city could reach the target (depending on the density ring) of four to seven acres per thousand population, though the valley systems of the Hatchford Brook, the Cole, the Rea (with the Bourn Brook and the Chad Brook) and the Tame (with the Hockley Brook and other tributaries) promised linear strips of green walkways.

The development plan was submitted to the Ministry in 1952 for approval. A public inquiry was held in February 1954. A total of 450 objectors was whittled down to about 200; all recorded complaints about matters of detail, and there was no opposition to the general principles. The Minister's criticism of the plan focused on the industrial land allocation, claiming that the increase was too great; subsequently the Ministry would press for some industry to move out of the city. By this time of course the problem was complicated by the initiation of a housing overspill programme, much earlier than anticipated; if industry did not move to the overspill areas people would decline to live in them. The issue was never really resolved, Birmingham's Labour leaders largely antagonistic to industry leaving the city, particularly when unemployment began to edge upwards. Industrial derating in 1958 substantially increased the amount paid in rates on industrial premises and this further encouraged resistance to the blandishments of regional planning. The Minister did in fact reduce the city's allocation of industrial land when the development plan was approved in 1960, but by then it was already becoming out of date.

The development plan covered the city as a whole; other plans such as for comprehensive redevelopment areas were also prepared. One which was not proceeded with concerned the central area. In 1939 the City Council had decided to prepare a town planning scheme for the central districts. But during the early war years, when the public works committee had reached an advanced stage in preparing a scheme for the inner ring road, Manzoni's advice was that with the freehold of all the Corporation Street land and the judicious purchase of sites along the projected line of the new road, development in the city centre could be easily controlled, to the extent that a plan for the central business area was not required. Nearby Coventry, where an ambitious central area plan would form the basis of a new pedestrian shopping area, demonstrated a very different planning example, allowing professional protagonists to hint at the malign influence of engineers on post-war redevelopment.

The city's development plan was not particularly far-sighted; it was essentially a rationalisation of conflicting land uses, while proposed changes largely reflected known requirements for housing. Much depended on the detail to be fitted in later. One such area was Edgbaston where the Calthorpe Estate became the only private agency allowed to carry out a major town planning scheme. In 1950 the estate was asked to settle the lines of its future development for inclusion in the development plan. Bournville Village Trust was commissioned to prepare a scheme. Following negotiations the estate agreed to sell to the corporation around 100 acres in four fringe areas for municipal housing; accordingly the private areas retreated into an enclave between Hagley Road and Bristol Road. A detailed redevelopment scheme was prepared in 1957 by a Birmingham architect, John Madin; having eliminated the commercial development near Five Ways he then divided the residential area into three density bands: detached houses with very large gardens, medium-density small flat blocks and terraced houses, and multi-storey flats, particularly along Hagley Road. In the event there was a significant retreat from multi-storey housing after 1964, a change in fashion reflected elsewhere in the city at the same time. The implementation of the plan enhanced Edgbaston overall and the area remained an environmental jewel in the city's crown.

By this time the city was exercising greater planning and redevelopment powers than ever before; planning now represented a major feature of City Council work. The Town and Country Planning Act 1947, together with a number of local Birmingham Corporation Acts, provided the means whereby the city's post-war redevelopment and change could be guided. Building by-laws, which also regulated development, were locally determined until 1961, after which there was a national code, obligatory on all local authorities. New building regulations, drawn up in 1965, were administered by the public works committee.

A natural concern with the city as a whole, in which the strategic issues of overspill and industrial location loomed large, still left a whole raft of planning matters which turned on the detail of particular projects. We have dealt with redevelopment schemes and the building of new housing estates, and we consider central area matters in the next chapter, but there were other important new developments which were added to the planning agenda. The redevelopment of the city's wholesale markets was one project which took over 20 years to unfold.

The markets were grouped in a series of late 19th century buildings adjoining the Bull Ring, to the south east of the central shopping district. After the war the public works, and markets and fairs committees prepared a plan for a new market precinct to be built on the site of the existing markets, for which land was allocated in the development plan. As in London and other major cities, traffic congestion generated by the markets' activities was a serious inconvenience (in this case around Edgbaston Street and Digbeth). It was a case of either relocation or improvement on site and it was some time before the matter was resolved.

The first intention was to transfer the abattoir and meat market to Castle Bromwich and to this end a large site was acquired in 1948. But the markets and fairs committee increasingly favoured retaining an improved Bradford Street abattoir even if it meant a much larger markets precinct. An acrimonious dispute with the public works committee ensued and it required a majority vote in City Council in 1960 to determine that both the abattoir and the meat market should be located within the precinct. In the event a 28-acre precinct was designated as an area of comprehensive development, and in 1969 plans were prepared for a multi-storey development to accommodate the wholesale markets for fruit and vegetables, poultry, fish and meat, as well as an abattoir, warehousing, cold stores, offices and provision for parking. The whole area, officially opened by the Princess Royal in 1976, now marks a distinctive quarter at the edge of central business zone; it may be functional and lively during the day but at night it is an alien, empty district which one hurries through.

Educational precincts were developed to form important land use nodes in three parts of the city. In the case of the University of Birmingham it was a major extension of a campus dating from the beginning of the century; the course of progressive site planning from the founding of the institution is traced by Whitehand (1991). The University commissioned a new layout in 1957 from Sir Hugh Casson and Neville Conder. Using the commanding position and gently sweeping contours of the site, they took over the architectural fantasy of Aston Webb and opted for an 'inward looking complex of buildings as self-centred and secluded as a hill-top monastery' (Casson and Conder, 1958). A courtyard layout approach, replaced the axial treatment of the earlier layout, and a new library was built across the old axis to enclose a central pedestrian area. New buildings followed in rapid succession, including one tower block (Muirhead) which attracted architectural acclaim, though it was scarcely user-friendly in its inability to deflect wind and rain and to transport staff and students up twelve floors at congested peak hours (I write as an occupant of some years' standing). Much more lasting in commendation were the halls of residence, attractively grouped round a lake to the north of the main campus, contributing to a major environmental enhancement of Edgbaston.

In 1966 the College of Advanced Technology at Gosta Green was granted university status and the new University of Aston prepared plans for the comprehensive development of more than 30 acres encircled by Aston Street, Corporation Street, the Inner Ring Road, Jennens Road and the Digbeth Branch Canal. The development, approved as an amendment to the city development plan, involved the demolition of the first municipal dwellings in Lawrence Street and Ryder Street. The Aston campus, completed by the beginning of the 1980s, is very different from its Edgbaston rival, but is equally successful in its own way: small, compact with a hard 'urban' feel to it, cheek by jowl with the city centre. More recently, the Birmingham Polytechnic (since 1992 the University of Central England) site at Perry Barr has shown welcome signs of landscape improvement designed to knit together an interlocking series of buildings, but this campus is still raw and does not yet proclaim distinctiveness.

Twenty years after the submission of the city development plan the Council approved its successor, the structure plan, a new strategic document introduced by the Town and Country Planning Act 1968. It was a sign of the times that the public consultations which attended the preparation of this plan attracted little interest; the professional language of its authors had grown more arcane by the years, and disillusionment was widespread with a planning process which had failed to deliver the beautiful city and contented communities that had been promised. Nonetheless the structure plan did provide the opportunity of reassessing city objectives: there was emphasis on fostering the growth and prosperity of the local economy, suburban shopping centres were given a more explicit role in retail distribution patterns, provision for improved road and rail links was made, and measures to stimulate urban renewal in the middle ring of suburbs promised to contribute to environmental upgrading in these areas.

New priorities were beginning to emerge in city planning perspectives. One related to a growing awareness of the importance of historic buildings, propelled by a powerful conservation lobby. Many buildings were lost before the full force of public opinion could be mobilised. Snow Hill station was a case in point. One Birmingham observer (Bird, 1970) wrote with a mixture of anger and wistfulness:

> One January afternoon in 1970 I watched practically the entire dignified façade of Snow Hill station knocked down while I waited for a 32 bus. The tears in my eyes sprang half from the dust, half from the sad-sweet memories of assignations beneath the clock in the booking hall, a favourite place for lovers' meetings in bygone years. (p. 224)

Other buildings, the loss of which were much lamented, included the late Victorian pub. Crawford and Thorne (1975), for the Birmingham Group of the Victorian Society, listed some of the city's surviving turn-of-the-century pubs, noting those earmarked for demolition because of road widening schemes or redevelopment. An architectural style was being swept away.

Controversy surrounded plans to demolish the 108-year old Reference Library, and with it the unique Shakespeare Memorial Library; following a public inquiry it was demolished in 1974 to allow for central area road proposals, but the Memorial Library was later recreated in the new Library Exhibition Hall. A development scheme for the General Post Office site was similarly contentious; built in 1891 it formed part of a group of historic buildings around Victoria Square, though the demolition of Galloway's

Corner at the western ('top') end of New Street was already a loss to enclosure. A long-running saga ended with a new 'chateau' frontage and office buildings at the rear. Crucial to the retention of individual buildings is the 'listed buildings' procedure. Buildings listed on the grounds of their architectural importance are subject to revision and updating – sometimes with surprising results: in March 1993 the University of Birmingham learned that the Ashley and Strathcona Buildings (1961–4) and the Minerals and Physical Metallurgy Building (1966) had been listed.

Meanwhile preservation rather than demolition had become a popularly-supported option, and under the powers of the Civic Amenities Act 1967 the city began a programme of designating areas of special architectural or historic interest. Conservation areas were defined for a range of areas including the hearts of villages long-engulfed (Northfield, King's Norton (Figure 10.1), Yardley and Harborne), the distinctive Bournville Village and Moor Pool Estate of the turn of the century, part of Edgbaston, and Colmore Row (and environs, including Waterloo Street) in the heart of the city. Conservation replaced comprehensive redevelopment as policy for an improved Jewellery Quarter and over the years the range of the city's conservation areas was extended to sites including: St Paul's Square, Aston Hall and Church, High Street, Sutton Coldfield, Lee Crescent, the St Agnes area of Moseley, and the canal side district of Warwick Bar. Yardley Old Village was upgraded in status to 'outstanding', Colmore Row was enlarged and in Edgbaston the area designated was increased to one square mile to make it one of the largest in the country, second only to London Mayfair's Grosvenor Estate.

While such different environmental priorities were being addressed, planning in the city was obliged to deal with a different set of contending issues from another quarter. As part of the reorganisation of local government, introduced in 1974, Birmingham became a Metropolitan District Authority in a new West Midlands County Council which extended from Wolverhampton to Coventry. The marginal adjustments made in 1964 and 1966 when Birmingham made a net gain of under 200 hectares in exchanges with adjoining authorities, were nothing compared with the disputed addition of Sutton Coldfield to the city and the loss of functions to a higher authority. Birmingham was no longer master in its own house, though it was allowed to retain its 'city' designation; it relinquished some of its planning role to the County Council and lost powers over water supply and sewerage to the Severn Trent Water Authority.

Birmingham's political culture had changed a great deal since the heady years of the previous century. Newton (1976) could point to a statistically 'average' city. Collecting information regarding 52 social, economic, political and financial variables for the city and for all English and Welsh county boroughs (pre-1974), he found that in only seven out of the 52 was Birmingham statistically different from the mean and all of these had very

Figure 10.1 King's Norton conservation area. The Saracen's Head and St Nicolas Church, 1964.

obvious connections with sheer size. Tracing a total of 4250 formally organised voluntary associations in Birmingham, he thought that the city's political system could be considered a pluralist democracy. One consequence could be seen in that 'the mood of the council membership is generally cautious, conservative and suspicious of change of any kind' (p. 241). The City Council in the 1970s was struggling to keep in touch with changing circumstances, let alone take definitive leads.

The city's needs were changing and the City Council was slow and uncertain in adaptation. The immediate post-war period had come to an end: war damage had been made good, redevelopment had been implemented, the inner ring road (the jewel in the crown) had been completed, and a massive housing programme had run its course. A planning scenario extending over a quarter of a century had been fulfilled. For much of the time one chief officer, Manzoni, had held the reins of power in a remarkable balance of political and professional will. His successor, Neville Borg (1973) reviewed the years of post-war change with no little admiration for how it had been accomplished:

> The results are a product of a system so loose in its central control as almost to be called a Code of Practice, under which political initiative, in certain directions, was combined

with official energy and inspiration. Men and companies with a keen instinct for the opportunity in which to take decisive action . . . were able to do so because a powerful authority followed the advice of a few men. Amongst these was one whose intuitive grasp of the relationship between social need and political solution enabled very great material advances to be generated, if not as a by-product, at least as a secondary objective; this was Sir Herbert Manzoni. (p. 76)

The situation would change abruptly: political uncertainty, not helped by professional prevarication faced with the onslaught of the social sciences on the prescriptive policies of the planning machine, ushered in a period of 10–15 years in which Birmingham's command of the planning system weakened considerably.

The county proceeded to prepare its own structure plan which imposed certain strategic policies on the city. No planning input could have been starker in its political context (Struthers and Brindell, 1983). There were acknowledged differences in outlook between Birmingham and the county authorities; there had been long-standing antagonisms over overspill both of people and jobs; the urban authorities in the conurbation had already prepared structure plans; and there were allegiances to other organisations, notably the West Midlands Planning Authorities Conference, which operated as a regional study team, and the West Midlands Passenger Transport Executive, which had certain responsibilities for planning public transport. These problems were scarcely eased by what followed.

Elections were held in 1973 for the new Metropolitan County. Labour, the majority party, was led by the previous leader of the Birmingham City Council, Sir Stan Yapp, and was dominated by members from Birmingham, the Black Country and Coventry. In 1977 there was a total change; the Council went Conservative with a leader from Solihull. In 1981 it reverted to Labour. The structure plan for the county was prepared against the background of these shifting political majorities and changing planning fashions (dispersal *versus* inner city regeneration and road building *versus* conservation, for example). The conflict between the conurbation and its neighbours went unresolved, but an unsatisfactory period of political and planning uncertainty came to an end when the County Council was abolished in 1986. The metropolitan districts became structure plan authorities and Birmingham's unitary status was restored.

More significant in the long term was the city's internal reorganisation of its departmental and committee structure. A separate planning department was established, and a new Officer, Graham Shaylor, was appointed in 1974. The public works committee was replaced by a planning committee and an environmental services committee. After Shaylor's retirement in 1990, he was succeeded by Les Sparks, former City Planning Officer of Bath. Conservationists felt encouraged.

Roads

We have already traced the origins of the Council's and the Chief Officers' fixation with the inner ring road. The 'kind of loop' referred to in 1917, enclosing an area almost exactly equivalent to the built-up extent of Birmingham in 1780, became an indispensable measure for post-war reconstruction. A Corporation Act gave powers for acquisition of the land.

By this time inner ring roads were conventional wisdom for the planning of large cities (Tripp, 1942) and this was reflected in Government advice (Departmental Committee, Ministry of War Transport, 1946). But immediate action was not forthcoming. There were other priorities, not least the maintenance and repair of existing roads which had been neglected during the war years, and in any case Government would not sanction expenditure on a scheme noticeably more ambitious than that for any other provincial city. There were a number of improvement schemes which were considered urgent, quite apart from the inner ring road. The first was the widening of Digbeth, for which the Ministry of Transport finally gave permission in 1953; the new Digbeth was formally opened to traffic in July 1955 by the Minister, John Boyd-Carpenter.

The next 20 years saw a frenetic period of road building, fully reflective of the auto-oriented culture of the city. Better road communications were demanded by Birmingham industry. It was argued that the interdependence of local firms required a constant transfer of components and partly finished goods from one factory to another, by road. In the Chamber of Commerce transport was a major policy interest. The importance of the vehicle assembly industry made Birmingham a car city in outlook; representations for better roads and parking space readily took priority among political parties. The low importance accorded to suburban railway lines meant that the municipal motor transport services could also apply pressure for road improvements. Meanwhile even in broader planning terms, the road was more than a highway scheme: it would facilitate the extension and partial redevelopment of the central shopping district. All these factors conspired to lend weight to a powerful public works committee and its principal chief officer, Herbert Manzoni; the inner ring road scheme was swept along by the irresistible force of a municipal bureaucracy geared to a fixed objective; no wonder Manzoni's portrait, taken when he was President of the Institute of Civil Engineers, shows him holding plans of the road in his hands.

Transport Minister Boyd-Carpenter centred his priorities on arterial and motorway schemes, but his successor Harold Watkinson allowed more scope for urban roads and in early 1956 approved the commencement of the first section of the inner ring road, with 75% grant. Plans for the road were reshaped to include underpasses and flyovers; the first two sections were started in 1957 and 1959 and Government approval was obtained for the remainder. Work first began on the section between Horse Fair and the entrance to New Street Station. Smallbrook Street disappeared, and with it the Scala Cinema, one of the first cinemas to be built as such (1914) in the city centre, and Smallbrook Ringway took its place. The first section of the inner ring road was officially opened in March 1960 by the new Minister of Transport, Ernest Marples. The next section extended the line beyond the Bull Ring to Carrs Lane and by 1964, the year after Manzoni's retirement, the internal link from Snow Hill to Lower Priory had been constructed. The northern section followed, from Holloway Circus to Lancaster Place, and this became the major through route for traffic from south west to north east; a half-mile length of tunnel linked Suffolk Street to Great Charles Street. An inner ring road had become an urban motorway. The complete circuit was finalised in 1971 and officially opened by the Queen in April; the inner ring road of 2¼ miles, now renamed Queensway, had finally come to fruition after twenty-five years (Figure 10.2). Manzoni's successor, his previous Deputy, Neville Borg proved faithful in completing the task.

Meanwhile there were other developments elsewhere. To tackle an increasing traffic problem several car parks were built and in 1962

Figure 10.2 Central Birmingham, 1973. The Inner Ring Road complete. Smallbrook Ringway runs left-right in the centre of the photograph.

Figure 10.3 Gravelly Hill Interchange (Spaghetti Junction), under construction.

Birmingham became the first provincial city in the country to adopt parking meters. There was another first, too: the opening of the Birchfield Road underpass was the first in the provinces. This was part of a city-wide scheme which envisaged the gradual improvement of the city's twelve main radial roads linked by three ring roads – inner, middle and outer. Construction of the middle ring road began to take shape in the programme of slum clearance and redevelopment; the first stretch was completed between Spring Hill and Five Ways between 1967 and 1972 and others followed during the 1970s and 1980s. In a different scheme the Aston Expressway, opened in 1972, linked the city centre to M6 at the Gravelly Hill Interchange, locally dubbed 'Spaghetti Junction' (Figure 10.3).

New situations

The planning and development machine had a remarkable capacity for a remorseless implementation of Council plans. It was less good at dealing with the finer points of changing conditions in social and economic affairs. The statutory planning system was geared to land use considerations; the framers of post-war legislation had not bargained for cities where problems

203

stemmed from circumstances very different from those of buildings and their replacement. The physical aspects of planning were increasingly replaced by the social and economic.

The Newcomers

The 1951 census indicated that Birmingham's population totalled 1113 000, an increase of 110 000 over that of 1931. But by 1971 the figure showed a reduction to 1 013 000, virtually the same as 1931. The decline began to gather pace after 1961, and during that decade, and remorselessly thereafter, the city population fell. During these years the number of people living in the outer suburbs of the city rose, hence the decline was concentrated in the inner districts. The processes of redevelopment led to a net population loss, compounded by overcrowding levels falling generally in the areas of older properties.

But for a while the main focus of attention lay not in geographical shifts of population within the city or losses overall to a wider region of dispersal, but in newcomers to Birmingham and their distinctive source of origin. Between 1951 and 1961 the number of overseas immigrants to Birmingham nearly doubled (51 500 to 100 000). The largest group was from Ireland (both north and south) with 22 000, but it was the other groups which attracted most attention: 15 500 West Indians (500 to 16 000), 7000 Pakistanis and Indians (3000 to 10 000) and 2000 others from the rest of the Commonwealth (3000 to 5000).

The population composition of the city took on a totally new dimension due to the sustained in-migration of people between the mid-1950s and the early 1970s, a movement which affected most large cities in Britain. The essentially rural communities of the West Indies, India and Pakistan found employment prospects in Britain greater than in their own countries (so too did the Irish), and the unskilled, for which Britain had a high demand, were attracted by higher wages. Commonwealth subjects naturally turned to Britain; all such immigrants had free access to this country until the Commonwealth Immigration Act of 1962. West Indian immigration into the United States, which might have been expected to increase, was restricted after legislation there in 1952 tightened immigration controls. So it was that the social scene in British cities changed dramatically. The younger sons of Asiatic families were financed by relatives, and West Indians found assistance from travel agents who provided credit. Once in Birmingham they flooded into jobs often left behind when the engineering and motor industries absorbed the indigenous workforce. The more unpleasant manufacturing processes, the service trades and the transport and building industries were open to the newcomers. Subsequently the immigrant service sector expanded in the retail trade, warehousing and catering.

Quite quickly, different geographical areas for particular community groups were apparent: Handsworth for the West Indians (Afro-Caribbean) and Sparkhill for Indians and Pakistanis. A discontinuous ring of districts of ethnic concentrations had emerged even by the 1961 census (Jones, 1967). The rising numbers and their spatial concentrations inevitably attracted social tensions, particularly regarding housing (as we have seen in Chapter 9), education and employment where a white host community felt particularly threatened. Yet political agitation was contained, and 'race relations in Birmingham were still placid enough in 1970 to be envied by many other areas' (Sutcliffe and Smith, 1974, p. 398), though this is an observation curiously at variance with that of Rex and Moore (1967) in connection with their study of Sparkbrook. Numbers increased and areas of population concentration solidified into highly distinctive cultural districts. The Handsworth riots of 1985 exposed the fragility of community peace when long-standing resentment over discrimination erupted over a local issue of drugs and allegations as to police action. At the time of the 1991 census Birmingham was home to 206 000 people from ethnic minority groups, the largest total for any local authority in the country, and 21.5% of the city population. There were of course higher percentages elsewhere (typically in the London Boroughs, topped by Brent (44.9%) but Leicester (28.5%) was the only other provincial city to exceed Birmingham in terms of ratio).

Inner city problems

We have already seen that economic conditions in the city deteriorated after the mid-1960s and severe employment problems, which marked the 1970s, recurred throughout the next two decades. The older, inner parts of the city bore the brunt, just as did the older parts of the conurbation, though for many years Telford New Town also suffered badly prior to the relative improvement during the 1980s when new investment was attracted. The issues raised, while dependent on economic failure, were complex and multi-faceted; they included housing, and social and environmental matters. While it would be quite wrong to suggest that inner city districts solely reflected a rising tide of community problems (some peripheral municipal estates also became blackspots), inner city concentrations did become particularly marked. A broad, crescentic swathe of deprivation was identified running across the north and east of the city centre from Handsworth to Lozells, Nechells, and Sparkbrook. The situation in Birmingham, of course, was little different from that in other big cities at that time, where several problems were manifest all at once: demographic and industrial decline, concentrated poverty and deprivation. The literature of the 1980s was replete with analysis and prescription: Hall (1981),

Donnison and Middleton (1987) describing Glasgow's experience, and Robson (1988) highlighting Greater Manchester exemplify the range.

Faith in the City, the Report of the Archbishop of Canterbury's Commission on Urban Priority Areas, was published in 1985. This study, concerned with the whole of England, was followed by *Faith in the City of Birmingham*, set up by the Bishop's Council of the Diocese of Birmingham on the initiative of Bishop Hugh Montefiore, and published in 1988. The commission was charged 'to examine and report upon the social and economic problems and opportunities facing the City of Birmingham together with the problems and opportunities which face its Churches'. Its analysis looked in detail at the urban priority areas of the city (and Birmingham had the heaviest concentration of all dioceses) and the nature of their urban deprivation. The report observed:

> Unemployment levels are high; housing conditions are deteriorating; crime rates are above average; incomes are lower and many are dependent on State welfare benefits. There is often a high incidence of single parent families and of old people living alone. Educational performance and health standards are generally lower than the average. These factors are often aggravated by racial prejudice. (p. 5)

In a sense a number of these characteristics were far from new. The late Victorian city also exhibited concentrations of poor housing and social distress and they remained throughout the 20th century. But a number of factors conspired to re-emphasise the problem, compounded by disappointment at the failures of the post-war world. Many decades of social welfarism, particularly after 1945, had seemingly failed: poverty, poor housing, and social disadvantage had not been eradicated; indeed in relative terms the imbalance of national disparities had scarcely been altered. The country had failed economically; a growth economy could not be sustained and when the full blast of international competition came along in a new technological revolution the industrial heartland crumbled. Social services were overwhelmed. The educational system was found wanting. Post-war housing disappointed, and municipal provision and standards of estate maintenance were heavily criticised. The quality environment promised by post-war planning failed to materialise and the population exodus, which by virtue of its selectivity, whereby the unskilled, the elderly and powerless groups are left behind, contributed to a downward spiral of community confidence; the problem could be seen as a consequence of an *intended* decrease in population density levels. As for local employment, planning had also contributed to the problem by being party to the process of redevelopment, the impact of dislocation being too great for many of those affected. With regard to ethnic mix, Birmingham's 'placid' race relations had been shattered by the Handsworth riots of 1985, strangely anticipated by Radcliffe's (1981) research which offered some rather gloomy predictions as to employment problems and intergenerational conflict.

By the mid-1980s the Birmingham inner city problem was all too obvious, the scale of inner city deprivation levels greater than in any other English city. Between 1971 and 1981 the inner city residential core had lost 17.6% of its population (still leaving a total of 272 000 people). More than two fifths (43%) were in households where the head was born in the New Commonwealth or Pakistan (compared with 15% for Birmingham as a whole and 4.5% for Great Britain). In mid-1986 the unemployment rate was 33.5% (21.1% in Birmingham and 11.9% in the UK). The proportions of households receiving supplementary benefit were high. Additionally the problems were compounded by a persistent housing crisis; although the population was falling, there was an increasing demand for dwellings, and homelessness was rising sharply.

A downward spiral of confidence affected the whole city, and into this new situation town planning was thrust – an activity which, in most local authorities until the 1960s was confined to matters of land use and development, both its promotion and control. But a profession, originally dependent on the disciplines of the built environment, had now to be equally reliant on those of the social sciences, and for some time it found an involvement with community and economic issues difficult to handle. A local authority bureaucracy also found new power relationships and community sensitivities taxing the old procedures.

In order to deal with the inner city problem, and its related social, economic and political questions, a new set of institutional arrangements at central as well as local level had to be forged. Government interest in urban problems was slow to take focus but after 1970 the newly created Department of the Environment under Secretary of State Peter Walker began to take more of a lead. In 1972 three inner area studies were commissioned, one of which was for Small Heath, Birmingham; the other two were for Liverpool and Lambeth. The reports were published in 1977, that for Birmingham under the telling title *Unequal City* (Llewelyn-Davies *et al* 1977). Couched in the language of the time, it marks a critical departure from previous approaches to land planning. Consultants and politicians now had a concept of a 'total' approach to urban renewal. The authors of the report recognised that low incomes were at the centre of inner area problems, hence solutions should begin with policies for maintaining and improving incomes. Explicit income support measures were required to reduce individual household poverty. With regard to housing, greater sensitivity was required on the part of those who govern to the needs of the governed. Resources were not limitless, therefore the principle of positive discrimination should be adopted in favour of those in greatest need, both to individual households and to the areas in which they lived. There should be greater coordination of local services, and action was necessary in the fields of community organisation, political representation and education. Urban renewal had previously been seen as a process of clearance and building construction; now the focus was on social and economic regeneration, though the political implications of what was being advanced would soon be diluted.

The Government White Paper *Policy for the Inner Cities* (1977), fore-shadowed new legislation, the Inner Urban Areas Act 1978, which gave additional powers to local authorities in England and Wales with severe inner area problems. The provisions applied to three types of designated districts, and Birmingham belonged to the most important one where local/central government partnerships were set up to supervise the imple-mentation of annual urban programmes, on a rolling three-year basis. Con-siderable resources were channelled to the partnership throughout the 1980s.

Meanwhile, in the city there was a reorganisation of committee respon-sibilities; in May 1978, a property services committee was set up with powers over the acquisition and disposal of land and the management of the city's industrial and commercial properties. In September Tyseley was declared the city's first industrial improvement area, where industrial premises were refurbished. More followed after 1980: the Jewellery Quarter, Digbeth, parts of Bordesley Green and Moseley Road.

A new initiative came in 1986 when the Council designated East Bir-mingham a regeneration area where an Urban Development Agency (UDA) would be set up to tackle the problems of social deprivation and economic decline. The Council had no desire for an urban development corporation (an agency of which a number had been set up in the country following the launch of London Docklands and Merseyside in 1981); it did not wish to lose either its planning powers or control over its regeneration process. The Council succeeded in convincing the Secretary of State for the Environ-ment, Nicholas Ridley, that a private-sector-led organisation, with a work-ing relationship with the Council, could achieve the same ends. Support came from the Birmingham Chamber of Industry and Commerce; with 5000 members it is the largest chamber of commerce in the UK, and its influence was crucial.

Birmingham Heartlands Ltd was established in March 1988, with five major construction companies (Bryants, R. M. Douglas, Galliford, Tarmac and Wimpey) forming the private-sector foundation of the company. It received no government grant; rather its function was to be an enabling agency, to promote and coordinate regeneration. Within the 2300 acres a Waterlinks scheme is a proposed mixed development for business, industry and housing in a new environment making use of the canal water space. Bordesley Village will be a new residential community; in the Nechells Green/Bloomsbury area there will be housing improvements with new industrial development in the east. The national economic recession has meant a slower start to these schemes than envisaged; there was some success, but Birmingham Heartlands found that it was unable to attract as much private-sector investment as had been hoped. It simply did not have the funds to acquire major sites or pay for the scale of reclamation works required.

Organisational change seemed inevitable when Birmingham's bid for the newly instituted 'City Challenge' funding for 1991/92, for that part of the city which included a portion of Heartlands, failed. In October 1991 the Council and the Heartlands Board decided to seek urban development corporation status for Heartlands: a complete U-turn after five years of independence from government. In January 1992 Secretary of State Michael Heseltine agreed. Funding is still not commensurate with the levels hoped for, and so far the redevelopment actually undertaken falls short of making the impact on East Birmingham that had been anticipated. Nonetheless there is a fascinating area here in course of physical and community change, as the historical sketch by Frostick and Harland (1993) reminds us.

11
The City Centre

This final chapter on post-war change deals with the transformations encountered in the central area. We have already considered the inner ring road and its effect, both in creating new sites for development and in acting as a restrictive collar to a tightly confined commercial core. We have also noted the circumstances leading to the redevelopment of the wholesale markets area, immediately adjoining the central district. The conservation movement and the impetus given both to the restoration of architecturally important and historic buildings and the protection of whole areas of distinction, particularly over the last twenty years, affected the whole city, but we have seen how the city centre was well represented during this period. Finally, we have also noted the proposals for the economic regeneration of the Heartlands area, the western tip of which has a bearing on the city centre by virtue of its proximity.

However, there is still an important story to be told which has not yet been included in the chronology of the years since 1945: the renewal and reshaping of the commercial, administrative and retail core of the central area. The account falls conveniently into three parts: the first phase covering development up to the end of the property boom, round about the end of the 1960s; the particular saga of the civic centre; and the final phase, beginning with the stagnation of the 1970s and early 1980s, followed by more lively years marked by a succession of new projects around the turn of the 1990s and evidence of a more sensitive, caring hand towards central area townscape by the local authority.

Over a period of approaching half a century Birmingham's central area assumed a definitive shape and internal structure, largely taken from decisions arrived at many years earlier. The building of the Town Hall and the Council House subsequently attracted an amalgam of uses and spaces which today form a district for civic administration, and it was natural that the International Convention Centre found a ready home in association with it. Birmingham's two main railway stations sought central locations and abandoned Curzon Street; even a third, Moor Street, is equally central. Had the railway companies decided to remain with Curzon Street the whole of the central area would have been pulled eastward; it is ironic that British Rail have had under recent consideration a major city station in Heartlands, even further to the east. In fact over a century and more the city's commercial and retailing core has proved remarkably durable in its essential spatial distribution, with no dramatic withdrawal from any one area to another. The essential spines remain: New Street, Corporation Street, High Street, with the southern hub of the Bull Ring, and only with the Broad Street developments, emphasised by the Brindley Place project, does the long-established nucleus threaten to become distorted.

The first phase

Early in the post-war period Birmingham acquired a remarkably privileged status in terms of its land holdings in the central city. It became ground landlord of blitzed properties and a swathe of land marking the line of an inner ring road with a lucrative frontage depth. In the event, because of building restrictions, it was eight years before the first post-war building was completed in the central area; this was the seven-storey Shell-BP office block (1953), now Grosvenor House, designed by the Birmingham firm of Cotton, Ballard and Blow, on the corner of New Street and Bennett's Hill. Shopping development followed, just along New Street where a new C&A's department store and a replacement for the war-damaged Marshall and Snelgrove's were built. This frontage was incorporated into a much larger project extending over the bomb damaged site at the corner of New Street and High Street; here, the buildings had been removed and wartime exhibitions and a circus used the vacant land. The Big Top site, as it had become known, was redeveloped from 1954 onwards by the same architects as for Grosvenor House, as a complex of retail units and a central, 12-storey office block. It was the city's first major shopping development. New Street (Figure 11.1) continued to command attention with the new Woolworth Building and Winston Churchill House, built on the site of the demolished Theatre Royal, again by the same architects. Corporation Street received a major new building with Rackham's store designed by T. P. Bennett in 1960.

Elsewhere the early developments were linked to the inner ring road. Three large sites on Smallbrook Ringway were advertised in 1957 and one of the bidders, John Laing, proposed the joint development of all three. A long site of limited depth produced a scheme (by a local architect, James

211

Figure 11.1 New Street, 1952. The days of vehicular shopping streets, kerb-side parking and shop awnings.

Roberts) with a continuous frontage of five storeys running along the southern side, and buildings of similar scale and design complemented by an hotel, The Albany, on the north. The continuity of shopping frontage, reflected the style of the Big Top development and imparted a distinctive architectural stamp to the city's early post-war appearance: it was conservative and rather undistinguished. Smallbrook Ringway did receive peer group acclaim, but Pevsner called the Big Top development 'a bad joke' (Sutcliffe and Smith, 1974, p. 464).

The fact was that Birmingham had no great architectural tradition to claim and had failed to produce any strong school of local architects. There were perhaps reasons for this. The city was not a mercantile centre and so had produced no distinguished commercial buildings, reflective of trading prestige. It had no stock of factories or warehouses of a scale which commanded architectural embellishment. Even in Edgbaston where private wealth was concentrated, layout and landscape took precedence over architecture. So there was not much to live up to, merely a collection of grand civic buildings including the Town Hall and Council House, some strong late Victorian architecture including hotels, public houses and schools, a fashion for buff terra cotta as in the Victoria Law Courts, and the more recent 'jazz' architecture in cinemas, for Oscar Deutsch's Birmingham-based Odeon chain, designed by Harry Weedon. So the field was open for new contributions, a place filled with distinction from the 1960s by local architects John Madin and James Roberts.

By the time the Smallbrook Ringway scheme was underway the national property boom was affecting Birmingham. The city's size and prosperity made it the first provincial city to be open to the new speculative mania for property development. It is somehow appropriate that one of Britain's best known property developers at this time, Jack Cotton, was Birmingham born. The original leases of the Council's Corporation Street estate were beginning to fall in, and in 1957 and 1958 the Council granted new leases for redevelopment blocks.

The biggest initiative, however, was in respect of the leasing in 1958 of three interlinked sites near the Bull Ring and the Market Hall to JLG Investments Ltd, a local company headed by Jo Godfrey, a developer who had been associated with Laing's Smallbrook Ringway scheme. A critical decision was taken to demolish the mid-19th century Market Hall so that a larger area would become available for redevelopment, whereupon Jo Godfrey and the architect James Roberts put forward a scheme for a multi-level shopping centre, retail market, car park, offices and bus station. With remarkable speed the public works committee approved the project in principle, in January 1959. But haggling ensued over ground rents; Godfrey offered £50 000 a year, whereas Birmingham wanted £75 000. Negotiations were broken off and in September that year the site was offered to developers by public tender. From eleven tenders Laing Investment Co. won with a ground rent of £109 000 a year. The scheme was similar to Roberts' earlier submission, though this time by a different architect. The similarity was almost inevitable since the specifications for the scheme had been derived from Roberts' work and his protracted negotiations with British Rail, Midland Red Omnibus and various other interests. There was consequent criticism in architectural circles that competitions of this kind should be better regulated.

The Bull Ring was finished in late 1963. But most of the shops were unlet and there was a distinct possibility of adverse publicity retarding profitability during the early years. The opening (by the Duke of Edinburgh) was delayed until May 1964, by which time sharply reduced rents had produced an 85% letting figure. Even so the Birmingham public did not immediately flock to the new centre and it was some time before trader resistance was overcome. Matters improved when British Rail completed its rebuilding, permitting the link into New Street Station.

Before its redevelopment the Bull Ring was 'a traditional cheap and vigorous mixture of barrow boys and shops, the most celebrated of old Birmingham's street markets' (Marriott, 1967, pp. 222–3). Closely adjoining the assembly of national retailers and department stores in High Street, New Street and Corporation Street the Bull Ring formed an integral part of the central retail core and 'varied the conformity of the multiples' neon with a welcome down-at-heel hubbub' (p. 223). The new complex was certainly different in appearance, composition and spatial organisation. On a 23-acre site a total of 140 shops was built covering 350 000 square feet of retail trading space, under one roof and at different levels.

Visually it had all the anonymity of 1960s commercial architecture; with no message proclaimed, it compared unfavourably with the old Market Hall. Only the splendid bronze bull placed at the end of a long wall gives any sense of local drama. Thirty years on, it is a period-piece which has not travelled well; it has all the foibles of 'functional' architecture where people came second. In a complex of five different layers of shops, the bus station at the bottom leads into the market hall, which itself opens into an open market precinct adjoining St Martin's Church. Also from the bus station there is access to two main floors of shops above; alongside these is a huge Woolworths store. Other shops are on a level with the ring road. Higher levels of shopping lead to a bridge across the road and into New Street Station. Pedestrian circulation also makes use of a sunken traffic island, where in a public garden Sir Herbert Manzoni is honoured, and a flight of steps ascends to the shopping streets to the north. Marriott (1967) concludes that the originator of the structure was 'a highly sophisticated designer with a Meccano set, tied down to a restrictive brief' (p. 227).

The 1960s closed with other additions to the Birmingham scene. The 25-storey Rotunda office block was erected in 1964, dominating the Bull Ring. A public house on the ground floor unhappily received the attention of IRA bombers ten years later. Opposite the Rackham's development Commercial Union House provided a new pedestrian shopping precinct (Martineau Square) in the same year, linked to the Littlewoods development which had opened two years earlier, covering a block bounded by High Street, Bull Street and Union Street. New Street Station was completed in 1967, with a further shopping centre, later known as the Pallasades, opening in 1970. Also by the beginning of the 1970s Richard Seifert's ATV tower (Alpha Tower) at Paradise Circus was complete, with the Holiday Inn nearby. But other things had gone: none more regrettable or shortsighted than the closure of Snow Hill Railway Station, the site of which then became the subject of numerous plans and proposals.

Overall, a distinctive new appearance had been imparted to central Birmingham in little more than a decade; there was an 'almost transatlantic modernity' (Sutcliffe and Smith 1974, p. 468) which set it apart from any other provincial city. Much had been swept away and old landmarks removed in an orgy of redevelopment, all without the benefit of a master plan for the city centre. Moreover the City Architect was scarcely involved in architectural advice. It all took place according to Manzoni's long-term schemes, the inner ring road providing the major opportunities for rebuilding. The public works committee was responsible for the leasing of inner ring road sites, while the estates committee handled sites in Corporation Street and elsewhere. The remarkable thing is that it happened at all, but the power of a municipal bureaucracy with a considerable hold of land ownership, aided and abetted by a speculative surge in the property market, proved irresistible. The niceties of planning and architectural quality were put on one side, and the backlash of public disappointment would follow later.

The Civic Centre

We have already noted the emergence of a distinct quarter in central Birmingham devoted to civic buildings. The Town Hall, the Council House, the Central Library, the Reference Library and Art Gallery all provided a core assembly before the close of the 19th century at the apex of the northern end of New Street and the western end of Colmore Row. After the Great War a properly planned civic centre for additional municipal offices and public buildings was proposed as a westward extension, beyond Easy Row and fronting Broad Street.

There could be no early start to building but the corporation started to buy up property; in the meantime Council offices were spread throughout the city centre in rented premises. The Hall of Memory was built during the years 1923–4 and this became a fixed point of reference for future development in the area. The Masonic Temple (now Central Television) and the Municipal Bank (now the Trustee Savings Bank) fronted the southern side of Broad Street. An open competition for a civic centre layout was organised in 1926, but the prize-winning scheme (by Maximilian Romanoff of Paris) was judged too ambitious for the city to implement. Instead, an 'in house' scheme was drawn up in the form of a layout plan based on a vast square surrounded by buildings, for which Council approval was forthcoming in 1934. A further competition, held for the design of particular buildings, was won by a Nottingham architect T. Cecil Howitt, and he was engaged for the first municipal office block: Baskerville House, ready for occupation in 1940.

The notion of a civic centre fitted in well with wartime reconstruction plans and in 1945 Council approved a new layout scheme, this time by a local architect William Haywood. One can only be grateful for the fact that it came to nothing. A central parade ground of over eleven acres was proposed, with the setting of formal gardens, and around the square would be offices, halls, a planetarium and colonnade and other buildings which could be used for library, museum and art gallery purposes. In the middle of the square a 140ft column was proposed, topped by a sculpture.

Circumstances conspired to deflect the Council from its approval of this gigantic scheme. A combination of perceived impracticalities, new design fashions and a reliance on incrementalism as opposed to a grand manner plan set Birmingham on quite a different course. In 1947 the Council acquired the shell of a private office block, Bush House, in Broad Street; on the western edge of the civic centre area it could always be incorporated into the wider scheme. It was not ready for occupation until 1954, but it showed that rented accommodation could be an acceptable solution to the office problem for some time. In any case, the new City Architect, Sheppard Fidler, was by now suggesting some very different design solutions for the civic centre site, favouring a step-by-step approach to the design of individual buildings over time, rather than a slavish adherence to a monumental axial-style layout. Notionally, a pattern of interlocking spaces replaced the big central square, rather, as we have seen, akin to the break-up of the old University layout in favour of precincts. Meanwhile certain developments around Broad Street occurred piecemeal; a fountain in the Hall of Memory Gardens was installed in 1954 as a Golden Jubilee commemoration of the Elan Valley water scheme, and a new Register Office opened on the south of Broad Street.

Vacillation and caution over financial prudence marked the period from the late 1950s to the end of the 1960s, but at least by the end of that decade a number of developments had established some fixed points for the future. When the Birmingham Chamber of Commerce decided to discontinue the engineering and hardware sections of the British Industries Fair at Castle Bromwich after 1957, enthusiasm was generated for the provision of new exhibition facilities in the city centre. The ageing Bingley Hall, formerly the residence of Charles Lloyd, the banker, was no longer adequate and Council proceeded to seek Parliamentary powers to build a new hall on a site to the south of Broad Street; the site was acquired in 1960. Meanwhile Sheppard Fidler's scheme included four 14-storey blocks for municipal offices, and when the City Architect indicated that one could be ready in four years, approval was given in principle in January 1960. But building was postponed and finally abandoned in 1965. Furthermore the exhibition hall proposal was aborted in 1968 when the site was leased to Associated Television for a broadcasting and entertainment centre (to come to fruition as the ATV Tower). The final twist to this part of the story came with government approval to the National Exhibition Centre scheme beyond the city boundary at Bickenhill.

While the proposals for the hall and the office block meandered to negative conclusions, other developments did proceed with positive consequences. During the early 1960s it was agreed that the civic centre should house a new school of music, the Birmingham Athletic Institute, a drama centre and accommodation for youth organisations, in addition to the new central library. Possibilities were realised when rapid progress on the inner ring road required the demolition of the central library; a new library was approved in 1967 (and opened in 1973), straddling the road in tunnel at this point, and adjoining buildings were added to the complex immediately west of Chamberlain Square. Meanwhile the four office blocks on the northern boundary were replaced by multi-storey flats; completed by 1969, they incorporated a public promenade on the banks of the nearby canal.

Further definition to the civic centre came with the building of a new Repertory Theatre. The old repertory theatre, founded in 1913, ran into financial difficulties during the 1950s, and indeed for many years profound problems attended the futures of both the Hippodrome and the Alexandra in spite of the loss of the Theatre Royal in 1956. The principle of municipal subsidisation was a nettle grasped both during the war and immediately afterwards, but it was not until the early 1960s that the solution to rehouse the old 'Rep' in a new, municipally-built theatre was seriously considered. For many years the Council (particularly the leadership of the Labour Party) had entertained the notion of a 'theatreland' in the Smallbrook Ringway area, but in 1963 a site for a new theatre had been earmarked in the civic centre. Restrictions on capital spending in the mid-1960s retarded the scheme, but building began in 1969 and the theatre's opening production was in October 1971.

After this flurry of development a decade of extensive construction activity came to an end. The 1970s marked the gradual withdrawal of cranes and scaffolding from the central area skyline, and the impression of living in a vast building site was eased. We shall return to this point in the next section, but for the civic centre the same context applies: with the building of the Repertory Theatre development in this particular sector of Birmingham came to a halt. The city caught its breath and seemingly took stock. From a planning point of view it was soon caught up in other fashions (conservation for example) and engaged in other concerns (including a response to a deepening disillusion with the product of the previous decade on the part of the citizenry and professional observers in architecture and planning). Above all the city found itself in increasingly difficult economic times, with inevitable consequences, particularly in the need for tight control over public sector expenditure. Meanwhile the national speculative property boom had overreached itself and there was a dramatic cut-back in activity; Birmingham no longer looked the attractive investment area it once did. Finally, a successful National Exhibition Centre development at Bickenhill turned the spotlight of attention away from further civic centre expansion, to leave the Broad Street area an unfinished backwater, uncomfortably situated between the ring road in the east and the Five Ways Shopping Centre in the west.

A change came in the 1980s when the decision was taken to construct an International Convention Centre in Broad Street. A substantial European Community grant made it possible to contemplate a major 'flagship' scheme, so beloved during the decade, to signal the revival of a city badly hit in the recession of 1981–84 and of a region undergoing profound economic change. Site clearance was underway by late 1986 for a scheme which both rounded off and gave new definition to the large civic space earmarked for so long in this area. The major elements are now in place: a major open space (Centenary Square); the ICC complex (Figure 11.2)

Figure 11.2 The International Convention Centre. The National Arena is to the rear, the Repertory Theatre to the right and Centenary Square in the foreground.

with its many halls, one designed to double as a concert hall, a replacement for the cold and uncomfortable Town Hall; a Hyatt Regency Hotel on the south side of Broad Street; and a National Indoor Arena north of Brindley Place. The framing of the square is provided by new and existing buildings; the composition is restless and lacks obvious harmony, but the paving, water features and landscaping of the open space itself is good quality and may rescue the scheme as a whole, although the sculpture by Birmingham-born Raymond Mason, depicting the city's people and their history, has not been well received. The pedestrian link to Victoria Square in the newly utilised space underneath the Library works particularly well.

It was argued that flagship developments of this kind, in this case designed to capture an important share of the national, European and international convention and business tourism market (which the ICC did brilliantly in hosting the EC leaders in 1992), would stimulate commercial activity in adjoining areas through some kind of trickle-down, filter effect. One can see some evidence of this in the activity which has become attracted to the renovated water front of the adjoining canal space at Gas Street Basin (well done, incidentally), in the new Novotel further down Broad Street and in the conversion of the former offices of Tube Investments to the Swallow Hotel at Five Ways. But work on the Brindley Place scheme, immediately adjoining the ICC, designed for further retail development, craft and heritage workshops and entertainment facilities only started in September 1993 after many years 'on hold' and the site remains part of a rather uncomfortable, down-at-heel fringe to the western sector of Birmingham's central district. We are a long way yet from the water-side development as seen in Sydney's Darling Harbour or the water front at Baltimore, prototypes perhaps for up-market urban renewal projects.

The second phase

In our chronological overview, we have already established that the city's first central area redevelopment boom had come to an end by the close of the 1960s. We must now look at the next twenty years or so and chart the events and circumstances of a very different period. Economic gloom and depression replaced the buoyancy and vigour of the earlier years; confidence was lost and with it came a disenchantment with the progress that had been made. There had been no qualitative improvement to city centre shopping; indeed as the years went by, and old established stores withdrew, Birmingham was thought to have fallen back as a regional shopping magnet. Some of this of course was due to changes in the wider geographical distribution of retail trade, and in its structure, considerations which were affecting all British cities, but such explanations were not readily appreciated by public opinion. More focused perhaps was the growing dislike of forms of monolithic architecture which dominated the central scene and the technocratic solution to road traffic whereby the pedestrian had come off second best, swept through underpasses, up ramps and stairs, and channelled along traffic-choked streets. The conservation movement, as we have seen, was an understandable reaction to the over-zealous destruction of the late 1950s and the 1960s, and helped to redress a balance towards a greater concern for a retention of the past.

By now the absence of a sensitive guiding hand for the component parts of the central area was obvious; some broad principles for the layout and appearance of the shopping, business and civic areas needed to be established, and arrangements made for the proper relationship and linkage between them. Very unfavourable comparisons could be made between Birmingham and some of its provincial rivals from the point of view of professional leadership and planning capability. Birmingham had been late to appoint a separate planning officer and for long the city had the reputation of an engineer-led authority – and its built environment reflected it. Nearby Coventry was quite different and always had been, but elsewhere in the country radical reviews of administrative and professional arrangements brought cities such as Newcastle, Liverpool, Manchester and Leicester to the fore as new planning authorities of imagination and purpose. Birmingham was in danger of being left behind.

Some early pedestrianisation work was undertaken early in the 1970s to include parts of High Street, Bull Street, Union Street, Cherry Street and Temple Row; the City Arcade between Union Street and Warwick Passage was restored and reopened; Chamberlain Square was pedestrianised and an amphitheatre (very successfully) created around the Memorial Fountain; and Victoria Square was (very unsuccessfully) partly landscaped (Figure 11.3). But Paradise Circus remained unfinished and for many years, until the late 1980s in fact, it presented a very alien waste ground adjoining the Library; a proposed bus station was abandoned, so too were plans for sports facilities. The overall city scene seemed little more than 'bits and pieces' compared with the environmental drama of earlier years. The erection of the Victorian clock in the High Street in 1979 was at least more tasteful than the huge sculpture of a gorilla ('King Kong') erected in Manzoni Gardens seven years earlier – mercifully, after six months it was taken away to a car sales premises in Camp Hill.

The 1980s proved a much more enterprising decade for the city centre. Economic recovery in the middle years led to a substantial investment flow for offices and commercial developments, and for some time the service sector flourished strongly. Property schemes returned. A site in Cannon Street and Needless Alley was developed for shops and offices: the City Plaza opened in 1988.

The Snow Hill Station site was also finally developed (the Colmore Court

Figure 11.3 The Council House. Victoria Square in 1975, then part of a traffic circulation system.

office blocks) and nearby, the demolition of the Gaumont Cinema in Steelhouse Lane and the old Wesleyan and General Insurance Building at Colmore Circus paved the way in 1988 for the insurance company's new large offices. Meanwhile Snow Hill was reopened for lines to the Black Country and to Stratford and Warwick (via the tunnel to Moor Street).

Paradise Circus was finally completed. The shopping arcade was opened as Fletcher's Walk. There were extensions to the Birmingham School of Music, and the additions of the Adrian Boult concert hall and Josiah Mason exhibition hall. Controversially the impact of the scheme will always be seen in the design of two buildings which flank the entrance way into the Library and provide part of the frame to Centenary Square: the black glass Chamberlain House office block and the Copthorne Hotel form a discordant and angular intrusion to their surroundings.

In 1984, a central area local plan (for the first time, such a document having been long resisted) set out objectives for the improvement of the physical appearance of the city centre. Considerable extensions to the network of pedestrian streets were proposed, and a careful identification of distinctive areas for special enhancement and emphasis advocated. All this represented a rather more positive, and certainly comprehensive view of central area planning. A city centre symposium ('Highbury Initiative') was held in March 1988, attended by national and international delegates from a range of professions and disciplines. The symposium broadly supported the city centre strategy; it emphasised the importance of pedestrian movement and suggested that the function of the inner ring road as a bypass should be transferred to the middle ring, releasing the inner ring from its barrier-like appearance. Unpopular subways could be eliminated and the pedestrian returned to the surface if the road were transformed into a city boulevard.

These plans are now being implemented and a major enhancement of the appearance of the city centre is taking place. A programme of pedestrianisation and pavement widening is transforming shopper comfort, and an altogether more agreeable assembly of spaces is emerging. The pedestrian route from Centenary Square to Chamberlain Square has been transformed by the relatively simple expedient of roofing over the central court of the Central Library, enclosing it in glass, creating a wind-free space and providing facilities for shops and restaurants. New Street is now wall-to-wall block paving, with mature trees established. Victoria Square has been completely refurbished in a large pedestrian circulation area where multi-coloured brick paving is sedate and relaxing. The centrepiece is a fountain, among the largest in any European city centre. Water springs from an immense, reclining bronze woman (by Dhruva Mistry). Other sculptures complete a very satisfying public space, backed by a renovated Council House.

The city's love-hate relationship with sculpture continues with controversy over Antony Gormley's 'iron man', commissioned by the TSB Bank, incongruous in its setting but, overall, this new civic square looks to be highly successful. A visually improved Colmore Row leads into St Philip's Churchyard Precinct, and with the Cathedral itself restored and 'face-lifted', this area now assumes a presence befitting city status. Work on Smallbrook Ringway is approaching completion as the first part of a massive scheme of changing levels and transforming the function of this section of the inner ring road.

Other improvements complement the successes of a very eventful last five years. The closure of the Co-op premises in High Street was followed by its redevelopment as a new shopping mall, the Pavilions clad in glass and chrome, with scenic lifts and the obligatory atrium. The refurbishment of the Hippodrome should help the revitalisation of Hurst Street and provide a more attractive street environment for the theatre. The Birmingham Shopping Centre above New Street Station was modernised and renamed the Pallasades.

In 1987 the Bull Ring Centre was targeted for redevelopment. Its commercial attractiveness had been diminishing for some years, the whole area acquiring a reputation for seediness. Plans were submitted by developers, the London and Edinburgh Trust; they envisaged the demolition of the Centre and the Rotunda in favour of a comprehensive scheme, known as the Galleries, extending east–west between the two Stations, Moor Street and New Street and north–south from the junction of New Street and High Street to Edgbaston Street. All existing buildings except Attwood House, adjoining the Rotunda, and St Martin's Church would be demolished. A storm of local criticism met the spectacle of a single, monolithic building enclosing three shopping levels and an indoor market, the solid massing of which would dwarf the church and split the Bull Ring from the rest of the main shopping area.

A body known as 'Birmingham for People', directed by John Newson, saw the Bull Ring proposals as symptomatic of the 'big is beautiful' ideology which had done so much damage to the city since the war. In 1988 a significant revision was proposed which allowed for a direct pedestrian route between the church and the junction of New Street and High Street; it also broke up the massiveness of the earlier scheme to incorporate a large semi-circular piazza around the church so as to accommodate the open-air market on its historic site. The proposals await an economic upturn for the massive investment to proceed.

So we are a long way yet from the city centre long promised. Much of the work undertaken in the last seven to ten years has been encouragingly good, a welcome relief from that thrust on the city in earlier years, but there are profound doubts about the sustained recovery of the central area property market, and its capacity to absorb the amount of shopping floor space entailed in current proposals. The long awaited Brindley Place scheme, the pull of the Snow Hill end of the city, the recovery potential of Lewis's, the much needed boost to New Street and the potential of a mega Bull Ring, all suggest a city caught in transition, and one does wonder whether a city centre, traditionally so cramped, and with its commercial drawing power increasingly sapped by developments elsewhere, can manage all these things at the same time. Meanwhile one hopes that the Council's new found concern for environmental sensitivities, attention to townscape detail and a basic regard for people's interests and foibles can be maintained. The Council's reputation in these matters is not high; the Council has always been more interested in big, eye-catching projects (and has sometimes done them very well), and history suggests that it has demonstrated a capacity to commit itself to some massive schemes with little forethought. The bigger the scheme the greater the risk of failure; the central area challenge is particularly daunting. We can but wish the Council well in its present endeavours; the improvements wrought over the past five years or so have already served to lift the spirits.

12
Reflections

Birmingham enjoys an uneven reputation in national esteem. It has never been one of Britain's loved cities; rather it has been derided or shunned. Dr Johnson of nearby Lichfield wrote to Boswell that 'we are a city of philosophers. We work with our heads, and make the boobies of Birmingham work for us with their hands' (quoted in Briggs, 1952, p. 5). At more or less the same time, the daughter of Hutton, the town's historian, ridiculed Birmingham as 'a place celebrated neither for fashion nor taste' (Stephens, p. 209). The social structure of the town depended on its manufacturing base, and in some quarters the absence of a capitalist aristocracy, with all its ramifications in terms of society and social connections, was keenly felt.

Into the 19th century novelists carried a repugnant image of Birmingham in their work. Jane Austen in *Emma* (1816) has Mrs Elton lament to Mr Weston about a family named Tupman recently settled nearby: 'encumbered with many low connections, but giving themselves immense airs ... how they got their fortune nobody knows. They came from Birmingham, which is not a place to promise much ... One has not great hopes from Birmingham. I always say there is something direful in the sound ...' (chapter 36). Charles Dickens in *The Old Curiosity Shop* (1841) has Little Nell flee London with her grandfather; in their wanderings they reach a part of the country which scholars suppose can only be Birmingham and the Black Country from the allusion to waterways, furnaces, coal and manufacturing towns. Descriptions are reminiscent of the fictitious Coketown in *Hard Times*, with scenes of ugliness and inhumanity. Passages conjure up images of an industrial and urban wasteland, contrasting squalid strife with life in peaceful country places: 'They were but an atom, here, in a mountain heap of misery, the very sight of which increased their hopelessness and suffering' (Chapter 44). Into the 20th century it took a regional novelist, Francis Brett Young, in *White Ladies* (1935) to portray Edgbaston (the fictional Alvaston) in glowing terms, as a leafy, attractive suburb in an industrial North Bromwich (Birmingham).

Lister's (1991, p. 53) observation that '(Birmingham's) reputation as a sprawling, blighted, industrial zoo whose citizens sported a collective inferiority complex dating back more than 300 years' surely goes too far. He makes too much of the entry for 'Brummagem' in the *Shorter Oxford Dictionary* which reads: '(contemptuously) an article made in Birmingham . . . with allusion to counterfeit groats, plate, etc; counterfeit, sham; cheap and showy, 1681'. The city deserves to be regarded in a more understanding light; after all, the history of Birmingham is closely bound up with the history of the nation. Particularly during the period when Birmingham grew as a manufacturing town, and then consolidated its position as an industrial city, this capital of the West Midlands contributed significantly to national life and thought. We can readily point to Birmingham's scientists and industrialists, as exemplified in the Lunar Society, its political leaders such as Attwood and Chamberlain, those divines who shaped the civil gospel in the second half of the 19th century, and the captains of both local industry and local government in the 20th century. Birmingham as a city offers a wonderful test-bed for understanding the course of English social history over the last century and a half, particularly from the point of view of the development of mass politics and the growth of large-scale municipal administration. With regard to town planning there is probably no better city in Britain from which to observe the course of 20th century urban growth (particularly the processes of suburbanisation) and the application of planning policies to post-war redevelopment, housing and roads.

These are the matters which have figured large in previous chapters, and which contribute to an understanding of the city from the points of view of its appearance, social and economic life, and culture. The story of Birmingham has been told in such a way as to capture the spirit of the city. We have found it helpful to do this by following a chronological narrative and by employing the particular disciplines of geography and history to provide both a cultural geography and a planning history of the city. The principal focus has been on the physical appearance of Birmingham and its urban form and function, informed from time to time, on an appropriately selective basis, from the insights of economic, social and political history. But the attention given to physical form and structure has not been at the expense of the community dimension; to understand Birmingham one has to look at the people as well as the places. Birmingham is socially as well as physically distinctive. Demographically the city has become racially mixed.and its population intones a common dialect. The 'Brummie' can readily be set apart from his Black Country neighbour, and the cultural gradation to the shire counties beyond the urban heartland is a sharp one.

As a University teacher I have experienced little difficulty in relating geograpy to planning through historical perspectives; students are usually curious about their environmental (urban or rural) past and their keen interest can soon be aroused when explanations of present form and appearance are attempted. Who can resist the call to imagination extended by Gill and Robertson's (1938) reminder of the Birmingham of old?:

> It seems strange to picture a little hamlet of peasants' huts grouped around the green, which became the Bull Ring; to see a small Norman Church where St Martin's stands today; to set in place of the Town Hall the corn field which was there in the sixteenth century, or by Needless Alley the potato field of the eighteenth century; to furnish Cherry Street with its orchard or to replace St Philip's Cathedral by Mr Phillip's barley close. It is almost more difficult to believe that after 1800 pleasure boats were taken from Deritend Bridge to tea gardens beside the upper river'. (p. 9)

Almost 50 years on we reconstruct the recent past with calls to remember the impact of the blitz and the course of post-war reconstruction.

We can look at particular districts and trace the past from various features on the ground, including street lines and boundaries from former field and ownership patterns. Even the most mundane objects can tell a story: street names, for example, where the compilation drawn up by Bird (1991) can be used to good effect. In the area around Small Heath Golden Hillock was a field name on a 1760 tithe map and Golden Hillock Farm is commemorated in Golden Hillock Road; Garrison Lane refers to the barracks constructed on four acres of land at Ashted in 1792; Armoury Road saw the birth of the Birmingham Small Arms Co. in 1863, the factory being built on condition that the Great Western Railway provided a station nearby ('Small Heath and Sparkbrook'); Muntz Street takes its name from George Frederick Muntz, a Birmingham MP from 1840 till his death in 1857.

From districts to buildings: the story of Aston Hall (Fairclough, 1984) illumines the course of urban change in that part of the city. A large early 17th century mansion (completed in the 1630s) for the Holte family lay less than three miles from the centre of Birmingham. The ancient village of Aston has been totally destroyed, the last of its houses (medieval in origin) demolished in 1977; only the Hall and the Parish Church remain. The Hall is now surrounded by Victorian terraces, post-war housing and industrial premises; five-sixths of the park have been built over. Aston Villa FC's ground, Villa Park, occupies the Hall's barnyard, fish pond and kitchen garden. The Aston Expressway today passes within 500 yards of the house. Purchased by Birmingham in 1864, it became the first country house to be opened to the public by a municipal authority.

Much can be made of such detail. But a framework and a context is necessary too. One such setting is the development of English society (particularly for our story) between 1830 and 1914, and the different traditions established by key provincial cities, of which Birmingham was one, during that period. Smith (1982) highlights two contradictions which featured in these years of transition. One was that 'the growth of industrial capitalism in England was favoured by and in turn threatened the existence of a decentralised state apparatus dominated by a commercialised country-house aristocracy'. The increasing power of urban business men and public officials gradually diverted social and political power away from the local to the national level. The second contradiction was that 'the fruits of ingenuity and labour were appropriated to a disproportionate extent by a relatively small class of property owners and their associates, but the persistence of these arrangements depended upon the complicity of the many who were excluded from most of the benefits' (p x). Hence there was both conflict and compromise between members of status groups and social classes. But all cities were different and worked out their own forms of industrial society. To take the six largest provincial cities in 1851, Liverpool and Bristol were centres of commerce and sea-trade; Manchester and Leeds were manufacturing centres with large textile factories; Birmingham and Sheffield concentrated on metal working largely carried out in small workshops. Birmingham developed its forms of internal organisation and processes of class formation in a distinctive manner, albeit the general tendencies which were at work in the country as a whole. Birmingham today retains the imprint from the past particularly in its economic structure and complex division of labour. Neither has it yet shed the consequences of a political power struggle which brought about a new network of civic institutions, dramatically the town council and school board as new monopolies of power, but with commanding influence elsewhere as in voluntary associations such as the Birmingham and Midland Institute, and in university education.

Another setting for the rise of Birmingham has to be seen against the course of western urbanism over the last 200 years. Lawton's (1989) recent synopsis is a useful starting point. The industrial and commercial revolutions brought about a concentration of capital and production. The ability to harness motive power to mass production progressively destroyed the world of handicraft workers and drew a surplus army of labour to new points of manufacture at sources of power and raw materials, and around transport nodes. In due time larger industrialists moved to the periphery of cities and new patterns of metropolitan industrial location emerged. The 20th century, particularly the second half, saw the rise of the salariat, the growth of a service economy and the segmentation of labour markets. Very recent decades have witnessed the decline of manufacturing employment, an economic collapse of the central core of cities, revolutions in transport and high technology leading to decentralisation and a complexity of spatial patterns over a dispersed regional city. All this, in broad outline, is Birmingham too.

Hence we can argue that when history and geography are fused, useful insights are gained about the nature of urban form and spatial patterns over time. This volume demonstrates that; Birmingham provides a template for other cities to follow. But we have introduced another dimension, one in which Birmingham offers so much: planning. When history and geography are further informed from this direction, the explanatory model derived *via* planning history becomes even more helpful. So this volume is also an excursion in planning history applied to a particular city. I have written elsewhere (Cherry, 1993) that planning history is as rewarding as an archaeological dig. We strip away the circumstances attending a particular plan, policy or strategy; we expose the influence of key actors; we reveal the pressure of competing interests; and we dust away the preconceptions and the biases which override rationality. New truths emerge: because the practice of planning is ultimately a matter of transaction and negotiation between competing interests, the outcome of executive action relies not so much on the merits of a particular plan or scheme, but on the force, or power of persuasion of the various actors concerned with its success or failure. Planning history teaches that all problems have origins and all policies have consequences; hence the development process takes shape over time, in context with the various social, economic, technological, political and institutional determinants of the day. Birmingham confirms these observations remarkably faithfully.

What emerges from the narrative of the earlier chapters is a city of inconsistencies, and occasionally opposites, in the way in which a particular image or characteristic develops over time. In a surprisingly large number of respects, that which can be captured as a formative 'flavour' of Birmingham, perhaps at one period of time, can be discounted by a different condition at another. The city's geographical location, and the subsequent shift in geographical values which impacted on that location, is a case in point. Originally in a peripheral setting, finally central to its region, Birmingham took root in an undistinguished backwater, but in its fruition became the centre of things. The Birmingham Plateau was inhospitable territory for Anglo-Saxon settlers and the River Rea an unpromising gateway to the heaths and woodlands to the south and west. The Domesday survey suggests that other neighbouring settlements had rather more to offer, while in any case meaningful town life existed at the edge of the plateau rather than within it. There was no sudden reversal of geographical values, no overnight discovery of strategic significance. It took until Tudor times for Birmingham, simply a one-street township, to consolidate its economic hegemony over the district and perhaps another two centuries to supplant Coventry as the principal manufacturing town in the region. The 18th century finally established the town as of national importance and, with the industrial transformations from mid-century onwards, Birmingham's centrality was reinforced. It would be no better marked than in successive transport revolutions, as a result of which Birmingham became a canal, rail, road and motorway hub. From a position of peripheral importance, to commercial node of a major metropolitan region, Birmingham's transformation was complete.

The key to Birmingham is to regard it as a city of process and dynamic change. Poorly endowed geographically, it took eight centuries for a township to emerge, a growing settlement which owed little to local natural resources or immediate strategic advantage. Over the next two centuries the growth of Birmingham turned a past geography on its head, becoming the focus for its region and creating its own conditions for expansion and total transformation; it became restless and thrusting, presenting a series of images to itself, the region and the nation. These images and symbols formed part of an emergent urban culture, expressed in the appearance of the town, the conduct of its people and the performance of its institutions. The tumultuous events of the last two centuries make it unlikely for the cultural traditions of Birmingham to run smoothly, or be well-grounded in a long history. Hence the inconsistencies and opposites to which we have referred. It all makes for a situation in which the city today might be regarded as inconsequential, ephemeral, overly concerned with the 'here and now', and inconstant in outlook because it has relatively little to guide it. But there is more to Birmingham than this, and its uneven projection in inconsistencies and opposites produces a city of surprises. The 'spirit of the place', which the editors of the series wish to see explored, can usefully be grounded in three aspects which this volume has touched on in earlier chapters: in its socio-cultural dimensions, as a city reflected in image and form, and in its 20th century town planning performance. We can refer to each of these in turn.

The spirit of the place

Important socio-cultural factors reflect some interesting opposites over time. The town proclaimed an open society, relatively free from extremes of wealth and social position because of the fluid interrelationship between small master and workman, particularly in the prevalent metal trades. The capitalists were not the landed aristocracy. There was also an absence of monopoly structures, whether guilds or religious exclusivity. It was a society which could boast assimilation, not only of people, but also of ideas and trade. Yet the town's history would be punctuated by some ugly instances of intolerance and easily manipulated rebellion, such as the Priestley riots, political agitation both in the French Revolutionary wars and again in the 1830s, and, coming more up to date, in labour disputes in the 1970s and Handsworth's 'race riots' in 1985.

An open society (periodically flawed as we have seen) was a sturdily

independent one with dissent from established political and religious positions readily in evidence. Birmingham was on the side of Parliament in the
Civil War (and was sacked for its pains). In the 19th century it took up a
stance of belligerent advocate of political reform under Attwood; the high
drama of the Reform Bill, and, later, Chartism was played out, at least in
part, on the streets of the town. Later, Joseph Chamberlain captured the
banner of the civic gospel and mobilised mass support for his policies
through the discipline of a political party. In terms of religion the established Church of England was long challenged by non-conformity. The
Quakers had influential adherents in commerce and manufacturing industry; the town became a centre for Unitarianism, with a hold on many leading families; Methodism flourished after John Wesley first preached in
Birmingham in 1743. The 1851 census on church attendance suggests that
we should not overplay the town's characteristic of dissent, but it was
strong enough in key social sectors to impart a key feature to the town.

Today the position is rather different. Political independence has largely
been diverted by a 20th century adherence to the dictates of national party
politics. Opportunities for political independence have been greatly diminished. Indeed since 1945 both Conservatives and Labour in the city have
shown a remarkable pragmatism in dealing with local issues and no little
convergence on some key policy issues, notably housing, planning and
roads. Perhaps the role of long serving, strong chief officers is a major
factor here. In terms of religion the position is also largely different in a
secularised late 20th century. The Selly Oak Colleges remain an interesting
bastion of nonconformist and ecumenical activity, black African churches
have grown vigorously, and substantial communities are adherents of
Islam, Hinduism and Sikhism. Birmingham's religious scene today is one
of inter-faith dialogue in a very different set of circumstances from a
century ago. The city's religious communities have introduced a new,
dynamic element into the local culture; the city is heterogeneous and more
vibrant as a result. The full consequences have not yet unfolded, but the
impact of Islam may prove to be the most enduring on the host community:
with 14 Moslem city councillors, 50 mosques and a substantial trading
representation in economic life, Pakistan's contribution to Birmingham in
socio-political terms is already pronounced.

The principal social structures of Birmingham have been fashioned by
the area's form of economic development. The 19th century manufacturing
town was not dominated by mills or factories, and the gulf (seen elsewhere
in the country) between mill and factory owners and their workforce was
largely absent. Birmingham was essentially a town of small workshops,
contracting work within the various metal trades was extensive, and an
elite, capital-owning, entrepreneurial class had a much reduced role compared with other industrial centres. Skilled craftsmen formed a much
broader section in the town's occupational structure, with socio-political

consequences that were felt long after organisational and technological change transformed Birmingham's industrial landscape. By the end of the 19th century factories were replacing the workshop as engineering supplanted handicraft. In the 20th century industrial processes confirmed the trend, particularly in vehicle and engine manufacture where huge factories were established, yet overall Birmingham retains a characteristic for small and medium-sized establishments.

Birmingham's rise to economic pre-eminence continued virtually unabated for 200 years, from the 1770s to the 1970s. Staple trades which had run their course were soon replaced by new manufacturing interests, as an inventive workforce proved highly adaptable and resourceful. Both town and city provided economic conditions for its labour to be well paid, and for employment to be reasonably regular and sustained. Birmingham survived the economic recession of the 1920s and 1930s remarkably well (as it had done in the 1870s and 1880s). Recovery in local domestic spending was based, at least in part, on local manufacture. An enviable reputation, however, was marred in the post-1970s period when a dramatic reversal of fortunes occurred and the past vigour of a manufacturing and industrial centre collapsed. An industrial heart, which once made it the workshop of the world, faltered and gave way to factory closure, unemployment and landscape dereliction. A city, with an ingrained expectation of continual expansion and prosperity, and with proven experience of adaptation, found it hard to take.

We argue that Birmingham's social and economic structures have helped to establish a cultural response from its community. We have already seen how an absence of style and fashion caused the town to be poorly regarded in national circles, yet in the middle of the 18th century there was a reading population and the scientific cliques represented by the Lunar Society were truly remarkable. In the 19th century cultural organisations flourished, though not to any greater extent than in other leading centres; the Midland Institute, the Reference Library and the Art Gallery were not exceptional. Perhaps the frenetic capacity for work, noted by many observers, led to the reputation for Birmingham being a cultural desert. Yet the late 20th century rejoinder has been to firmly reject that caricature. The Repertory Theatre, dating from 1913, and the City of Birmingham Symphony Orchestra founded in 1920, have been followed by the building of new premises for both drama and music and the refurbished Hippodrome now houses the Royal Birmingham Ballet. In October 1993 the city's new Art Exhibition Centre at the Gas Hall Exhibition Gallery was opened by the Queen.

We can also comment on attitudes struck between Birmingham and its neighbours during the centuries of its growth. Birmingham as a settlement began life with no great advantages; other settlements nearby had superior resources. Yet the town grew to usurp all competitors. However, it was never able to do this independently; there always had to be a reciprocal relationship with the regional community of which it was part. We saw this in the late 18th century when Birmingham's town life took on a recognisable identity, but it was one which the district as a whole shared. During the 19th century the economy of the town, while distinctive, was fused with that of the Black Country, and the canal and rail transport revolutions tied Birmingham inescapably to a wider frame. In the 20th century the city's annexations may have suggested greater independence, but in planning terms regional inter-dependence could not be denied. The final irony was when, between 1974 and 1986, the city found itself embedded in a new local government unit greater than itself. Birmingham's history is of a creative tension with its neighbours.

If we turn from social, economic and cultural matters to consider Birmingham as a city, we can see again how opposites can easily prevail. For example, Birmingham patently is not a historic city, in the sense that Chester, York and Lincoln are, yet our image of Birmingham is conditioned by our impression of what it was, as much as what it is. We think of the Birmingham of Matthew Boulton and James Watt, of scientific discoveries, of flights of canals, waterside archaeology, jewellery workshops, brass bedsteads and gun manufacture, of steam trains billowing their smoke under the vaulted roofs of Snow Hill and New Street, of Joseph Chamberlain's crusade for civic improvement and Cadbury's factory in a garden at Bournville. This combination of powerful and romantic images portrays Birmingham in a reassuring light. Street nameplates in cast iron remain a proud reminder of an industrial past, and from certain vantage points the office towers of central Birmingham suggest the vitality of a transatlantic townscape. Contrast these mildly reassuring symbols with other mid-and later- 20th century pictures: suburban sprawl, city centre traffic congestion, anonymous post-war redevelopment, high-rise building, and city districts abandoned to a new population whose cultures are still uncomfortably juxtaposed with those of a host society. Birmingham remains a city in transition, but with some exceptions the attractive symbols and meanings are still those which belong to the past rather than the present.

As a manufacturing town Birmingham was late to gain municipal status. For long it was governed through the institutions of a rural parish and latterly by a succession of improvement commissioners. When it did receive a Charter in 1838 the Town Council was largely impotent for some time, and not until 1851 did local government in Birmingham make an effective start – for a town with tightly delineated boundaries and a population of approaching a quarter of a million. After some further years of Council quiescence due to parsimony in public expenditure, a surge in public activity occurred. By the end of the century it was enjoying the reputation of being the best governed city in the Empire: from nowhere to pole position in little more than 30 years.

The City Council continued to attract councillors of merit and energy, and to appoint chief officers of professional stature. Neville Chamberlain, successively chairman of the town planning committee, mayor, founder of the Municipal Savings Bank and, following his election to the House of Commons at the relatively late age of 50 and rapid Parliamentary promotion, twice Minister of Health (and thereby in charge of local government), belonged to a generation which could still have a touching faith in the work of a local council. At the time of his Local Government Bill in 1929 he observed:

> Local government comes so much nearer to the homes, and therefore to the hearts of the people, than any national government can. To them it is something friendly, something familiar, something accessible. It is all that to them, and yet it is above them. They regard it as standing as a guardian angel between them and ill-health or injustice, and they look upon it, too, as something in the nature of a benefactor and a teacher in want. They come to it for advice. They feel confidence in its integrity. They look to it because it has ideals which they understand, and that they approve, and because it is always helping and teaching them to rise to higher things. (Cherry, 1980, p. 173)

Another generation would regard these sentiments with cynicism, but this was the Birmingham he knew and the city in which his network of socially-conscious paternalism contributed to its local affairs. Much has changed, not least in the way that a professional bureaucracy has taken over. For example, in the story that we have recounted, the force of Herbert Manzoni in planning for roads and redevelopment cannot be exaggerated. Officer replaced the enthusiastic, though committed, amateur. The balance was not redressed until the later 20th century style of caucus politics and disciplined party groups re-established a form of political leadership.

As town and city Birmingham achieved economic status by the sheer scale of its manufacturing output. To begin with, the home market absorbed the bulk of countless articles for domestic consumption, but in the second half of the 19th century Empire trade proved an indispensable outlet, as Chamberlain's conversion to protectionism and Empire preferences rather suggested. Competition from Germany, especially in iron and steel products, gave an early indication that Britain's economic might was facing serious challenge, but that the colonies could secure the country's favoured position. It is ironic that nearly 100 years on, of all British cities, Birmingham is now more European-oriented than most. It has gained massively in EC aid, its Convention Centre the most visible witness to European investment; in return, the EC logo appears on many Council publications.

If we turn to town planning in Birmingham we can see the same sort of unexpected twists and turns. Consider the irony of sequential trends in inward and outward population movement. As town and city, its population grew by absorption. From the middle of the 17th century when the number of its inhabitants began its spectacular, sustained increase, an inward migration from rural to urban supplemented the natural increase of births over deaths. The housing for its growing numbers of people spread to its borough boundaries and beyond. Around the turn of the century boundary changes gave the city room for expansion, massively after 1911, and between the wars and after 1945 the city's municipal estates and private suburbs transformed a former rural hinterland. Until this time net population movements were essentially inward to a Greater Birmingham, successive boundary extensions creating the largest, single-tier unit of local government in the country.

From the 1950s a planned dispersal of population took Birmingham people far afield. Town expansion schemes for places from Aldridge-Brownhills to Daventry and from Tamworth to Droitwich reversed the trend of centuries. Meanwhile private, voluntary overspill confirmed the new trend; whereas Birmingham had been a magnet of attraction, it became a pole of dispersal. Within the city itself the inner districts progressively lost population to the middle and outer suburbs; from Birmingham as a whole people sought suburbs further distant, or free-standing country towns beyond. Only the annexation of Sutton Coldfield in 1974 kept the city population above the million mark. However, the long standing capacity to absorb people from outside the city continued with the reception of immigrations from the new Commonwealth, notably the West Indies and the Indian Subcontinent.

In terms of town planning Birmingham got off to a spectacular start in the years before 1914. The city was the principal local authority in the country to espouse town planning, Councillor J. S. Nettlefold providing a homespun philosophy well suited to the Birmingham situation and in tune with emergent fashions, nationally: low density, private (not municipal) housing on cheap land, in the suburbs, with good transport connections. The city took up legislative powers with enthusiasm to prepare town planning schemes for its suburban areas. Much of inter-war Birmingham received their distinctive stamp. The city maintained an authoritative hold on town planning in preparing for post-war reconstruction, but after 1945 it was unable to keep its professional prestige. Architecture in the city disappointed, planning in the city was 'public works' oriented, the University of Birmingham failed to establish either a town planning or architecture school (though Aston and the Polytechnic did), and London and other cities in the country (best exemplified perhaps in Coventry initially) took the lead in town planning affairs. Post-war planning in Birmingham failed to live up to its early promise and not until the 1980s were there signs of recovered ground.

The same reversal of roles (in town planning aggressively prominent to disappointingly mundane) can be seen with regard to housing policy in the city, though in this case the trend went from negative to highly positive.

Birmingham began with a rooted hostility to the building of municipal housing. The Council's early experiments in the 1880s and 1890s went no further; political support was simply not forthcoming. A national change of mood, as the country faced up to reconstruction problems after the Great War, led to local authority house building being adopted after 1919 to deal with the question of a national housing shortage. After a slow start Birmingham adopted the council house with vigour, building 50 000 by 1939, more than any other city in the country. Huge swathes of north, east and south Birmingham became inter-war municipal estates, with their distinctive stamp of layout, design and social occupance.

Between the wars the Council was lukewarm if not hostile to flats. Again, its own experiments had attracted much criticism, though by the later 1930s the pendulum of acceptability had begun to swing somewhat. Manzoni's redevelopment proposals focused the debate on density and housing preference; meanwhile, nationally, wider considerations, ranging from architectural fashion, methods of building construction, anxieties about saving land, to subsidy arrangements, threw up the solution of high-rise dwellings in city-wide housing programmes. Birmingham changed course dramatically: a city with virtually no municipal flats proceeded to build more than 400 tall blocks and punctuate its landscape with residential towers. The view of Castle Vale, with its nest of tower blocks, from the M6 is testimony to the way in which a local authority house-building machine can adopt a particular design solution in a mega-project, which would have been unthinkable ten years earlier, or, indeed, ten years later.

Another planning feature shows more consistency, though there has been some departure by virtue of a late modification of attitudes: roads. Twentieth century Birmingham became a car city: producer, consumer and road builder. It seemed entirely apt, though environmentally horrifying, for its roads to be given over for a while to Super Prix motor racing. While the Council's particular Odyssey was the inner ring road, a host of other, hotly pursued objectives such as radial road widening to generous widths, dualling, roundabouts, one-way systems and a variety of traffic management projects, made Birmingham more road-oriented in its development than any other British city. Professionally, the town planner, usually regarded as creative designer and functional architect of form and space, was subservient to the road engineer. Not until the 1970s did the Council undertake some minor pedestrianisation work, but in very recent years a radical reappraisal of policy has resulted in some welcome changes. Central area streets, notably New Street and Victoria Square, are now pedestrianised and the function of the inner ring road itself is being recast with Smallbrook Ringway the first section to undergo a transformation.

However, we can point to one area of relative consistency in Birmingham's planning performance: the fact that a powerful local authority has proved adept in using development powers to boost its own civic image. Joseph Chamberlain's Corporation Street, Manzoni's inner ring road, the National Exhibition Centre, the Airport and the successive civic centre schemes which ultimately led to the International Convention Centre and Centenary Square, all share the same lineage; in recent years only the Olympic bid for 1992 came to naught. However imaginative the projects, such use of planning and planning-related powers is no more than opportunist. For most of the time, except perhaps at the outset and in very recent years, Birmingham's deployment of the planning system has been little more than regulatory and uni-directional. It has dealt with the big issues of house building and road construction, and has responded to development pressures as they occurred, on occasions succumbing to the grand and the brash.

But after nearly 50 years of post-war endeavour it cannot be claimed that the 'value-addedness' of the statutory system has yet created a city of distinctive identity, with an abiding appeal to its citizenry. Birmingham's townscape is still a matter of 'bits and pieces'; its city centre especially disappoints, though is recovering fast from the ravages of neglect and missed opportunities. Its main pleasures lie in its suburbs – environmentally privileged as in Edgbaston and Bournville, attractively mixed as in Harborne and Moseley, but with many areas of new housing surrounding reminders from the past, as at Northfield and Yardley.

However, it is encouraging that the city is renewing its sense of civic identity. Its townscape is undergoing 'repersonalisation' through the creation and enhancement of public spaces, including streets from which traffic has been banished. The public image is improving: twenty years ago an alien Spaghetti Junction might have been the country's impression of Birmingham, but today's picture is more likely to be formed by the International Convention Centre and the National Indoor Arena. But television pictures are one thing; the reality of personal experience is another. A city takes on a real identity when a community's values, pleasures and aspirations are reflected in its built environment – its buildings, its spaces, its sights and its sounds. There are parts of Birmingham which achieve this, some suburbs, certain historical districts and occasional parts of the central area, but elsewhere they are largely private rather than public. The city's attractiveness and sense of identity will be fostered when people and their living townscape have a closer affinity; at the present day, Birmingham is on the edge, still poised to secure the premier position more than a thousand years of history have promised.

References

Abercrombie, P. (1945) *Greater London Plan 1944*, HMSO, London.

Abercrombie, P. and Jackson, H. (1948) *West Midlands Plan*, Ministry of Town and Country Planning, mimeo.

Aldcroft, D. H. (1986) *The British Economy, vol 1, The Years of Turmoil 1920–1951*, Wheatsheaf Books, Brighton.

Allen, G. C. (1929) *The Industrial Development of Birmingham and the Black Country, 1860–1927*. Reprint, Frank Cass, London, 1966.

Atkins, P. (1989) The Architecture of Bournville 1879–1914, pp. 35–48 in Tilson, B. (ed.) *Made in Birmingham: design and industry 1889–1989*. Brewin Books, Studley, Warwickshire.

Austen, Jane (1816) *Emma*.

Barlow, M. (1940), Royal Commission on the Distribution of the Industrial Population, *Report*, Cmd 6153, HMSO, London.

Barnsby, G. J. (1989) *Birmingham Working People: a History of the Labour Movement in Birmingham 1650–1914*, Integrated Publishing Services, Wolverhampton.

Bird, V. (1970) *Portrait of Birmingham*, Robert Hale, London.

Bird, V. (1991) *Streetwise: street names in and around Birmingham*, Meridian Books, Warley.

Birmingham Social Survey Committee (1942) *Nutrition and the Size of the Family: report on a new housing estate*, Birmingham.

Black, H. J. (1957) *History of the Corporation of Birmingham, Vol VI, 1936–50*, City of Birmingham.

Booth, C. (1889–1903) *Life and Labour of the People of London*, Macmillan, London.

Borg, N. (1973) Birmingham, pp. 30–77 in Holliday, J. (ed.), *City Centre Redevelopment*, Charles Knight, London.

Bournville Village Trust, *When We Build Again* (1941), George Allen and Unwin, London.

Bournville Village Trust (1955), *The Bournville Village Trust 1900–1955*, Birmingham.

Braithwaite, L. (1986) *Exploring British Cities*, A. & C. Black, London.

Brannan, J. and F. (1992) *A Postcard from Bournville*, Brewin Books, Studley.

Brazier, R. H. and Sandford, E. (1921) *Birmingham and the Great War 1914–1919*, Cornish Bros, Birmingham.

237

References

Briggs, A. (1952) *History of Birmingham, Vol II, Borough and City 1865–1938*, Oxford University Press.

Briggs, A. (1963) *Victorian Cities*, Chapter 5, Birmingham: the making of a civic gospel, Odhams, London. Pelican Books, 1968, Harmondsworth, Middlesex.

Briggs, A. (1964) Social History Since 1815, pp. 223–45, in Stephens, W. B. (ed.) *A History of the County of Warwick. Vol VII, The City of Birmingham*. Oxford University Press.

Briggs, A. (1988) *Victorian Things*. B. T. Batsford, London. Penguin, Harmondsworth, 1990.

Broadbridge, S. R. (1976) *The Birmingham Canal Navigations*, Vol I, 1768–1846. David and Charles, Newton Abbot.

Bunce, J. T. (1885) *History of the Corporation of Birmingham, Vol II*, Cornish Bros, Birmingham.

Burnett, J. (1978) *A Social History of Housing 1815–1970*. David and Charles, Newton Abbot.

Cadbury Bros Ltd (1943) *Our Birmingham*, Bournville, Birmingham.

Cadbury, G. (1915) *Town Planning with Special Reference to the Birmingham Schemes*, Longmans Green, London.

Cadbury, P. S. (1952) *Birmingham – Fifty Years On*, Bournville Village Trust, Birmingham.

Cadbury, P. S. (1966) *The Lunar Society of Birmingham; bicentenary*, University of London Press.

Cadbury, P. S. (1968) *The Expansion of Birmingham into the Green Belt Area*. Report to the Directors of Cadbury Bros, accompanied by Report by Wise, M. J., 30 September.

Camden, W. (1586) *Britannia*.

Cannadine, D. (1980) *Lords and Landlords: the aristocracy and the towns 1774–1967*, Leicester University Press.

Cannadine, D. (1990) *The Decline and Fall of the British Aristocracy*. Yale University Press.

Casson, H. and Conder, N. (1958) Proposed development for Birmingham University, *The Town Planning Review* **29**, 7–26.

Chamberlain, N. (1913) Town Planning in Birmingham, pp. 175–82 in *Handbook*, British Association for the Advancement of Science.

Cherry, G. E. (1970) *Town Planning in its Social Context*, Leonard Hill, London.

Cherry, G. E. (1974) *The Evolution of British Town Planning*, Leonard Hill, Leighton Buzzard.

Cherry, G. E. (1976) Aspects of Urban Renewal, pp. 53–71, in Hancock, T. (ed.) *Growth and Change in the Future City Region*, Leonard Hill, London.

Cherry, G. E. (1980) The Place of Neville Chamberlain in British Town Planning, pp. 161–79 in Cherry, G. E. (ed.) *Shaping an Urban World*, Mansell, London.

Cherry, G. E. (1982) *The Politics of Town Planning*, Longman, Harlow.

Cherry, G. E. (1988) *Cities and Plans: the shaping of urban Britain in the nineteenth and twentieth centuries*, Edward Arnold, London.

Cherry, G. E. (1993) Milestones and Signposts in Twentieth Century Planning, *Town and Regional Planning* (Journal of the South African Institute of Town and Regional Planners), **34**, 3–9.

Chinn, C. (1991) *Houses for People: 100 years of Council Housing in Birmingham*. Wheaton Publishers Ltd, Exeter.

Chinn, C. (1993) *Keeping the City Alive: 21 years of urban renewal in Birmingham 1972–93*, Birmingham City Council.

City Development Department (1989), *Developing Birmingham: 100 years of city planning*, Birmingham City Council.

Conway, H. (1991) *People's Parks: the design and development of Victorian parks in Britain*, Cambridge University Press.

Court, W. H. B. (1938) *The Rise of the Midland Industries 1600–1838*, Oxford University Press.

Crawford, A. (ed.) (1984) *By Hammer and Hand: the arts and crafts movement in Birmingham*, Birmingham Museums and Art Gallery.

Crawford, A. and Thorne, R. (1975) *Birmingham Pubs 1890–1939*, Centre for Urban and Regional Studies, University of Birmingham.

Crompton, D. and Penketh, L. (1977) Industrial and Employment Change, pp. 111–26, in Joyce, F. (ed.) *Metropolitan Development and Change: the West Midlands, a policy review*, The University of Aston in Birmingham, Teakfield Ltd, Farnborough.

Cullingworth, J. B. (1975) *Environmental Planning 1939–1969, Vol I. Reconstruction and Land Use Planning 1939–1947*, HMSO, London.

Darby, H. C. (ed.) (1973) *A New Historical Geography of England*, Cambridge University Press.

Daunton, M. J. (1987) *A Property-Owning Democracy?*, Faber and Faber, London.

Dent, R. K. (1878–80) *Old and New Birmingham*. Reprinted 1973 by E. P. Publishing Ltd, East Ardsley, Wakefield.

Dent, R. K. (1894) *The Making of Birmingham*.

Departmental Committee set up by the Minister of War Transport (1946), *Design and Layout of Roads in Built-up Areas*, HMSO, London.

Department of Economic Affairs (1965), *The West Midlands: a regional study*, HMSO, London.

Design of Dwellings Sub-Committee of the Ministry of Health Central Housing Advisory Committee (the Dudley Report) (1944), *The Design of Dwellings*, HMSO, London.

Dickens, Charles (1841) *The Old Curiosity Shop*.

Diefendorf, J. M. (ed.) (1990) *Rebuilding Europe's Bombed Cities*, Macmillan, London.

Donnison, D. and Middleton, A. (eds) (1987) *Regenerating the Inner City: Glasgow's experience*, Routledge and Kegan Paul, London.

Doughty, M. (ed.) (1986) *Building the Industrial City*, Leicester University Press.

Dowling, G., Giles, B. and Hayfield, C. (1987) *Selly Oak Past and Present*, Department of Geography, University of Birmingham.

Dugdale, W. (1730) *Antiquities of Warwickshire*.

Dyos, H. J. and Wolff, M. (eds) (1973) *The Victorian City: images and realities*, 2 vols, Routledge and Kegan Paul, London.

Edwards, A. M. (1981) *The Design of Suburbia: a critical study in environmental history*, Pembridge Press, London.

Elrington, C. R. and Tillott, P. M. (1964) The Growth of the City, pp. 4–25, in Stephens, W. B. (ed.) *A History of the County of Warwick, Vol VII, The City of Birmingham*, Oxford University Press.

Engels, Frederick (1845) *The Condition of the Working Class in England*, 1969 edn, Panther Books, London.

Englander, D. (1983) *Landlord and Tenant in Urban Britain 1838–1918*, Oxford University Press.

Eversley, D. E. C. and Keate, D. M. R. (1958) *The Overspill Problem in the West Midlands*, The Midlands New Town Society, Birmingham.

Fairclough, O. (1984) *The Grand Old Mansion: the Holtes and their successors at Aston Hall, 1618–1864*, Birmingham Museum and Art Gallery.

Faith in the City (1985) Report on the Archbishop of Canterbury's Commission on Urban Priority Areas, Church House Publishing, London.

Faith in the City of Birmingham (1988) Report of a Commission set up by the Bishop's Council of the Diocese of Birmingham, Paternoster Press, Exeter.

References

Flinn, M. W. (1965) An Introduction to Edwin Chadwick, *Report on the Sanitary Condition of the Labouring Population of Great Britain*. Edinburgh University Press.

Frostick, E. and Harland, L. (1993) *Take Heart: people, history and change in Birmingham's Heartlands*, Birmingham Museum and Art Gallery, Hutton Press.

Gale, W. K. V. (1948) *Soho Foundry*. W. & T. Avery, Birmingham.

Gardiner, A. G. (1923) *Life of George Cadbury*, Cassell, London.

Gauldie, E. (1974) *Cruel Habitations: a history of working class housing*, Allen and Unwin, London.

General Survey Sub-Committee, City of Birmingham, 8 December 1911.

Giles, B. D. (1976) High status neighbourhoods in Birmingham, *West Midlands Studies*, **9**, 10–33.

Gill, C. (1952) *History of Birmingham, Vol I, Manor and Borough to 1865*, Oxford University Press.

Gill, C. and Robertson, C. G. (1938) *A Short History of Birmingham*, City of Birmingham.

Gledhill, A. (1988) *Birmingham's Jewellery Quarter*, KAF Brewin Books, Studley.

Green, F. and Wolff, S. (1933) *Birmingham and District*, Souvenir Magazines Ltd, London.

Hall, P. *et al* (1973) *The Containment of Urban England*, 2 Vols, George Allen and Unwin, London.

Hall, P. (ed.) (1981) *The Inner City in Context*, Final Report of the Social Science Research Council Inner Cities Working Party, Heinemann, London.

Hall, P. and Hay, D. (1980) *Growth Centres in the European Urban System*, Heinemann, London.

Hardy, D. (1979) *Alternative Communities in Nineteenth Century England*, Longman, Harlow.

Harris, J. R. (1986) Michael Alcock and the transfer of Birmingham technology to France before the Revolution, *The Journal of European Economic History*, **15**, 7–57.

Harrison, M. (1991) Thomas Coglan Horsfall and 'The example of Germany', *Planning Perspectives*, **6**, 297–314.

Harvey, W. A. (1906) *The Model Village and its Cottages: Bournville*, B. T. Batsford, London.

Hasegawa, J. (1992) *Replanning the Blitzed City Centre: a comparative study of Bristol, Coventry and Southampton 1941–1950*, Open University Press, Buckingham.

Haywood, W. (1918) *The Development of Birmingham: an essay*, Kynoch, Birmingham.

Hennock, E. P. (1973) *Fit and Proper Persons: ideal and reality in nineteenth century urban government*, Edward Arnold, London.

Hill, J. and Dent, R. K. (1897) *Memorials of the Old Square*, Achilles Taylor, Birmingham.

Hopkins, E. (1989) *Birmingham: the first manufacturing town in the world 1760–1840*, Weidenfeld and Nicolson, London.

Hopkins, E. (1990) Working class life in Birmingham between the wars, 1918–1939, in *Midland History*, **XV**, 129–50.

Horsfall, T. C. (1904) *The Improvement of the Dwellings and Surroundings of the People: the example of Germany*, Manchester University Press.

Housing Committee Reports, Speeches, etc., City of Birmingham, 1901–07.

Howard, E. (1899) *Tomorrow: a peaceful path to real reform*, Swann Sonnenschein, London. Revised as *Garden Cities of Tomorrow* (1902).

Hutton, W. (1782, 1783, 1793, 1809) *An History of Birmingham*. Reprinted, E. P. Publishing, East Ardsley, Wakefield, 1976.

Jones, J. T. (1940) *History of the Corporation of Birmingham*, Vol V, 1915–35, City of Birmingham.

Jones, P. N. (1967) The Segregation of Immigrant Communities in the City of Birmingham, 1961, Occasional Papers in *Geography*, **7**, University of Hull.

Kellett, J. R. (1969) *Railways and Victorian Cities*, Routledge and Kegan Paul, London.

Kennedy, A. (1993) *Inter-War Suburbia: patterns of private housing development in south Birmingham*. Unpublished B. A. dissertation, Department of Geography, University of Hull.

Kinvig, R. H. (1950) The Birmingham District in Domesday Times, pp. 113–34 in *Birmingham and its Regional Setting: a scientific survey*, British Association for the Advancement of Science.

Langford, J. A. (1868) *A Century of Birmingham Life: 1741–1841*, 2 vols, E. C. Osborne, Birmingham.

Lawton, R. (ed.) (1989), *The Rise and Fall of Great Cities*, Belhaven Press, London.

Lees, A. (1985) *Cities Perceived: urban society in European and American thought, 1820–1940*, Manchester University Press.

Leland, J. (1538) *Itinerary*.

Lister, D. (1991) The Transformation of a city: Birmingham, pp. 53–61, in Fisher, M. and Owen, U. (eds) *Whose Cities*, Penguin, Harmondsworth.

Little, B. (1971) *Birmingham Buildings: the architectural story of a Midland City*, David and Charles, Newton Abbot.

Llewelyn-Davies, Weeks, Forestier-Walker and Bor (1977), *Unequal City: Final Report of the Birmingham Inner Area Study*, Department of the Environment, HMSO.

Long, J. R. (ed.) (1961) *The Wythall Inquiry: a planning test case*, The Estates Gazette, London.

Macmorran, J. L. (1973) *Municipal Public Works and Planning in Birmingham, 1852–1972*, Public Works Committee, City of Birmingham.

Manzoni, H. J. (1939) *The Production of Fifty Thousand Municipal Houses*, City of Birmingham.

Marmaras, E. V. (1992) *Central London Under Reconstruction Policy and Planning, 1940–59*. Unpublished PhD, Department of Economic and Social History, University of Leicester.

Marriott, O. (1967), *The Property Boom*, Hamish Hamilton, London.

Martin, S. and Pearce G. (1992) The internationalisation of local authority economic development strategies: Birmingham in the 1980s, *Regional Studies*, **26**, 499–503.

Marwick, A. (1965) *The Deluge: British Society and the First World War*, The Bodley Head, London; Pelican, Harmondsworth, 1967.

Masterman, J. H. B. (1920) *The Story of the English Town: Birmingham*, SPCK, London.

McCulla, D. (1973) *Victorian and Edwardian Birmingham from old Photographs*. B. T. Batsford, London.

Miller, M. (1992) *Raymond Unwin: garden cities and town planning*, Leicester University Press.

Millward, R. and Robinson, A. (1971) *The West Midlands*, Macmillan, London.

Ministry of Health, Ministry of Works (1944) *Housing Manual 1944*, HMSO, London.

Ministry of Health (1949) *Housing Manual 1949*, HMSO, London.

Ministry of Housing and Local Government (1958) *Flats and Houses 1958: design and economy*, HMSO, London.

Money, J. (1977), *Experience and Identity: Birmingham and the West Midlands 1760–1800*, Manchester University Press.

Muthesius, S. (1982), *The English Terraced House*, Yale University Press.

Nettlefold, J. S. (1908), *Practical Housing*, Garden City Press, Letchworth.

Nettlefold, J. S. (1914) *Practical Town Planning*, St Catherine Press.

Newton, K. (1976) *Second City Politics: democratic processes and decision-making in Birmingham*, Clarendon Press, Oxford.

Nockolds, H. (1976) *Lucas: the first hundred years*, 2 vols, David and Charles, Newton Abbot.

References

Norris, J. (1960) *Human Aspects of Redevelopment*, Midlands New Town Society, Birmingham.

Oliver, P., Davis, I. and Bentley, I. (1981) *Dunroamin: the suburban semi and its enemies*, Barrie and Jenkins, London.

Orbach, L. F. (1977) *Homes for Heroes: a study of the evolution of British public housing, 1915–21*, Seeley, Service, London.

Paris, C. and Blackaby, B. (1979) *Not Much Improvement: urban renewal policy in Birmingham*, Heinemann, London.

Pelham, R. A. (1950) The Growth of Settlement and Industry c. 100–c. 1700, p. 158 in *Birmingham and its Regional Setting: a scientific survey*, British Association for the Advancement of Science.

Perkin, H. (1989) *The Rise of Professional Society: England since 1880*, Routledge, London.

Policy for the Inner Cities, (1977) Cmnd 6845, HMSO, London.

Pompa, N. D. (1988) *The Nature and Agents of Townscape Change: south Birmingham 1970–85*, Unpublished PhD, Department of Geography, University of Birmingham.

Power, N. S. (1965) *The Forgotten People*, Arthur James, Evesham.

Priestley, J. B. (1934) *English Journey*, William Heinemann, London.

Radcliffe, P. (1981) *Racism and Reaction: a profile of Handsworth*, Routledge and Kegan Paul, London.

Rex, J. and Moore, R. (1967) *Race, Community and Conflict: a study of Sparkbrook*, Oxford University Press.

Robson, B. (1988) *Those Inner Cities*, Clarendon Press, Oxford.

Rodger, R. (1989) *Housing in Urban Britain 1780–1914*, Macmillan Educational, London.

Rowlands, M. B. (1987) *The West Midlands From AD1000*, Longman, Harlow.

Ryan, M. J. (1976) *Comprehensive Redevelopment in Birmingham: the work of the Corporation with special reference to the Town and Country Planning Act, 1944*, Unpublished MPhil thesis, Centre for Urban and Regional Studies, University of Birmingham.

Schofield, R. E. (1963) *The Lunar Society of Birmingham: a social history of provincial science and industry in eighteenth century England*, Clarendon Press, Oxford.

Skipp, V. (1979) *The Centre of England*, Eyre Methuen, London.

Skipp, V. (1980) *A History of Greater Birmingham – down to 1830*, Victor Skipp, Birmingham.

Skipp, V. H. T. (1983) *The Making of Victorian Birmingham*. Victor Skipp, Birmingham.

Slater, T. (1981) *A History of Warwickshire*, Phillimore, Chichester.

Smith, B. M. D. (1964) Industry and Trade, 1880–1960, in Stephens, W. B. (ed.) *A History of the County of Warwick, Vol VII, The City of Birmingham*, Oxford University Press.

Smith, B. M. D. (1977) Economic Problems in the Core of the Old Birmingham Industrial Area, pp. 148–78 in Frank Joyce (ed.) *Metropolitan Development and Change: the West Midlands, a policy review*. The University of Aston in Birmingham, Teakfield Ltd, Farnborough.

Smith, B. M. D. (1989) The Rise, Fall and Minimal Survival of the Birmingham Motor Cycle Industry, pp. 179–92 in Barbara Tilson (ed.) *Made in Birmingham: design and industry 1889–1989*, Brewin Books, Studley, Warwickshire.

Smith, D. (1982) *Conflict and Compromise: class formation in English society 1830–1914, a comparative study of Birmingham and Sheffield*, Routledge and Kegan Paul, London.

Special Housing Inquiry Committee, *Report* (1914), City of Birmingham.

Spencer, K. *et al* (1986) *Crisis in the Industrial Heartland: a study of the West Midlands*,

Clarendon Press, Oxford.

Stedman, M. B. (1958) The townscape of Birmingham in 1956, *Transactions, The Institute of British Geographers*, **25**, 225–38.

Stedman, M. B. and Wood, P. A. (1965) Urban Renewal in Birmingham, *Geography*, 50, 1–7.

Stephens, W. B. (1964) Social History Before 1815, pp. 209–22 in Stephens, W. B. (1964) *A History of the County of Warwick, Vol VII, The City of Birmingham*, Oxford University Press.

Stephens, W. B. (ed.) (1964) *A History of the County of Warwick, Vol VII, The City of Birmingham*, Oxford University Press.

Stewart, A. (1981) *Housing Action in an Industrial Suburb*, Academic Press, London.

Stratton, M. (1989) Architectural Terracotta in Birmingham, pp. 21–34 in Barbara Tilson (ed.) *Made in Birmingham: design and industry 1889–1989*, Brewin Books, Studley, Warwickshire.

Struthers, W. A. K. and Brindell, M. J. (1983) The West Midlands: from reconstruction to regeneration, pp. 62–95 in D. T. Cross and M. R. Bristow, *English Structure Planning: a commentary on procedure and practice in the seventies*, Pion, London.

Sutcliffe A. (1974) A Century of Flats in Birmingham, 1875–1973, pp. 181–206 in Anthony Sutcliffe (ed.) *Multi-Storey Living: the British Working Class Experience*, Croom Helm, London.

Sutcliffe, A. and Smith, R. (1974) *History of Birmingham, Vol III, Birmingham 1939–1970*, Oxford University Press.

Swenarton, M. (1981) *Homes fit for Heroes: the politics and architecture of early state housing in Britain*, Heinemann, London.

Thomas, A. D. (1986) *Housing and Urban Renewal*, George Allen and Unwin, London.

Thompson, F. M. L. (ed.) (1982) *The Rise of Suburbia*, Leicester University Press.

Thoms, D. (1989) *War, Industry, and Society: The Midlands, 1939–45*, Routledge, London.

Thorpe, H. (1950) The Growth of Settlement Before the Norman Conquest, pp. 87–112 in *Birmingham and its Regional Setting: a scientific survey*, British Association for the Advancement of Science.

Tilson, B. (ed) (1989) *Made in Birmingham: design and industry 1889–1989*, Brewin Books, Studley, Warwickshire.

Tiptaft, N. (1945) *I saw a City*, Cornish Bros, Birmingham.

Tripp, H. A. (1942) *Town Planning and Road Traffic*, Edward Arnold, London.

Tudor Walters Report (1918) of the Committee appointed by the President of the Local Government Board and the Secretary of State for Scotland to consider questions of Building Construction in connection with the provision of dwellings for the working classes in England and Wales and Scotland and to report upon the methods for securing economy and despatch in the provision of such dwellings, Cmd 9191, HMSO, London.

Unequal City (1977) Final Report of the Birmingham Inner Area Study, Department of the Environment, HMSO, London.

Unwin, R. (1909) *Town Planning in Practice: an introduction to the art of designing cities and suburbs*, Fisher Unwin, London.

Upton, C. (1993) *A History of Birmingham*, Phillimore, Chichester.

Uthwatt, A. A., Expert Committee on Compensation and Betterment (1942) *Final Report*, Ministry of Works and Planning, Cmd 6386, HMSO, London.

Vince, C. A. (1923) *History of the Corporation of Birmingham, Vol IV, 1900–15*, Cornish Bros, Birmingham.

Vincent, E. W. and Hinton, P. (1947) *The University of Birmingham: its history and significance*, Cornish Bros Ltd, Birmingham.

Walker, G. (1950) A Survey of the Industrial Population of Birmingham and the Black

References

Country, pp. 249–68 in *Birmingham and its Regional Setting: a scientific survey*, British Association for the Advancement of Science.

Walters, J. C. (1902) *Scenes in Slumland*, Birmingham Daily Gazette.

Warwick, G. T. (1950) Relief and Physiographic Regions, pp.3–14 in *Birmingham and its Regional Setting: a scientific survey*, British Association for the Advancement of Science.

Waterhouse, R. E. (1954) *The Birmingham and Midland Institute 1854–1954*, Birmingham.

Wates, N. and Knevitt, C. (1987) *Community Architecture*, Penguin, Harmondsworth.

West Midland Group, *English County: a Planning survey of Herefordshire*, Faber, 1946.

West Midland Group, *Land Classification in the West Midland Region*, Faber 1947.

West Midland Group (1948) *Conurbation: a planning survey of Birmingham and the Black Country*, The Architectural Press, London.

West Midland Group, *Local Government and Central Control*, Routledge, 1956.

Whitehand, J. W. R. (1987) *The Changing Face of Cities: a study of development cycles and urban form*, Basil Blackwell, Oxford.

Whitehand, J. W. R. (1991) Institutional Site Planning: the University of Birmingham, England 1900–1969, *Planning History* (13)2, 29–35.

Whybrow, J. (ed.) (1972) *How Does Your Birmingham Grow?*, John Whybrow Ltd, Birmingham.

Whybrow, J. and Waterhouse, R. (1976) *How Birmingham Became a Great City*, John Whybrow Ltd, Birmingham.

Wise, M. (1982) An Early Experiment in Suburban Development: the ideal village, Birmingham, pp. 151–56 in Grant, E. and Newby, P. (eds) *Landscape and Industry*, Middlesex Polytechnic.

Wise, M. J. and Johnson, B. L. C. (1950) The Changing Regional Pattern During the Eighteenth Century, pp. 161–86 in *Birmingham and its Regional Setting: a scientific survey*, British Association for the Advancement of Science.

Wise, M. J. and Thorpe, P. O'N. (1950) The Growth of Birmingham 1800–1950, pp. 213–28 in *Birmingham and its Regional Setting: a scientific survey*, British Association for the Advancement of Science.

Wise, M. J. (1951), On the Evolution of the Jewellery and Gun Quarters in Birmingham, *IBG Transactions*, XV; 59–72.

Wood, P. A. (1976) *The West Midlands*, David and Charles, Newton Abbot.

Woods, R. (1978) Mortality and Sanitary Conditions in the 'Best Governed City in the World' – Birmingham, 1870–1910, *Journal of Historical Geography*, 4, 35–56.

Wyatt R. J. (1981) *The Austin 1905–1952*, David and Charles, Newton Abbot.

Yelling, J. A. (1992) *Slums and Redevelopment: policy and practice in England, 1918–45*, UCL Press, London.

Young, F. B. (1935) *White Ladies*.

Young, M. and Willmott, P. (1957) *Family and Kinship in East London*, Routledge and Kegan Paul, London, Pelican, Harmondsworth 1962.

Zuckerman, J. and Eley, G. (1979) *Birmingham Heritage*, Croom Helm, London.

Index

Index